THE DALMATIAN

Coach Dog • Firehouse Dog

June Harrah bronze of Ch. Tally Ho Last of Sunstar from the collection of Mr. Wendell Sammet.

THE
DALMATIAN
Coach Dog • Firehouse Dog

by

ALFRED and ESMERALDA TREEN

FIRST EDITION
Third Printing 1982

HOWELL BOOK HOUSE Inc.
230 Park Avenue
New York, N.Y. 10169

Library of Congress Cataloging in Publication Data

Treen, Alfred.
  The Dalmatian, coach dog—firehouse dog.

  SUMMARY: Describes the history of the Dalmatian dog,
its care, breeding, training for various uses, and its
record as a show dog.
  1. Dalmatian dogs. (1. Dalmatian dogs.   2. Dogs)
I. Treen, Esmeralda, joint author.   II. Title.
SF429.D3T73   636.7'2   80-10650
ISBN 0-87605-109-3

Contents

About the Authors

ALFRED AND ESMERALDA TREEN have been "in Dalmatians" for more than 30 years.

They began breeding Dals in 1947. Their home-bred American and Canadian Champion Coachman's Chuck-a-Luck was the only Best in Show Dalmatian to sire two Best in Show sons. He sired 27 champions.

Alfred has judged the breed since 1965. He is currently eligible to judge all the breeds in the Non-Sporting and Toy Groups and all but seven of the Hounds. He judged the national specialties of the Dalmatian Club of America in 1970 and 1977.

He has served the Dalmatian Club of America as a governor, treasurer, vice president and president and is a member of its Standard Committee. He developed the DCA Regional Club Council and served as its chairman for several years. He is now chairman of the DCA's Judges Education Committee. In 1979 he was appointed to the Board of Directors of the American Kennel Club.

He has been the only president of the Waukesha Kennel Club since it was founded in 1961 by the Treens with the help of friends. He is currently its delegate to the AKC.

He was also vice president of the Houston Kennel Club and served as a show committee member and chief ring steward of the Mississippi Valley Kennel Club.

Esmeralda Treen apprenticed as a judge of Dalmatians in 1969. Since then she has become eligible to judge ten of the breeds in the Sporting Group.

She judged the national specialties of the Dalmatian Club of America in 1973 and 1979.

In 1967 Mrs. Treen became co-editor of *The Spotter,* the newsletter of the Dalmatian Club of America. As editor in 1971 she turned it into a quarterly magazine which is now an award-winning club bulletin.

She helped inaugurate the Houston Kennel Club's obedience training program in 1953. In 1957 she became a judge of obedience trials and in 1960 she qualified for Utility class judging.

Both Treens are members of the British Dalmatian Club and the Chicagoland Dalmatian Club. Mrs. Treen belongs to the Association of Obedience Clubs and Judges as well as the Dog Writers Association of America.

The Treens have judged dog shows in five countries and from coast to coast and border to border in 40 of the 50 states. They are students of all things canine. They have taken courses in genetics to plan breedings and in drawing to sharpen their eyes for judging. They have collected a large library of dog publications.

In preparation for writing this book the Treens visited every major art gallery in London including the Queen's Gallery in Buckingham Palace. They spent five days in the Reading Room of the British Museum. Some years earlier they did research in the archival print room of the British Museum. Their investigations also included visits to Yugoslavia and the Dalmatian coast.

The Board of Governors of the Dalmatian Club of America appointed the Treens as official delegates to the British Dalmatian Club World Congress in London in April 1980.

Mr. Treen's vocation has been personnel and industrial relations. In 1935 he was employed by U. S. Steel in Chicago and in 1946 by the AOSmith Corporation to assist in the development of its corporate personnel function and the decentralization of its operations. Other AOSmith assignments gave him experience in Houston TX, Granite City IL, in the St. Louis area and Milwaukee.

The Treens reside in Sussex WI and have a son and daughter.

Acknowledgments

WE ARE GRATEFUL to the many people and organizations that helped us in our search for information. The Library Staff of the American Kennel Club, the Reading Room of the British Museum, the Library of Congress, the John Crear Library in Chicago, the Milwaukee Art Center and the Chicago Art Institute libraries, the Milwaukee Public Library, the Minneapolis Public Library, and the Barbara Sanborn Library in Pewaukee, Wisconsin and, through it, the Wisconsin State Library Service, were particularly helpful. The private library collections of John S. Best, Francis P. Fretwell, John T. Marvin and George S. Pugh, coupled with their insights and suggestions, were most valuable. Similarly useful was the guidance of the Rev. Mr. Philip Talmage, Reference Librarian of Marquette University, who led us through some of the complexities of church history which related to the Dalmatian's own background. Ellen McCallister, Librarian of Mount Vernon Ladies' Association of the Union, cooperated in the matter of George Washington's coachdogs. Mary Folse, Ph.D., with her great knowledge of classical antiquities and her use of Greek, Latin and Sanskrit, was particularly helpful. She and her husband, Gregory L. Hutchison, presented us with some challenging ideas from their frame of reference as serious students and world travelers.

Within the breed, material contributed by breeders, exhibitors and judges was received with enthusiasm. Two members of the Dalmatian fancy deserve special thanks. Walter Johnson's statistical contributions will be of great interest and value to the fancy. Robert Slater's drawings should enable the newcomers to visualize both the quality to be sought and the defects to be avoided. They should enable thoughtful judges and exhibitors and breeders to evaluate specimens of the breed with greater understanding.

Alfred and Esmeralda Treen

Oil painting of Boy on Horseback with Dalmatian. From the collection of Mrs. George Ratner.

Famous Reinagle (1749 - 1833) drawing of the Dal. Note cropped ears.

1

Origins

THERE is no O in Dalmatian!

There are no Dalmatians in Dalmatia!

We believe it is important to start with first things first. The spelling of the breed name should be correct. It is DalmatiAn. It is NOT DalmatiOn! And if you feel this is nit-picking and superfluous, some of the local breed clubs, many of the magazines published for the dog fancy, and hundreds of people who have occasion to use the word misspell it frequently.

DalmatiAn. It should be simple. The word is formed by adding a final N to the word Dalmatia, the name of an ancient country now a province of Yugoslavia. Many people believe that the Dalmatian originated in Dalmatia and that is how the breed got the name. Many canine authorities place the origin of the dog somewhere around the Adriatic, and while there is no absolute proof, this is probably where the forerunners of the breed emanated or developed. While it isn't literally true that there are no Dalmatians in Dalmatia it is almost a proven fact. Very few of these dogs exist in what is supposed to be their native land. Allegedly these are British imports or descendants of imports. And it is quite possible that the dogs did originate in that part of the world. It is almost a fact that the breed did come from somewhere near the Mediterranean or the Adriatic. There are various little clues pointing to this as the original area: for instance, the discovery of the statue of a spotted dog in the Mycenea ruins mentioned in the *Penguin Book of Lost Civilizations*. This factor indicates that a dog similar in outline to our Dalmatian, and also spotted, did exist at a very early time in this area, but perhaps it was a spotted mastiff.

Some of the theories concerning the origin of the Dalmatian can bring endless discussions. For instance the theory that the Dalmatian was the product of breeding the Istrian pointer with the Harlequin Great Dane can evoke near shouting matches. It is well known that the Dane was not always as large a dog as we know him today. Youatt refers to the Dalmatian as the "lesser Danish dogge." No less a breeder of Harlequin Danes than Antonia Pratt has reported that sometimes litters of Harls are born with rounded spots rather than the desired (in Danes) torn patches. This idea, however, was rejected vociferously by the Great Dane Club of America as being the worst sort of canard. It is up to you to decide if it could possibly be the origin of the Dalmatian.

As to why or how the breed was called Dalmatian, no one really knows. There are a number of theories, most of them quite logical, and anyone may believe any one of them. They are, however, still theories, not facts. Some of them have been around for a long while.

A young poet, Jurij Dalmatin (1546-1589) who lived in Serbia, another province of Yugoslavia, received some dogs from the Bohemian Duchess Alena Meziricska Lomnice in 1573. In a letter to the Duchess, Dalmatin wrote, "The interest in my Turkish-dogs grows in all Serbia . . . I have presented several tens of them . . . these dogs are so popular that they call them by my name—Dalmatin. This new name is already more and more ingrained . . ."

At the time Dalmatin wrote his letter about his "Turkish" dogs the entire area was under the domination of Turkey. The Turks overran the Balkans and pushed on into Europe where they were finally stopped by the Viennese in 1683. The Turkish rule of Bulgaria and other Balkan areas ended in 1827.

His name, Jurij, is another form of George and Dalmatin is obviously a place name, probably Dalmatia. In those years people did not have surnames. They had a first name and then something to distinguish them from all others with the same first name, either son of someone, or from a city, a village, a country, or whatever. So Jurij, living in Serbia, was named Dalmatin because he came from that area. The word for the breed in Italy is Dalmatina.

Certain theories as to why the dogs were called Dalmatians are so much conversation. For instance we have read that the dogs were named Dalmatians because the spots resembled the bubbles in the volcanic rock found along the coast of Dalmatia. There is no volcanic rock along the coast of Dalmatia. The mountains are all layered limestone. It is true that spotty vegetation on some of the limestone mountains might give one the idea of spots but that is too far-fetched.

The barrenness of the hills of Dalmatia is not a quirk of nature by any means. During the time of the struggle between Hungary and Venice for domination of this land the forests, which at one time covered the hills, were destroyed to build ships. After Venetian dominance was established, the hacking away at the forests continued to such an extent that timbers intended to be used in building ships were left at the water's edge to rot.

Reforestation is not the easiest thing to accomplish, besides which the peasants knew very little about such things. The constant winds off the Adriatic have resulted in scrubby looking forest and vegetation all along the Dalmatian coast.

If these hills resemble the spotted dogs, it is because one's imagination wills them to do so. This seems, on the surface, a far-fetched reason for naming the breed Dalmatian; it would have been more realistic to name zebras Dalmatians.

That they were called coach dogs long before they became known as Dalmatians is true. According to the authority William Arkwright, the hounds were first in the development of the dog as we now know it. Then through refinement in breeding, man developed the pointer. Hunting dogs were important to put meat on the table. Arkwright also places the origins of the hounds and pointers somewhere around the Mediterranean. He favors Spain as most writing indicates that hounds and pointers were used there very early on. Topsell wrote in his *Historie of Four-footed Beastes* that there was a new variety of hunting dog found in Italy that became very popular among the Italians, "especially the white and yellow spotted dogs." This history, published in 1607, was based mainly on other authorities.

Dalmatians do not really exist in Dalmatia today. In 1930 the late Mr. Bozo Banac introduced Dalmatians to the country. He brought them to his home near Dubrovnik from England in 1930. Locally they were referred to as the "English Dogs." About 25 years later someone visiting the lovely countryside discovered the last Dalmatian in Dubrovnik. He was descended from the "English Dogs" which Mr. Banac had imported. In the summer of 1977, we visited the old town of Dubrovnik. We inquired about Dalmatians everywhere. The concierge at our hotel was the only one who said there were Dalmatians in Dalmatia. "Many, many . . . yes, yes." We asked other questions and all answers were happily favorable. His apparent reaction to any question was to answer with whatever he thought we wanted to hear. If we had asked if the dogs had pink spots, I feel sure he would have said, "many, many . . . yes, yes."

We did see one Dalmatian in Dubrovnik. It was a young bitch owned by a man from Switzerland visiting Dubrovnik on his summer holiday. We also visited the island of Korcula but found no dogs there.

Actually, there are several serious breeders in Yugoslavia. They are located in Zagreb and Zupanja and they imported their breeding stock. Dalmatia is a region of Croatia, one of the six socialist republics of Yugoslavia. Zagreb and Zupanja are situated in Northern Croatia.

"The Dalmatian Dog" pictured in *Dog in Health & Disease* by Stonehenge. 1859.

Mr. Fawdry's Dalmatian dog Captain, a top winning dog in England, 1874 - 77. Reproduced in Freeman Lloyd's *Dog Breeds of the World.*

A print of "Spotted Dick" from Hugh Dalziel's *British Dogs.*

14

After the Trojan War Achilles' son, Pyrrhus Neoptolemos, settled in Epirus where he either conquered or married into the family of an eponymous hero named Molossus. Molossus gave his name to the famous Molossian hounds of antiquity, which are mentioned in many classical works in Greek and Latin. These were a mastiff type of dog.

Since Epirus, according to classical atlases, was the area immediately south of the Keraunian Mountains, directly east of Corfu and the Roman Dalmatia was north of these mountains, there is every possibility that these dogs were taken into Dalmatia by the ancients, and caused historical confusion. They were used as shepherd dogs and as dogs of war, guarding the mountains for their masters.

Harry Glover, the British authority, suggests that the Dal may have been confused with a spotted Mastiff, a larger more powerful dog. His suggestion of the mastiff type lends credence to the possibility that the spotted dog of Dalmatia is not a Dal at all but an Epirote or Molossian mastiff.

The earliest known pictures portraying dogs which could be an original form of Dalmatians can be found in a fresco (circa 1360) in the Spanish Chapel of Santa Maria Novella in Florence. This church is under the Dominican Order of Friar Preachers whose habits are white with a black over cape. We shall never forget the smile on the face of the Dominican priest in the Sacristy of that church when we asked where we could find the frescoes of the Spanish Chapel with the Dalmatians. His face lit up and he said, quite proudly, "Domini Canes!" The dog of God.

In the early days the Church and the State were the institutions which controlled mens' lives. The Church came to be represented in painting and literature by various allegorical figures. We find symbolism in art throughout history. Somewhere along the line the black and white dog became the main representative of the Church. This grew out of the Inquisition, that fearful state of affairs which held everyone in its thrall during the fifteenth century and even into the sixteenth century. The order of the Dominicans was in charge of the Inquisition. So paintings, posters and other art forms used the Dal to represent the Dominican order. This has been considered an artistic and ecclesiastical joke through the years.

During the Cromwell years (1649-1660) in England, spotted dogs were used in antipapal tracts and leaflets as a symbol of Roman rule of the British church. Political woodcuts of that period can be found in the British Museum showing this, which tends to establish the breed in Italy at that time.

There is a mosaic frieze at the church of Saint Francis, in Lima, Peru, which shows a Dalmatian. Based on the information provided by a tour guide and sent on by Benito Vila, the tile for the frieze was shipped from Spain to Peru in the late sixteenth century. It was not erected until 1620, because the Viceroy had difficulty in locating anyone qualified to do the work. This is another instance of the white dog with black markings being used in an ecclesiastical setting, but this time in the western hemisphere.

It is very difficult to say when the word Dalmatian actually came into use to describe the spotted dog we know. According to the *Oxford Dictionary of the English Language,* the word was first used in 1824. We were able to prove the Oxford Dictionary in error as Thomas Bewick, in his first edition of 1790, shows a drawing of the dog and a description of the dog and it is clearly labeled "The Dalmatian or Coach Dog." Probably the first printed use in English of "Dalmatian" to designate our breed was in 1780, when a translation of Buffon's *Natural History* was published in Scotland.

There is no mention of the Dal in *The Boke of St. Albans* (1480) and nothing in any of the published works on dogs written by Gesner (1587). Dr. Caius, who wrote *DeCanis Britannicus Libellus* in 1560, later translated by Abraham Fleming in 1576 and called *Of English Dogs,* has a doubtful reference. Edward Topsell published a two volume *Historie of Fourfooted Beastes* in 1607 basing most of his knowledge on the Gesner and Caius and Fleming books. He did, however, state that the Italians were very pleased with a new variety of hunting dogs, "especially white and yellow spotted dogs."

The famous Dutch painter, Gerard ter Borch, painted a scene from The Congress of Munster in 1647. A detail of this painting shows the Dauphin of France with his Dalmatian. This is definitely a Dalmatian. The typical tri-color found in the old prints and paintings of the Dal is shown in a painting by Pieter Boel (1632-1647), which hangs in the Kennel Club in Clarges St., London. The Hunting Party, by Jan Fyt (1609-1661), includes a heavily marked Dalmatian type along with several Spaniels and a Greyhound. Hunting Dogs and their Attendants, painted by Francesco Castiglioni probably about 1700, shows a Dalmatian trying to be a lap-dog, something those of us who have had the breed will understand completely.

Throughout Europe we can find paintings with Dalmatians in them painted later than those mentioned above. That these dogs were favored by royalty is undeniable.

In the 1800's writers mentioned the dog frequently. Buffon, the great French naturalist, in 1772 proclaimed the Dal as the Harrier of Bengal. He offered no proof of his statement. When we visited the Kennel Club in London, Commander Williams, upon finding out that we were doing research on the origins of the breed, stated, "Ours came from India!"

Many theories prevail on how the dog could have migrated from the Indian area, through Europe and so to England. Could the Gypsies have brought the dogs to Europe and to England? The Gypsies, forced to migrate to the Middle East as early as the fifth century, established settlements in the Balkans and Eastern Europe before the end of the fourteenth century. They

1855 print of Dalmatian Dog from James
Cowles Prichard, *Natural History of Man.*

17

came from the Upper Himalayas of north India, where they had been part of a loose federation of nomadic tribes. In Western Europe, Gypsy groups continued a nomadic life, their ranks being increased by migration from the Balkans as the Turks moved in late in the fifteenth century. They were hunters. They wandered through Europe as blacksmiths, horse traders and entertainers (musicians and fortune tellers). Their true origin was unknown by medieval society. Whether they furthered the development of the Dalmatian because of the influence of their religious beliefs is pure speculation. White angels and black devils were featured in their doctrine of war between light and dark. There is a considerable bibliography of material on the migrations of the gypsies, but it does not get into dogs.

Perhaps the dogs migrated with the Roman legions? Caesar and Pompey fought their civil wars in the area now known as Yugoslavia. All that impedimenta one reads about the Gallic wars were not necessarily merely machines of war but included complete households. There were camp followers in Caesar's day, too, and perhaps spotted dogs.

Another theory concerning the name of the Dalmatian is an ecclesiastical one. There is a vestment, a tunic-type garment, beltless but with sleeves. Early ones were made of a soft white wool found on sheep from the mountains of Dalmatia. The garment has ornamental bands running from the shoulders to the lower hem. Many of these can be seen in the Museums of the Vatican. As the church progressed in importance in the world the Dalmatic, as this vestment is called, became more ornate. The ornamental bands became ermine. Weaving has always been an occupation in Illyria and Dalmatia. At one time the weavers of Illyria turned out the uniforms for the Roman Army as well as fabric for civilian use. Writing in *Black Lamb and Grey Falcon,* Rebecca West says, "No matter what bestial tricks history might be playing, there were always looms at work in Illyria."

Tying the Dalmatic vestment to the area of Illyria and Dalmatia is quite simple. In the Capitoline Museum in Rome, there is a statue of Augustus holding a shield which has a figure of an Illyrian wearing a Dalmatic. This is the first knowledge of the garment. But during the third century the Pope dictated a rule that all martyrs would be buried in this type of garment. All deacons and officiating bishops in the Western church wear the Dalmatic and the monarchs of England also wear a Dalmatic at their coronation.

Is it possible that the ermine decorations on the Dalmatic reminded people of the spotted dog and thus the name came from a church vestment, which apparently originated in Dalmatia rather than because the dog originated there? It is impossible to prove that he did.

2
Chronology of Ancestry Lore

In RESEARCHING canine history for clues of the Dalmatian's origin, we found that the facts were few for the effort involved. We did not keep score.

Very few written records in English on any subject exist earlier than the tenth century A.D. Dogs did not become subjects to write about until much later. E. Gwynne Jones, a British librarian, researched some 12,000 references to produce his "Bibliography of the Dog" (London 1971). He located sources for 3986 books published in the English language during the years 1570 through 1965. Only 41 of these were produced before 1780, the year the term Dalmatian was printed in English probably for the first time to designate a breed of dogs in a translation from the French of Buffon's *Natural History*. Among those 41, only one refers to a breed of spotted dogs.

In our search, we located 80 items with some bearing on the origin of the breed. Frequently, these were repetitious or in conflict. For the reader's interest we have listed some facts or quoted or summarized each writer's conclusions in the chronology and bibliography which follow.

3000 BC——"There is a coloured painting from the tomb of Redmera at Thebes which depicts the tribute from various parts of Asia. Eight dogs form part of the tribute, among them a greyhound, a mastiff, and a large spotted type not unlike the Dalmatian hound." H. Epstein, *The Origin of Domestic Animals of Africa*. (Gwatkin 1933-34)

2000 BC——The Tablet of Antefaa II, from the Tomb in the valley of El Assasif, includes four dogs complete with collars. William Youatt, *The Dog*

Was the Dalmatian known in Egypt?

Needlework picture attributed to a member of the Juvenal family of Philadelphia. Embroidered in silk and chenille on silk, it represents Lady Jane Grey visiting with her friends, Mrs. J. Ramsey van Roden and Howell Barrett Pennell.

20

(1847), describes one as resembling a Dalmatian. Edward C. Ash, *Dogs: Their History and Development* (1927), however, says "It appears to me to be more of a great Dane and a mastiff cross than the famed carriage dog. It is significant that this type of dog is rarely, if ever shown in a hunting scene, suggesting that its main function was the guarding of property."

1700 BC——"I have seen at Tyrnia, the birthplace of Hercules, a fresco dating circa 1700 B.C. depicting a staghunting scene with a large number of dogs, clearly 'Dalmatians' though artistic license has given them red and blue spots." Vane Ivanovic, SPOTS OF NEWS (April, 1977).

1600 BC——"Spotted dogs were known and remarked upon in classical times, for mention is made of them by Greek and Roman authors, but unfortunately with insufficient detail to allow us to feel with any certainty that the dog mentioned as spotted was a Dalmatian. The discovery of a model of a dog of the Mycenaea period of Grecian history shows that at that time, 1600 years B.C., a dog with round black spots had been noticed or was desired. This model, in terra-cotta, has upright ears, the body is white, marked with black spots, and to some extent conforming with the standard description of the Dalmatian." Edward C. Ash, *Dogs: Their History and Development* (1927).

1253——A report of a Dutch visit to Dalmatia describes dogs found there. It does not mention color or suggest a spotted dog.

1480——There is no mention of a spotted dog in Dame Julliana Berners' *The Boke of St. Albans*.

1560—— "Recently (so fond are we all now of novelties), a new variety has been imported from France all white, with black spots; this is called the Gallican." Dr. Johannes Caius, (Edward IV's physician) *De Canis Britannicus Libellus*. This Latin treatise may be the first mention in print of a breed of spotted dogs.

1576—— "There is also at this day among us a new kinde of dog brought out of France (for we Englishmen are marvellous greedy gaping gluttons after novelties and covetous cormants of things that be seldome, rare, strange and hard to get). And they be speckled all over with white marble blew, which beautifies their skins and affoordeth a seemly show of comlinesse. These are called French dogs as is above declared already." *Of English Dogges* translated from *De Canis Britannicus Libellus* by Abraham Fleming, a student. Fleming's additions which may be inaccurate, certainly confuse and suggest a roan spaniel or a belton setter. We do not know whether he actually saw a Gallican or was paid by the word like a scrivener and let his imagination have full play.

1587——*Historiae Animalium* assembled by Conrad Gesner included Dr. Caius' description of British dogs along with the sentence on the Gallican.

1607——"In Italy they make account of the spotted one, especially white and yellow for they are quicker nosed." Edward Topsell, *The Historie of Fourfooted Beasties*.

1637——Aldrovandus, an Italian naturalist, captions an illustration, "A sagacious spotted dog for taking quail." Ash translates this differently, "Spotted sporting dog trained to catch game with English dog plant."

1649-1660——Anti-papal tracts and leaflets in the British Museum published during the Cromwell period utilized spotted dogs as a symbol of Roman rule.

1772——A Dalmatian figure captioned "The Harrier of Bengal" in *Natural History*, Count de Buffon (translated from French by Barr) may be first printed use of this term in English language.

1780——"The hound, the harrier, the turnspit, the water-dog and even the spaniel, may be regarded as one dog. Their figure and instincts are nearly the same; and they differ only in the length of their legs, and the size of their ears, which, however, in all of them are long, soft and pendulus. These dogs are natives of France; and I am uncertain whether the Dalmatian dog, or, as it is called, the harrier of Bengal, ought to be disjoined from them; for it differs from our harrier only in colour. I am convinced that this dog is not an original native of Bengal, or of any other part of India, and that it is not, as has been pretended, the Indian dog mentioned by the ancients, and said to have been produced between a dog and a tiger; for it has been known in Italy above 170 years ago, and not considered as a dog brought from India, but as a common Harrier." Count de Buffon, *Natural History, General and Particular*, Vol. IV. Translated from French and published in Scotland. May be the first printed use in English of the term Dalmatian to designate a breed of dogs.

1780——Riedel shows a spotted dog marked English.

1790——"The Dalmatian, or coach dog has been erroneously called the Danish Dog, and, by Mr. Buffon, the Harrier of Bengal; but for what reason it is difficult to ascertain, as its incapacity for scenting is sufficient to destroy all affinity to any dog employed in pursuit of the hare." Thomas Bewick, *A General History of Quadrupeds*. Possibly this was the first use of the term "Dalmatian" by a British writer to designate the breed. Bewick goes on to say, "It is very common in the country at present and is frequently kept in genteel houses, as an elegant attendant on a carriage, to which its attention seems to be solely directed. We do not, however, admire the cruel practice of depriving the poor animal of its ears, in order to increase its beauty."

1800-1803——"The common Coach Dog is a humble attendant of the servants and horses." Syndenham Edwards, *Cynographia Britannica*.

1804——"This particular race, of which so exact and beautiful a representation has been produced by the conjunctive efforts of the artists concerned, are by the earliest, and most respected writers, said to have been

"Le Braque de Bengale." This is the name given by Buffon. This picture is after a painting by Gilbert de Seve, born 1615.

The Dalmatian from a study by Thomas Brown, 1829.

"Spotted Sporting dog trained to catch game" from Aldrovandus (1637)

23

originally natives of Dalmatia, a district in European Turkey, bounded on the west by the Gulf of Venice; and from whence it is presumed, the breed was formerly transported to those countries, where by their prolific increase, they are now more universally known. Numerous as they become, and truly ornamental as they prove in the department to which they are so fashionably appropriate, less has been said upon their origin and introduction than upon any other distinct breed of the canine race.'' William Taplin, *The Sportsman's Cabinet*.

1820——"However he may have originated, he appears first to have been noticed in Dalmatia, a province of European Turkey, thence to have spread through Italy and the Southern parts, over most of the Continent of Europe, being generally esteemed a hound or hunting dog, notwithstanding his very universal different destination.'' John Scott, *The Sportsman's Repository*.

1829——"This dog has been erroneously called the Danish Dog by some authors, and Buffon and some other naturalists imagine him to be the Harrier of Bengal; but his native country is Dalmatia, a mountainous district of European Turkey. He has been domesticated in Italy for upwards of two centuries, and is the common Harrier of that Country.'' Captain Thomas Brown, *Biographical Sketches and Authentic Anecdotes of Dogs*.

1837——"Showy and interesting as it is, little that is interesting can be said.'' Thomas Bell, *A History of British Quadrepeds*. Pictured with a closed landaulette complete with Coachman.

1839-1840——Colonel Hamilton Smith commented on the possibility that the coach dog was derived from an Indian breed "with a white fur marked with black spots, small half-dejected ears and a Greyhound-like form.'' A print from India is in his notes in Naturalists' Library, Volume 10, Mammalia, edited by Sir William Jardine. It is captioned "The Parent of the Modern Coach Dog.'' Another illustration, called "Dalmatian or Coach Dog,'' is patched and carries its tail curved over the back.

1847——"The difference between these two breeds (The Great Danish Dog called also the Dalmatian or Spotted Dog) consists principally in size, the Dalmatian being much smaller than the Danish. The body is generally white marked with small round black or reddish brown spots. The Dalmatian is said to be used in his native country for the chace, to be easily broken and stanch to his work. He has never been thus employed in England but is clearly distinguished by his fondness for horses and as being a frequent attendent on the carriages of the wealthy. To that office seems to be confined, for it rarely develops sufficient sense or sagacity to be useful in any of the ordinary offices of the dog.'' William Youatt, *The Dog*.

1862——"Although Yougoslavia is considered by the F.C.I. to have been the original home of the Dalmatian, the breed has been developed and cultivated chiefly in England. When the dog with the distinctive markings was first shown in England in 1862 it was said to have been used by the frontier guards of Dalmatia as a guard dog. But nothing is definitely known about its origin. The breed has become widely distributed over the continent of Europe since 1920. Its unusual markings were often mentioned by the old writers on cynology." Dr. Erich Schneider-Leyer, *De Hunde Der Welt* (1960), translated from the German by Dr. E. Fitch Daglish, *Dogs of the World* (1964).

1867——First edition of *Dogs of the British Islands*, a series of articles and letter reprinted from "Field" John Henry Walsh, "Stonehenge," mentions neither the Dalmatian or the Danish dog.

1872—— "I am at a loss when I try to trace the breed to its source. By French writers it is called "Le Braque de Bengale," and so Buffon named it. In 1556 a print was published at Cadiz of a recently-imported Indian dog, somewhat intermediate in shape between the Greyhound and the Southern Hound, light and strong in frame, deep in the chest, shorter in head than the Greyhound, with small, half-falling ears. This dog was white, and entirely covered with small black spots. It was conjectured that it belonged to a breed possessed by the Mohammedan princess of the west coast, and without much doubt it was the parent of our present—or past—Coach Dogs. These facts, and a figure of the imported dog, will be found in the tenth volume of the 'Naturalist's Library,' nearly word for word as I have quoted them." Rev. Thomas Pearce ("Idstone"), *The Dog*.

1879—— "The origin of the Dalmatian is quite as obscure as that of other breeds . . . I think it reasonable to assume that he is a native of Dalmatia, on the eastern shores of the Gulf of Venice. This does not militate against the idea suggested by the motto at the head of the chapter (A newe kind of dogge brought out of Fraunce, and they be speckled all over with white and black.—Dr. Caius), which I have taken from Caius, that we had the dog from France." Hugh Dalziel, *British Dogs*.

1882——Stonehenge (John Henry Walsh) under a chapter heading, "The Dalmatian and Danish Dogs," concludes his description of the Dalmatian with "he has been long employed in England to accompany our carriages as an ornamental appendage, but this fashion has of late years subsided. Hence he is commonly known as the 'Coach Dog' but in his native country is used as a pointer in the field, and is said to perform his duties well enough.

"The small Danish dog is smaller than the Dalmatian, but being spotted in the same way, and characterized by the same fondness for horses, they are generally confonded under the term 'Coach Dog'."

1883— " In many of his points he pretty closely resembles a large Bull Terrier, but in head he is more like the Pointer." Gordon Stables, *Our Friend the Dog*.

A typical Dalmatian from *The American Book of The Dog,* 1891. by "Coquina."

A comparison of the Dane and the Dal.

Painted metal garden ornament, 19th century. National Gallery of Art, Washington, DC.

26

1891——"The Dalmatian, or Coach Dog, came from the Province of Dalmatia, in the southern part of Austria, bordering on the northeast shore of the Adriatic Sea, and from this province it derives its name. It is known in France as the 'Braque de Bengale,' and is there supposed to be an Indian variety." Major T. J. Woodcock, *The American Book of the Dog* (Edited by G. O. Shields ("Coquina")).

1894——"There is little doubt that our modern 'coach dog' originally sprang from Dalmatia, a province in the southern part of Austria, hence his name, but from there he might have gone over to Spain, or perhaps, in the first instance some Spaniard might have sent him out to Dalmatia, where the enterprising inhabitants soon claimed him as their own. However, it does not matter much what country first gave him birth." Rawdon B. Lee, *A History and Description of the Modern Dogs of Great Britain and Ireland (Non-Sporting Division)*.

1897——"Records of the sixteenth century describe such a dog as belonging to Spain. The latest authentic trace is to Denmark, where it was used for drawing carts. Resembles the pointer in form." H. W. Huntington, *My Dog and I*.

1901——" . . . probably indigenous to Dalmatia, a province of Austria, but records of the XVI century describe such a dog as belonging to Spain. The latest authentic trace is to Denmark, where it is used for drawing carts. It very much resembles the pointer in form." H. W. Huntington, *The Show Dog*.

1903——"The origin of the Dalmatian is not quite as obscure as that of many other breeds. There appears to be no valid reason to reject the origin suggested by his name, and, with no arguments against it that bear investigation, and suggestions to the contrary appearing to be mere fancies unsupported by proof, it is reasonable to assume that he is a native of Dalmatia, on the eastern shores of the Gulf of Venice, where, we have been assured, by some of the older writers on dogs, this variety has been domesticated for at least two hundred years." C. H. Lane, *British Dogs* (Edited by W. D. Drury).

1904——"As to the dog's origin there seems to be no precise data or information, but there is little or no doubt that he comes from Dalmatia, on the eastern shores of the Gulf of Venice." Theo Marples, *Show Dogs*.

1904——"A good deal of uncertainty as to the origin shrouds the undoubted antiquity of the Dalmatian dog. It has had attached to it in different countries and at different times such irreconcilable localisation as the Danish dog and the Bengal Harrier! Buffon presumed it to be an offshoot of the French Matin, transported to the northern latitude of Denmark; Dalziel thinks it reasonable to assume its native home was Dalmatia, on the eastern shores of the Gulf of Venice . . . Having thus drawn the track of the Dalmatian across two continents, from Copenhagen to Calcutta, I leave the choice of allocating its place of nativity to the wisdom or fancy of the reader." Herbert Compton, *The Twentieth Century Dog (Non-Sporting)*.

1905——"It is more probable that this variety of dog originally came from Dalmatia in the south of Austria, though there is nothing, so far as our knowledge goes, in proof of this." Frank T. Barton, *Non-Sporting Dogs— Their Points and Management*.

1905——"It is passing strange how such a man as Buffon came to name the Dalmatian the Bengal Harrier, and Youatt was as bad when he lumped him in with the Great Dane—the Danish dog, as he was called at that time—as only differing in size. The Dalmatian is a dog of ancient lineage and with as straight a record as almost any dog. He was the hound that came from Dalmatia, and there is little reason to doubt that he was of the same class of hound that the pointer emanated from. Even to this day they have very much in common, in appearance, habits and disposition, and the Dalmatian is by no means a bad shooting dog, when any attention is paid to his training." James Watson, *The Dog Book*.

1907——"Of the antecedents of the Dalmatian it is extremely hard to speak with certainty . . . The earliest authorities agree that this breed was first introduced from Dalmatia, and it has been confidently asserted that he was brought into this country purely on account of his sporting proclivities." F. C. Hignett, *The New Book of the Dog* (Edited by Robert Leighton).

1907——"A great deal has been written on this old breed as to its native land, some writers claiming it a Danish dog, others going so far as to describe it as the Turkish breed. However, there is no question in my mind but that Dalmatia, on the eastern shores of the Gulf of Venice, was the native home of this sporty breed." D. C. Sands, Jr., Secretary of the Dalmatian Club of America, *Dogs* (Edited by G. A. Melbourne).

1907——"Very little is known of the origin of this dog or what country first gave him birth." H. Fred Lauer, *The Dalmatian or Coach Dog*.

1908——"The Dalmatian—formerly known as the Carriage Dog; vulgarly as the Plum Pudding Dog—is of very ancient lineage. Regarding the origin of the breed, Buffon considered it an off-shoot of the French Matin; Youatt connected it with the Great Dane. In the writer's opinion, the dog probably originated from the same class of hound as did the Pointer. The earliest writers, including Dalziel, almost unanimously hold that the breed was introduced from Dalmatia—hence the name." Hebe Wilson-Bedwell, *The Kennel Encyclopaedia* (Edited by J. Sidney Turner).

1927——"According to old records, his native country is Dalmatia, a mountainous district on the Adriatic coast. He has been domesticated in Italy for upwards of two centuries and is the common harrier of that country." Mrs. Fred Kemp, *Pedigreed Dogs as Recognized by The Kennel Club*.

28

1927——"Many places, far apart, have been the supposed native land of the 'Dalmatian', 'Carriage Dog' or 'Plum Pudding Dog,' but Dalmatia is the country which most writers claim to be the correct one . . . It is a curious fact that no information can be gathered from the people of Dalmatia as to the origin of the dog in their country." Franklin J. Willock, *The Dalmatian*.

1927——"That the Dalmatian is an Italian breed we find supported in later times. During the stormy period of Cromwell's power, when anti-Roman Catholicism was rampant, many illustrated leaflets, often extremely vulgar, show Roman Catholicism depicted in the shape of a Dalmatian dog of the very same type as such dogs are today." Edward C. Ash, *Dogs: Their History and Development*.

1931——"Originally a product of Dalmatia, the breed was first introduced to these shores on account of their sporting proclivities, as they were capable of doing a good day's work in the field; although we find they at all periods prefer feathered to ground game, and though taking little notice of hares, would be happy working with the sportsman when pheasants and partridges were about." Arthur Craven, *Dogs of the World*.

1931——"The name, appearance and original vocation of Dalmatians have given play to various witticisms, some calling them Damnation Dogs, Carriage Dogs, Spotted or Plum-pudding Dogs. Attempts have been made, without being convincing, to divorce them from their association with Dalmatia, the pre-War province of Austria bordering the eastern side of the Adriatic. One writer in 1843 endeavoured to show their connection with the Bengal Harrier, whatever that was . . . In the absence of any better evidence I think we are safe in assuming that the breed did come from Dalmatia or neighbouring regions, and that it was used there and in Italy to do the work of pointers." A. Croxton Smith, *About Our Dogs, The Breeds and Their Management*.

1931——"Its origin is uncertain. It probably came from Italy. It is very unlikely that it originated from Dalmatia. Travellers who visited Dalmatia make no mention of any such dog. In 1253 a Dutch traveller visited the country and describes, amongst other things, the dogs he saw there as large, powerful dogs, that pulled carts, and were used by the sportsmen to face bulls and bait lions. It is certain that if white dogs covered with spots existed in the country they would have been mentioned and described, for the Dalmatian is not a dog that can be passed without notice. Later works, giving the experience of travellers and describing the country, the people, and the natural history, make no mention of such a breed of dogs." Edward C. Ash, *The Practical Dog Book*.

1932——"While it is generally conceded that the Dalmatian originated in Dalmatia—a rugged, mountainous 5,000 square mile part of Yugo-slavia on the Adriatic coast—from the following varied accounts of the writers accepted as the authorities of the seventeenth and eighteenth centuries it will be seen that the evidence in support of this supposition is neither based on definite facts nor is it in any way so conclusive as to establish the matter beyond doubt.

"What little data there is available is tantalisingly conflicting and in some cases is obviously mere conjecture on the part of the authors. The 'lifting of copy' being as rife then as it is today, it is not surprising to find that they stole each others opinions or 'facts' without crediting the source, and expressed them with enthusiasm and embellishments as their own. In this way any early sign-post which may, in the light of latter-day investigations, have pointed the right direction has been lost.

"Even so, it is upon such writings that the declared origin of many of our present-day breeds is founded, for the investigator who endeavours to trace their ancestry beyond 150 years or so soon finds himself enveloped in a veritable sea of confliction and lost in a cloud of obscurity.'' James Saunders, *The Dalmatian and All About It*.

1933——"No one seems to know when the breed began. There was once a story that he was part tiger and came from Bengal. That was a pretty idea but a poor invention. Far more plausible was the idea that he lived in Denmark and worked for the peasants as a draught-dog, but that theory has not much value, the dog used in Denmark being the harlequin Great Dane, which, being also spotted, no doubt was confused with the Dalmatian. Then, of course, we have the story that he came from Spain. Perhaps he did come that way sometimes with cargoes of brandy or wine, or precious metals. The only thing we know is that he has always been called the Dalmatian and he probably came direct from that part of Southern Europe. Possibly wandering gipsies brought him, as he seems to have been almost as valuable as a dancing bear in the way of amusing the squires and yokels of Britain and extracting gifts from the people who had money to give away. Once the gipsies, who roved all over Europe, learned that there was a trade to be done in these dogs, there would be a supply to meet the demand, and we know that even to-day there is a trade in horses carried on by gipsy tribes in parts of Europe and Asia.

"The curious thing is that the Dalmatian, so far as we know, is not the common dog of any country, so we have no evidence of that kind as to his place of origin.'' Rowland Johns, *Our Friend The Dalmatian*.

1934——"The origin of the Dalmatian is very uncertain; but there is one fact which stands out clearly. The breed has been known in England for over two hundred years at least. At the second recognized dog show held in this country, in 1860, only five breeds were scheduled. One of these was the Dalmatian. This is their first authentic appearance as a show dog.

"As far back as 1790, however, Dalmatians were mentioned in contemporary literature, and they also figured in early heraldry. One theory suggests that they originated in Dalmatia and were imported into this country during the eighteenth and nineteenth centuries by the gentlemen of the period who were making the 'Grand Tour.' They found them useful as guards as well as being ornamental. If this is their true origin it is curious that no trace of them remains in Italy. Another suggestion is that they were used as gun-dogs in Spain, but there seems little corroboration of this theory.'' Walter Hutchinson, *Hutchinson's Dog Encyclopedia*.

1935——''It is fair to imagine that the first of the distinctly spotted dogs came from Dalmatia, a country situated along the eastern Adriatic Coast, Europe.'' Freeman Lloyd, *Dog Breeds of the World*, American Kennel Gazette, March 1, 1935.

1935——''Nor can I understand the why and wherefore of this handsome dog's name, for when I was in Bosnia I made inquiries of natives, familiar with Dalmatia, and none seemed to have heard of the dogs in question, being indigenous to, or inhabiting, that country.'' Harding Cox, *Dogs of Today*.

1940——''The Pointer, who is the dog most like him and probably related to him, is a product of Spain, which is a great way from Dalmatia, and his traditional masters the Gypsies, know no homeland.'' Arthur Roland, *The Story of Pedigreed Dogs*.

1942——''The Dalmatian is truly a dog of mystery. Not only is its origin completely unknown, but even its birthplace is in dispute. Part of this confusion as to the original home of the breed may be due to the fact that the Dalmatian has been a favorite with gypsies. A wanderer like its Romany masters, it has been seen and known in various localities, but not located in any particular place. It is said that the breed originated in Dalmatia, a province of Austria on the eastern shore of the Adriatic. There is, however, no definite proof of this.'' Edwin Megargee, *DOGS*.

1945——''apparently indigenous to Dalmatia but not found there in any substantial strength . . . in fact quite a different type to the Dalmatians of Britain and the USA . . . originally used as a gun dog in the Balkans and Italy, then as a guard against highwaymen in France about the middle of the seventeenth century, and introduced from there into England at the end of the eighteenth century.'' Clifford L. B. Hubbard (''Canis''), *The Observer's Book of Dogs*.

1945——''This is another dog of questionable origin. He is considered to be indigenous to Dalmatia, but the breed was frequently found in the company of gypsies who roamed the Balkans.'' Felice Worden, *The Sketch Book of Dogs*.

1947——''The plum-pudding dog, Bengal harrier, Dalmatian, or as it is better known perhaps, 'the carriage dog,' is an old variety. Its name, 'Dalmatian,' is a mystery . . . there is considerable evidence that the

Dalmatian was an Italian variety.'' Denlinger, *The Complete Dalmatian.*

1948——''That they are a very old breed is beyond question . . . It is usually assumed that these dogs came from the country after which they are named, on the eastern shores of the Adriatic and in Italy they have been used for doing the work of pointers.'' Sigma, *The Book of the Dog*, (Edited by Brian Vesey-Fitzgerald).

1948——''The origin of the breed is obscure, as is its early history. Early references to the Dalmatian suggest it was a type somewhere between the Pointer and the so-called Lesser Danish Dog; Buffon described a spotted dog of similar size but called it the ''Bengal Harrier'' (Which was quite a safe title in the days when knowledge of dogs was so scant). Taplin considered it a relation of the Great Dane. From the author's researches, however, the Dalmatian appears to be a descendant of the Istrian Pointer which may at some past date have had a little Great Dane blood introduced to give depth of muzzle and tone to the colour; the Istrian Pointer is remarkably like the Dalmatian except that the markings are not in uniform spots nor so dark in color. It is well known that the Dalmatian was used as a gun-dog in Italy, Austria and other countries which dabbled in the affairs of Dalmatia, and not until about 1665 does any evidence appear of it being used in its now traditional role of coach dog.'' Clifford L. B. Hubbard, *Dogs in Britain.*

1957——''The origin of the Dalmatian is still obscure despite very many attempts at research into his early history. Practically all the early writers on dogs were completely confounded when dealing with this breed while the majority cribbed from each other and got into deeper messes by coining new names for the breed in support of their theories. A lot of trouble has resulted from these old names for the breed especially as they were for the most part names like Bengal Foxhound, Great Danish Dog, Lesser Danish Dog, Bengal Harrier, Spotted Dog of Holland, and so on . . . The The 'Old English Hound' is yet another breed mentioned as ancestor (the claim that Dalmatians were used to hunt in packs has been given us support for this). However, summing up I feel we are on quite the safest ground for the time being (for there is still much to learn of this breed) if we regard the basic stock from which the Dalmatian is descended as the Istrian Pointer (Istrianer Braque), himself carrying the blood of mid-European Pointers, and the old small type of Harlequin Great Dane.'' Clifford L. B. Hubbard, *The Dalmatian Handbook.*

1957——''There is no official record for the first introduction of the breed.'' Brian Vesey-Fitzgerald, *The Domestic Dog: An Introduction to its History.*

1958——''The early history of the Dalmatian has been traced, and closely linked to the gypsies of central Europe. As far as they wandered so did their dogs.

"The most likely site of origin of the breed was probably the small province of Austria known as Dalmatia, and the breed has been known as a Dalmatian for at least 200 years." Evelyn Miller, *Dalmatians as Pets*.

1958—"No compelling evidence proves that the Dalmatian coast was his first home, nor can any other region boast his birthplace . . .

"Some authorities think he sprang from spotted dogs of ancient India. Others say Egypt of the Pharaohs, Italy or what is today Yugoslavia. All admit the mystery surrounding his name. Perhaps easiest to believe is the idea that he first showed his telltale spots among bands of gypsies roving the Balkans." *Man's Best Friend* - National Geographic Society.

1959—"The spotted 'coach dog' has been a close companion of men and horses as far back as our historical records go . . . Ancient Egyptian paintings show a dog with a white coat and the distinctive black spots following a chariot, and during the centuries when man traveled by coach the Dalmatian is found running along with the carriage, usually trotting under the front or rear axle or between the horses.

"The Dalmatian was an early favorite with wandering Gypsy bands, who spread the breed throughout Europe. He received his name from the province of Dalmatia in Austria, where he was once bred on a large scale and where the breed was standardized to the present size and coloring." Arthur Liebers, *How to Raise and train a Dalmatian*.

1960—"Although Yugoslavia is considered by the F.C.I. to have been the original home of the Dalmatian, the breed has been developed and cultivated chiefly in England. When the dog with the distinctive spotted markings was first shown in England in 1862 it was said to have been used by the frontier guards of Dalmatia as a guard dog. But nothing is definitely known about its origin."Dr. Erich Schneider-Leyer, *De Hunde Der Welt* (Translated from the German by Dr. E. Fitch Daglish in 1964 as *Dogs of the World*). There is a footnote by Dr. Daglish, "The first Dalmatian club ever to be formed was the English club in 1890; in the same year this club published the Standard on which that of every other country is based."

1961—"The origin of the Dalmatian is shrouded in mystery. He has been traced back hundreds of years, but no particular country or place can be pinpointed as the site of his genesis." Evelyn S. Nelson, *Pet Dalmatian*.

1962—"The actual place or country of their origin is wrapped in mystery. It would seem that the most probable explanation is that several countries and perhaps as many distinct types of dogs have contributed in the past to their make-up." Catherine Gore, *Dalmatians*.

1963—"There are almost as many marks of interrogation in the history of Dalmatians as there are spots on the dog's body. The one thing that appears to be clear is that the breed has no definite connection with Dalmatia, although there may be a link with Italy.

"The suggestion that the Dalmatian may be of Italian origin rests largely on a painting of two typical Dalmatian heads by one of the Castiglione family and the fact that under Cromwell's regime in this country, the breed appears to have been a symbol of popery. The latter fact, however, does make it plain that these spotted dogs were known in this country in the seventeenth century." S. M. Lampson, *The Country Life Book of Dogs*.

1964——"... an ancient breed and we do not know its original home. Unlike so many modern breeds it is in no way man-made. It has come down to us as a heritage from the past, an original breed with its elegant shape and spectacular markings as curious and striking in their way as the stripes on the zebra.

"Many and varied theories about the origin of Dalmatians have been put forward but . . . little reliable evidence exists for any of them . . . This dog may have survived almost unchanged from the dawn of history." Eleanor Frankling, *The Popular Dalmatian*. (Revised and reprinted in 1969 as *The Dalmatian* with the 1964 history repeated.)

1968——"Dogs of the pointer type are of very ancient lineage. Today they are distributed throughout mountain areas between northern India and western Europe. Such are the dogs of the gypsy caravans and the Dalmatians—one distinctive breed of pointer—supposed to have been brought with the gypsies from India to Dalmatia, whence they reached Britain in the eighteenth century. Richard and Alice Fiennes, *The Natural History of Dogs*.

1970——"It may be that when the gypsies of India migrated to Europe, they took the animal from place to place, roving over the Balkans and settling temporarily in Dalmatia, a province of Austria. The gypsies made numerous uses of the breed, with bird hunting its main occupation." Beth Brown, *Dogs that Work for a Living*.

1971——"The most likely theory about the origins of the Dalmatian we know today seems to be that the breed was developed as a mid-European hunting dog. The name would seem to imply that they came from Dalmatia, now part of Yugoslavia; there is little evidence to support this, but we do know that a spotted dog very much resembling the Dalmatian has been widely distributed throughout Europe for the last four hundred years or more." Betty Clay, *The World Encyclopedia of Dogs*.

1971——"The Dalmatian, as the name implies, comes from Dalmatia, on the Adriatic coast. Even so, it is a breed which flowered in Great Britain in those now far-away times when the English aristocracy was expected to indulge in bizarre eccentricities.

"It is believed that specimens were brought back during the grand tours of Europe which were then a feature of the lives of upper-class Englishmen. They soon put the dog to work: it was to adorn their stately processions by

horse and carriage. This the Dalmatian did by trotting with the entourage.''
Maxwell Riddle, *The International Encyclopedia of Dogs*.

1973——"Many authors have written about the origins of this dog but very few are in agreement. His name should indicate his origin but this is not the case. The breed appears to be quite ancient, since the friezes discovered in Greece and the Middle East dating back to remote periods show dogs similar in lines and coat to the present Dalmatian.

"Some authorities think that he came from Denmark, a theory supported by the fact that he is called Dane in some countries. He is quite prevalent today in Denmark. Buffon believes that he is descended from the Mastiff which after having passed from England to Denmark and then to warmer climates, presumably produced the Turkish Dog. Besides these theories there are many others, all different, all somehow plausible, but none certain, while Angliola Denti di Pirajno, a well-known expert on the breed states: 'The hypothesis which seems to rest on the most solid base indicates that the Dalmatian has an Eastern origin.' '' Fiorenze Fiorone, *The Encyclopedia of Dogs*.

1973——"Despite his name, no trace of him has been found in Dalmatia. He is a dog of very ancient origins. One finds him represented on ancient Egyptian bas-reliefs and on Greek friezes. He was not classified as a breed, however, until the eighteenth century when a very similar but now extinct breed, the Bengal gundog was recognized in England.'' Gino Pugnetti, *The Great Book of Dogs*.

1977——"The breed is quite an ancient one, and it has been suggested that it was originally a guard dog, and even a war dog in Dalmatia or Croatia, though there is a possibility that here it was being confused with the spotted German Mastiff known at one time as the Tiger Dog, which was a hunting and fighting dog . . In Dalmatia where these dogs are said to have originated they were probably a small version of the spotted or harlequin Great Dane, and probably these were later crossed with Pointers to reduce the size and improve the markings.'' Harry Glover (Compiler and Editor). *A Standard Guide to Pure-bred Dogs*.

1977——"I myself come from Cartat in Dalmatia. My family, and in particular my step-father, Mr. Banac, a shipowner, were often asked about Dalmatians by visiting English friends. None of us knew of the origins of Dalmatian dogs. We then introduced Dalmatians to Dalmatia in the early thirties, Dr. Frankling has referred to this in her book.

"There are dogs in our part of the world to some extent similar, short haired pointers you could call them, occasionally with well defined black spots on a gray ground, not what one might call convincing evidence of the Balkan origin of Dalmatians.'' Vane Ivanovic, *Spots of News*, British Dalmatian Club.

At seven months of age, Coachman's Courbette and Coachman's Croupade wait patiently for Bill Fetner to harness the horse before going for a coaching drive. The wheels of the Brewster gig are approximately four feet in diameter.

Mrs. Lloyd Reeves and the late Mr. Reeves out for the morning ride accompanied by some of the Rabbit Run dogs.

3

The Coaching Dalmatian

THE DALMATIAN has had the knack of improving without changing. While he has lost the opportunity and joy of running with the carriage, the coach and four, the tally-ho and the fire engines, he still has the desire. He is still built to run hard for long distances. He may be the only true coach dog. At any rate he is the only dog that was traditionally bred and trained to run with the horse-drawn vehicles. When he has the chance he is still delighted to go with the horses. He may hock with a mounted horse, lead or follow a vehicle, or run under an axle. Historically, he is under the front axle, the closer to the horses' heels, the better.

Coaching has been the Dal's accepted role for more than three hundred years. In his *Dogs in Britain* (1948) Clifford Hubbard says, "Not until about 1665 does any evidence appear of it being used in its now traditional role of coach-dog. By 1670 it was certainly used in France as an accessory to travel by coach, and was invaluable as a guard against highwaymen."

That the Dalmatian considers guarding his owner's property part of the job of coaching is made clear in Major T. J. Woodcock's article in 1891. "A good Coach Dog has often saved his owner much valuable property by watching the carriage. It is a trick of thieves who work in pairs for one to engage the coachman in conversation while the other sneaks around in the rear and steals whatever robes and other valuables he can lay his hands on. I never lost an article while the dogs were in charge, but was continually losing when the coachman was in charge."

Woodcock also tells us, "In training for the carriage, it is usually found necessary to tie a young dog in proper position, under the fore axles, for seven or eight drives before he will go as required. Some bright puppies, however, require little or no training, especially if they can be allowed to run with an old dog that is already trained."

A research team from Harvard University in 1940 found that the tendency to run under a vehicle or to follow a horse was inherited but that it differed from dog to dog as to the exact position preferred if the dog had a choice. In their study of inheritance of position preference in coach dogs, Clyde E. Keeler and Harry C. Trimble worked with a large kennel of Dalmatians which for more than 25 years had trained Dals to follow horses and run under carriages. They reported, "This training usually began shortly after the dogs were six months old. In the beginning a pup would be taken out with its collar fastened to that of a trained dog and the pair led behind the carriage at gradually increased rates of speed. In most instances the leash could be omitted in a short time and the neophytes then were permitted to seek the particular position which suited them best. It has been observed throughout this long period that dogs did have individual preferences for particular positions and that they always sought those same places.

"Dogs of the Dalmatian breed have definite differences with respect to the eagerness with which they follow horses and carriages. Since approximately 70 per cent of the animals tested chose those positions which entitled them to be rated as 'good' coaching dogs, it is evident that this trait is well intrenched in the breed.

"Two of the dogs in the colony which were classed as failures from the coaching standpoint were also described as 'man-shy.' This description suggests the possibility of some relationship between natural timidity and poor coaching ability."

The study reached three conclusions. First, Dalmatian dogs trained for running beneath carriages have individual preferences for distance behind the horses. Second, something connected with these preferences appears to be inherited. Third, it is possible that "bad" coach following may be an expression of general timidity. The last may be one of the reasons shyness is considered a major fault in the Dalmatian standard.

In *"Teaching a Dalmatian to 'Coach' "*, an article in *Country Life in America* (1911), Eleanor Walton Yates quotes a DCA member who has driven with Dalmatians both here and in England. He says, "I find the most practical as well as the best English custom is for the dog or dogs to run directly under the front axle near the horses, but always clear of the horses' heels. Running between two horses and under the pole, the dog takes many chances and does not look as well as under the axle, when the trap is high enough to allow it. The dog must follow the pace of the horse and stick there. He must stay under until his master or the groom alights, unless he is trained to jump in the trap and keep watch over the robes, whip, etc."

The article continues, "Mr. J. Sergeant Price, the pioneer of the Dalmatian interest in this country, gives about the same version, and he has used these dogs under single, double, and four-in-hand traps.

"In judging, dogs are allowed 75 points for ability to keep with the trap, 25 points counting toward their trueness to standard.

"Running underneath the vehicle, or 'coaching' as it is called, seems to be a characteristic formed by heredity in a Dalmatian, as most of them take to this place themselves. Even puppies when only a few months old will go under the trap with little training, and being kept with the horses all the time and going with the team, will soon find their way up behind the horses' heels where one would think it impossible that the horses would not strike them on the head with their hoof every step they take. They delight to go fast—the faster the pace the better they seem to enjoy it. While most Dalmatians take to coaching themselves, others are like black sheep in a flock and will never learn."

One of the rules compiled by the DCA Road Trial Committee of 1912 stated, "That a four-wheel, one-horse trap should be used, and that the dog should travel with her shoulders under the front axle." This was an interesting development since pictures of the results of 1910 and 1911 road trials show Dalmatians running under a two-horse single axle trap.

At the close of World War II people were anxious to resume their normal activities and these included dog shows. However, the clubs which sponsored the shows were not all ready to rush into the business of giving shows and so there were not quite as many for the first several years of peace. They were hard to get to, many people having disposed of their automobiles, and it was an expensive hobby just at first, comparatively speaking.

Some Dal fanciers wanted to get back in the swim of competition and so revived the Road Trials which had been held in the past using driving horses and vehicles for the dogs to coach with. Now the trials were planned without vehicles.

Mrs. Alfred Barrett and Mr. and Mrs. Lloyd Reeves revived the sport in the New England area. Mr. Reeves rewrote the road trial rules to be used on horse-back instead of in a riding vehicle and the trials were held.

Mr. and Mrs. Meistrell held a Road Trial on Long Island. While both trials seemed to be most successful they were not continued probably because of the great expense. Conditioning of the dogs and horses was time consuming and expensive for the exhibitor who either had to hire a horse at hourly rates for training and on the day of the show or transport his own mount to the show site and condition both horse and dog for the trial.

Participants of a Dalmatian Road trial held in the late
1940's after World War II at Rice Farms, Huntington, L.I.

Roadcoach Frou Frou CD, owned by Wendell
Sammet, winner of a Dalmatian road trial.

In order to have a successful trial the judges and the stewards needed two horses each since they were riding thirty miles in following the exhibitors and moving along at a brisk pace most of the way.

At the trial on Long Island, held at Rice Farms in Huntington, the course was ten miles, circular, starting and finishing at Rice Farms polo field. The foot judge checked dogs at the start and finish, a mounted judge and steward rode along with each entrant. These last two alternated so that the horses could be rested in between.

Along the course were signs marked with the pace at which the rider was to go. The requirements included walk, trot, canter, hard gallop, with the dogs off lead, at the horses' heels throughout. The course went through sections of wood, high grass, open fields, across a main highway, (a sit-stay was ordered before crossing the road) past a farm yard with chickens, cows, goats, and a noisy but unaggressive farm dog. The course started on the polo field and ended there with a hand gallop past the foot judge, the dog still heeling.

The cost of the horses, the rental of a van to transport the horses, various and sundry other expenses were borne by the Great Neck Dog Training Center. No entry fee was charged at this trial as it was an experiment.

Many people today talk about reviving road trials. Mrs. Barrett points out that it is almost impossible to find an area for this activity which doesn't cross many roads and which, then, would require numerous stewards to watch for the normal automobile traffic on these roads and so direct the dogs and riders. The cost becomes prohibitive. Anyone wishing to try these trials can get all sorts of advice from Mrs. Barrett and Mrs. Meistrell, both well-experienced in riding and in Dalmatians.

The Road Trials in New England following the war were conducted along lines which had been set before the outbreak of hostilities. These road trials were designed to award points and a Road Trial Championship of Record would be awarded to a dog which acquired 10 points. The championship stakes would count whether the stakes were open or member stakes.

The distance of the trials was set for:

1 day	15 mile puppy trial
2 day	25 mile derby trial (25 miles each day)
3 day	25 mile all age trial (25 miles each day)

There were two judges on foot and one mounted judge. The mounted judge started riding with the first handler. Handlers were staggered at 10 minute intervals. The mounted judge rode for about ten minutes with each handler. The foot judges were posted at the most difficult sections on the trial so they could observe the dogs under the hardest working conditions. When the last dog passed the unmounted judges they were picked up by automobile and taken ahead to another point of the trail where the first handler was about to pass.

Much of the outline of the road trial rules was based on foxhound trials and information was available from a prominent MFH in the area.

The trials were run in Dover, MA, one time but abandoned because of the obvious disadvantages outlined before.

We can always hope that some brave soul will revive the road trials and manage to overcome the obstacles of space, traffic, and expense.

Painting of Mrs. Paul Moore by Franklin Voss.

4

The Firehouse Dog

IT WAS EASY for the Dalmatian to earn the nickname, "Firehouse Dog." He moved into the firehouses with the horses. Coach dogs readily became Firehouse dogs in America as the man-drawn volunteer fire brigade pumpers and hose carts became horse-drawn. The breed's built-in love for horses made it a natural. While other breeds and other animals also became firemen's pets and mascots, the more colorful spotted dogs which ran ahead to clear the way became traditional features of city life.

This was particularly true in New York City where Captain Joseph C. Donovan was a Dalmatian breeder and delighted in furnishing a pup to a new fire-station or one without a mascot. On at least one occasion a New York firefighter showed a winning Dalmatian at Madison Square Garden. This was Bessie of Engine Company No. 39 at the 1910 Westminster Kennel Club show. She was particularly fond of Lieutenant Wise who called her a natural born mascot. He said, "By instinct she would run ahead of the horses whooping it up and getting people out of the way for us."

Kate Sanborn, who interviewed Wise in 1916 for her book, *Educated Dogs of Today,* seemed to think Bessie knew what her boss was talking about as she got up and put her head near his hand. Both of them had been transferred to Murray Hill, Flushing soon after the mechanization of Engine Company No. 39.

"She knows I'm talking about her," Wise said. "If I died suddenly she would be in an awful fix. She'd keep looking for me. When we were at headquarters with three fine horses and plenty of work, she always followed

43

Answering the alarm!

Mike of New York Fire Company No. 8 with his travelling check and trophy.

me home on my day off. I was living up in the Bronx then and of course had to ride. Bessie would not stay in the engine house but would run after the car I had taken. Finally I got a street-car pass for her and I guess she is about the only dog in this city that could hop on and off a car without causing trouble with the conductor. Her fire department badge, a little brass helmet swinging from her collar and her pass from the Street Railway Company made her safe. She knew the right corner as well as I did and traveled the line alone if by any chance she missed me. Her son Mike has the pass now.

"I'm afraid she is the last of the mascots. The companies that have been motorized find their dogs will not run ahead of the gasoline engines and trucks. They miss the horses and I guess are afraid of the machine.

"Bessie would always follow me into a burning building in the old days and stay one floor below the fighting line, as the rule required. We had to establish that rule for fear a dog might cause a man to stumble if retreat was ordered. Bessie, I think, knew as much about the risks we ran as we did, but she stuck to the rules and always waited a floor below the men handling the nozzles."

Bessie's career had been doomed for a long time. When the first motor cars appeared on the roads in 1892 there was a cloud on the occupational future of the coach dog and the horse. Kate Sanborn reported, "For five and a half long years Bessie cleared the crossing at Third Avenue and Sixty-seventh Street for her company, barking a warning to surface-car motormen, truck drivers, and pedestrians, and during all that time she led the way in every one of the average of forty runs a month made by No. 39. Then like a bolt from the sky the three white horses she loved were taken away, even the stalls were removed, and the next alarm found her bounding in front of a man-made thing that had no intelligence——a gasoline-driven engine. Bessie ran as far as Third Avenue, tucked her tail between her legs and returned to the engine house. Her heart was broken. She never ran to another fire."

At the time Bessie was shown at the Garden the Westminster Kennel Club offered a special class for Dalmatians, dogs and bitches, owned by members of the New York Fire Department. The results of the show indicate that first place was won by Mike, owned by Mr. Dan M. Lynx, breeder-owner. Bess, owned by Lieutenant Wise, was second. Smoke II, owned by Hook & Ladder No. 68, came in third and another Bess, owned by Mr. Pierre A. Debaun was reserve.

As firefighting equipment became mechanized in the early 1900's many Dalmatians adapted to a less strenuous but still exciting role of riding to the scene of a fire on the equipment or stayed on guard at the station.

Today his modest role as mascot to firefighters continues. Occasional news reports from many parts of the United States feature some aspect of the Dalmatian linked with the firehouse. And Sparky, the Dalmatian wearing a fireman's helmet, is the usual symbol of fire prevention week. He is well known to almost all school children in this country as he is found on posters, in coloring books, and makes visits to schools with local fire departments in the interest of fire prevention.

Old fashioned horse-drawn fire engine pumper escorted by Dalmatian. Sketch by Harold Bruel, courtesy *The Chronicle of the Horse.*

No picture of Mount Vernon is complete without dogs.

5

The Dalmatian Comes to America

Wʜɪʟᴇ ᴡᴇ ʜᴀᴠᴇ ɴᴏ ᴋɴᴏᴡʟᴇᴅɢᴇ of the earliest date a Dal was brought to this country we do know George Washington bred coach dogs. We located two items which indicate this.

First, in a letter to his nephew, George Augustine Washington, August 12, 1787, George Washington wrote, "At your aunt's request, a coach dog has been purchased and sent for the convenience and benefit of Madame Moose: her amorous fits should theretofore be attended to, that the end for which he is sent may not be defeated by her acceptance of the services of any other dog." The original letter is in the Library of Congress collection.

Second, the Alderman Library at the University of Virginia has Washington's *Ledger B*. In it on August 14, 1787 he notes the amount he paid for the coach dog——15 shillings. Apparently the purchase was made in Philadelphia and charged to his cash account. Unfortunately he did not note the name of the dog's original owner.

According to the *Oxford Dictionary of the English Language,* no one used the term "Dalmatian" until 1824. We know this is in error as we found the first edition of Bewick published in 1790 uses the term "Dalmatian" and shows a picture of a Dal.

In more recent times than our first president, we find that the first Dalmatian to be registered by the American Kennel Club was known as "Bessie," 10519; whelped October, 1887; owned by Mrs. N. L. Harvey, San Francisco, CA., recorded as white, black and tan; breeder and pedigree unknown.

they shall go by the first conveyance that offers
as they are already purchased agreeably to Ma:
thews directions. — The hinges you will receive
in a bundle with the wimble bit agreeably to your
Aunts request in a former letter. — If the wimble
bit (which is a complete one) is given to Mathew
take a mem°. of the number and quality of the
pieces & make him sign it for I have suspicions
that many of my tools are converted after a
while to the uses of themselves & called their own

At your Aunt's request a Coach Dog.
has been purchased and sent for the conveni=
ence, & benefit of Madame Moose; her amo:
rous fits should therefore be attended to, that the
end for which he is sent may not be defeated
by her acceptance of the ~~~~~~~~~ services of any
other dog. —

With respect to the money which has
been called for by the Directors of the Potomk.
Company, the treasurer must wait till I return,
and this cannot be considered as any great
indulgence, as I have always been punctual
hitherto in my payments. — As I did not advise
to the annual meeting of the Comp y. myself &
did not receive your intimation of it till it
was too late I could not appoint a substitute
in time & must for these reasons be excused. —

If Fairfax does not chuse to stay on
his present lay, he must go — I like him very
well, but I do not chuse to give away my sub=
stance to Overlookers; who I am sure cannot
make so much in any other way. — He cannot I
should think have forgot, that his wages were
only £30 a year & that it was my own act
to add ten pounds more, long after the Bargain
was made, merely on acc t. of the trouble he w d.
have with the fishery. —

If M r. Lund Washington wants Dow's
money, he must have it, but really I see no more
than the man in the Moon where I am to get money
to pay my Taxes &c a. &c a. &c a. if I have made
no Crop, & shall have to buy Corn for my people.

You must endeavour to get stuff for
the Venitian blinds — one ready made goes by
the

We also know that after the time of General Washington the Dalmatian or coach dog didn't disappear from the face of America. In Alistair Cook's great book, *AMERICA,* can be found a picture of Southern slaves and bales of cotton they have picked. Lying at their feet is a dog which is definitely a Dalmatian. The general use of cameras seems to have developed about the time of the Civil War.

And writing of Strawberry Mansion, the stately white house which stands above the Schuykill River in Philadelphia, Joan Church Roberts, in an article in Architectural Digest, traces the history and development of the house. The established date of its beginnings is 1797–98 when the central portion of the house was named Summerville. It was built by a brilliant Quaker lawyer, Judge William Lewis. Judge Lewis lived in the home until his death in 1819.

In 1821 the property was sold at a sheriff's sale and was purchased by Joseph Hemphill, also a lawyer. Mr. Hemphill had two sons, Alexander and Coleman. The Hemphill family lived there for about ten years and it would seem lived extremely well. Coleman Hemphill "built a race track, raised Dalmatian dogs, and grew strawberries from "roots imported from Chile." Coleman had very little interest in business pursuits as in 1831 his father, in partnership with William Ellis Tucker, was involved in a china factory in Philadelphia where they produced Tuckerware, and he refused to become interested in the business. There is a story to the effect that Coleman brought his Dalmatians into the showrooms at 17th and Chestnut Sts., turned them loose, and the dogs had a field day romping about. They managed not to leave a single unbroken complete set of china.

Few people today would know the name of Alfred Maclay yet he was the first president of the Dalmatian Club of America. Harry T. Peters, father of the well-known and popular multi-group judge, Harry Peters of New York, was the first vice president. J. Sergeant Price, Jr., was the secretary-treasurer. Mr. Price remained a member of DCA until his death.

The original group of enthusiastic breeders started meeting in 1904 and organized the club in 1905. There were twenty-six members in the Club's roster including Howard Willets, Joseph B. Thomas, Jr., Mrs. C. F. Denee, Percy Drury, H. Fred Lauer, Dr. Henry Jarrett, and Miss Rachel Holmes. H. Fred Lauer is remembered for having written the first book about the breed in the United States. Copies of this original book (really a pamphlet by today's standards) are quite rare and exceedingly valuable on the antique book market.

In 1913 a young lady, Miss Flora McDonald, joined the club. Mr. Peters had moved up to president; Arthur Whitney, of the Rocksiticus Kennels was vice president and Theodore Crane was secretary-treasurer. Mr. Maclay was the delegate to AKC. Mr. Crane retired from the office of secretary-treasurer

Ch. Windholme's Market Rose, painting by G. Muss Arnolt, 1915, owned by Harry T. Peters. From the American Kennel Club collection.

The Dalmatian painted by Edwin Megargee 1942.

in 1915 and Miss McDonald was named to the post, a job she held until her death in January 1967. Miss McDonald later became Mrs. Leonard W. Bonney.

Another name change took place among the early members. Miss Holmes became Mrs. Fay Ingalls, which name is probably remembered by some of the people now active.

Early kennel names which appear in extended pedigrees of most of the dogs being shown at the present time include Gladmore (Mr. Franklin J. Willock); Head of the River (Mrs. Sanger); Tally Ho (Mrs. Bonney); Borrodale (Mrs. Gladding); Cress Brook (A. E. Bonner); Four-in-Hand and Le Mel (Leo Meeker); Tattoo (Mrs. Paula Orr, later Mrs. Hohmiller); Rabbit Run (Mrs. Reeves); Sarum, (Mrs. Maurice Firuski); Lorbryndale (Byron); Walls, (Mrs. Evelyn Wall); Strathglass (Hugh Chisholm); Stock-Dale (Sidney C. Stockdale); Whitlee, (Jean Whiting Verre); Hackney Way (Dr. & Mrs. Zane Feller); Whiteside Sioux (Mrs. Wilbur Dewell); and Regal.

In the late 1930's we find Roadcoach, (Mary P. Barrett); Tomalyn Hill (Evelyn Nelson White); Gren (Mrs. Wiseman); Reigate (George and Mary Leigh Lane, and Mrs. Close); Williamsview (William Hibbler); Kingcrest (Dr. & Mrs. George King); Sitts-In (Rudolph L. Sittinger); Dal Quest (Marjorie Van der Veer); and Green Starr (Dr. & Mrs. David Doane).

World War II placed a damper on dog activities for obvious reasons. Many shows were cancelled during the war and many of the great Dals were sent off to do their duty in the wartime effort. In the late forties another group of people came into the picture. We were introduced to Quaker's Acre, Ard Aven, Coachman, Colonial Coach, Pryor Creek, Dalmatia, Williamsdale, Dal Duchy, Rovingdale, Oz-Dal, and Brain-Tree. Many of the older kennels dropped out of sight while still others continued to breed and show. In the Valley Kennels became a well-known name. When Mrs. Ratner (then Sue Allman) purchased a fine dog from Roadcoach Kennels breed history was made. The dog was named Roadcoach Roadster. He was campaigned in a new and vigorous way which brought fame to the dog, to In the Valley Kennels, to Roadcoach Kennels, and to the breed.

The line of succession in the presidency of the Dalmatian Club of America shows that Mr. Whitney succeeded Mr. Peters and was followed by John C. Weekes. A few years later Franklin J. Willock became the president. When Mr. Willock retired Mrs. Alfred E. Barrett (Roadcoach Kennels) accepted the office and served for nineteen years. She was succeeded by Miss Evelyn S. Nelson. Within the last twenty years we have had a number of people at the helm. They include William W. Fetner, Jr. (Coachman Kennels), William Hibbler (Williamsview Kennels), Dr. David G. Doane (Green Starr), Alfred E. Treen (Pryor Creek), Robert Migatz, Dr. N. Sidney Remmele (Tuckaway), and John A. Austin (JaMar).

The original rules of DCA limited the membership to 50 people. This was changed in 1937 because of the growing interest in the breed. The interest was sustained and furthered by the hard-working Mrs. Hohmiller and Mr. Willock. Mrs. Hohmiller was the first *American Kennel Gazette* columnist for the club although Mrs. Bonney did write a number of early columns for the magazine.

In the early days of the Dal in the U.S. the largest and apparently the most important kennel was Gedney Farms, White Plains, NY, owned by Howard Willets. Another important breeding kennel was Halnor Kennels, Oak Ridge, VA, owned by Mrs. C. Halsted Yates. And Mr. Willock's kennel, Gladmore, was among those of prominence. It was through Mr. Willock's efforts that the DCA started specialty shows, the first one being held in 1926. Most of the entries were from his kennel, Mrs. Sanger's Head of the River, and from the very well-known Tally-Ho kennels of Mrs. Bonney. These people urged others to whom they had sold puppies to enter and make this a gala affair. A Mrs. West (later Mrs. Austin) had the honor of being the judge of the first DCA national specialty. The national scope of the club was actually limited to the eastern seaboard. Shortly thereafter a breeder in the Michigan area became very active. Cressbrook kennels are still to be found in many of today's pedigrees.

The DCA sponsored at least two road trials for coaching Dals. The first was at Wissahicock Kennel Club and the second was held at the York, Penna., show. Fred Lauer's description of the trials makes us wonder why we aren't holding these trials today. Most of the dogs still carry the coaching instinct. Lauer gives detailed information on the method of training dogs to coach. And we well remember the story of the Fetners, Coachman Kennels, St. Louis, receiving delivery on a newly refurbished vehicle, a gig, and deciding to try it out with their driving horse. They hitched up the gig and off they went for a drive in their immediate area. Suddenly they were aware that they were not alone. Coaching as though she had been trained to do it was a six month old puppy, Coachman's Quadrille, who had been curled up on the patio when they took off with the gig and the horse. Oddly enough, this bitch soon to become a champion had the call name of "Gig".

In the late thirties obedience was introduced to the sport of dogs and among the most prominent in our breed to participate in the obedience trials were the Meistrells. Lois and Tots trained their dogs well and seemed to win the trials with increasing regularity until the war brought a stop to it. They donated their dogs to the war effort, were active in dogs for defense, and helped to train dogs for the canine units.

The first Dal to receive a CD title was Meeker's Barbara Worth. The first CDX, UD and TD was Io, owned by Harland Meistrell. The first bench champion to win a CD was Ch. Byron's Penny, owned by Mr. Robert Byron.

The first champion CDX Dal was Mrs. Bonney's Tally Ho's Black Eyed Susan. Ch. Duke of Gervais, owned by Maurice Gervais, was the first champion UD in the breed. The first liver Dal to win in obedience was Virginia Prescott's Roadcoach Cocoa UD.

Shortly after World War II a number of kennels became established and many of them have continued to this day. Before the beginning of those hostilities we had Roadcoach, Four-in-Hand, Ard Aven, Reigate, Brain Tree, Of the Walls, Sioux, Williamsdale, just to name a few of the more prominent ones. Coachman Kennels, Colonial Coach, and Pryor Creek, all started at about the same time. Both Colonial Coach and Coachman are still producing fine Dalmatians. At Pryor Creek we are no longer active breeders.

The year 1950 is about the time that the breed started to proliferate. Oddly enough, a statistical study indicated that the percentage of Dalmatians being registered, shown, and bred has remained approximately the same as in 1950 in ratio to the over-all number of dogs being registered, shown, and bred because the entire dog fancy has had such extensive growth.

When DCA allowed its membership to be opened to more than 50 members the increase was very slight. As recently as the '60s the figures of 150 to 170 remained the top of the membership. By the end of that decade the number had grown to about 180. At this time the DCA lists more than 500 members.

The Dal standard has certainly changed since the beginning of DCA and the showing of the breed. Mr. Lauer in his book *The Dalmatian,* 1907, talks about the color in Dals. Having expounded on the number of black ears on Dals, black at birth, he states, "The reason we do not often see the jet black ear (the ear that was black when born) at a show is, that as a rule this dog is most too dark and poorly marked for a show dog and the owner does not show him. When you get a good spotted eared dog he is usually very lightly spotted over the body. A very good spotted dog in body has seldom a good spotted ear. How many litters are born in which there are not from one to four of the puppies with one black ear, or both, or with blotches on the face over the eye? Not many I presume. Therefore, I have no objections to the black ears, and we should not penalize a dog for black ears nor for tan spots on the legs and cheeks, for these we know to have been proper Dalmatian colorings from the very first of our information regarding the breed up to the time the English Clubs were started and there is no reason why the change has been made."

And Mr. Lauer has art on his side to prove his statements. One of the earliest prints of a Dal obtainable shows a Dalmatian with a distinct brown patch on its face.

Another reason for the solid or poorly marked ears is probably the old custom of cropping the Dals' ears. The ears were not cropped in the fashion of a Doberman, Boxer, Schnauzer, etc., as we know the process today. Instead

Ch. Crestview Lisa winning Best of Opposite Sex at Dalmatian Club of America 1961. Judge, Mrs. Alfred W. Barrett. Trophy presented by Arthur W. Higgins. Handler, Anne Hone Rogers.

the ears were cut off next to the head. There was a good reason for this. Being used as a guard dog with the coaches, the Dalmatian was subject to attack by wild animals and other dogs and the ear simply made a good place to grab. Without the ear leather the Dalmatian had less vulnerable areas to offer an attacker.

The famous Reinagle print of the Dalmatian shows a dog without any ear leathers.

In the early stages of development in this country the markings were not considered so terribly important by the exhibitors. Pictures in Lauer's book show dogs which would, today, be sold as pets and which would never see the inside of a show ring. Refinement of our spotting patterns have been an evolutionary process. Today we see beautifully marked animals. And with the emphasis on markings of 25 per cent of the standard, we also see some very unsound, poor types being named winners because they have such great spotting patterns.

In 1963 a check of the Dalmatian kennels advertising in the dog magazines showed Maranan, Tandem Acres, In the Valley, Sachsedals, Long Last, Dalwyck, Reigate, Greeneland, Blackpool, Crown Jewels, Hay Hill, Rustic Rail, Dal Haven, Tara Lou, Coachman, and Castle Coach. Coachman, Long Last Blackpool, Crown Jewels, and Maranan are still among the kennels actively breeding. Dal Haven is still in existence but does not carry on an active breeding program. Tandem Acres belonged to the late Virginia Prescott. In the Valley was Mrs. Ratner's kennel in Pennsylvania. Both George and Mary Leigh Lane have passed on and Reigate is no more. Mr. Greene is no longer breeding at Greeneland and Mrs. Corbly no longer breeds or shows the Rustic Rail dogs. The others have dropped from sight.

In recent years the catalog of the national specialty show has a list of kennel prefixes with the names and addresses of the owners, when that information is available, and the word "inactive" following the prefix if that kennel is no longer in existence. This has become an important feature of the catalog. At the DCA specialty show held in California in July 1978, there were more than 500 kennel names listed. Of those, 210 were founded in the last seven years. Some of them have had great success in the ring and others are simply names of kennels and owners.

A glance at the advertisers in the DCA quarterly magazine, *The Spotter*, shows the following kennels very active: Coachman, Melody, JaMar, Tuckaway, Albelarm, Green Starr, Whinemaker, Rolenet, Paisley, Roadrunner, Anchor Creek, Croatia, Reicrist, Indalane, Sunkist, Pic-a-Dilly, Firewag'n, Korcula, Firesprite, Star Seeker, Proctor, Dalwood, Mardot, Clockgate, Seaspot, Centurion, Diamond D, Deltalyn, Roughrider, Pepper Pike, Canalside, Long Last, Fireside, Snowcap, Summerhill, Montjuic, Weeway, and Paxson.

Ch. Rockledge Rumble winning Best in Show under Mrs. L. W. Bonney at Steel City Kennel Club, Gary, Ind. in 1966. This was Mrs. Bonney's last judging assignment before her death. The dog is owned by Mrs. Gloria Schwartz. Trophy presenter was George Swadener.

58

Early on the Dalmatian fancy was pretty much concentrated on the east coast, principally in New York and New Jersey, but extending from southern New England south to Virginia. The breed had been known in America for more than 100 years before a club to further its interests was formed in 1904 and chartered in 1905.

The relatively few prominent breeders and the limited number of dogs shown in the breed tended to create a Dalmatian gene pool which produced dogs fairly similar in type. As the breed grew in popularity Dalmatians began to appear in other parts of the country. Prominent local breeders developed. Other gene pools flourished. Availability in the various regions often prevailed over scientific breeding. Local winners became popular sires. Regional characteristics developed. Knowledgeable judges could almost be sure what part of the country a particular exhibit came from. This was not always complimentary.

Fortunately several factors developed which tended to improve the situation. More information both pictorial and factual became available within the dog fancy as the number of publications increased. "Where Fanciers Gather" in the AKC *Gazette* spread information from member specialty (parent) clubs which was thought to be authentic and of worthwhile importance. Over the years the Dalmatian fancy was represented by breed columnists Pauline Orr (later Mrs. Hohmiller), Mrs. L. W. Bonney (1927), Franklin J. Willock (1930), Miss Evelyn Nelson (later Mrs. Gerald T. White) and currently, Betty (Mrs. John P.) Garvin. Commercial aviation, air freight and the interstate highway system made it easier to visit prestige shows and to ship bitches to studs which hopefully might improve a breeder's line.

For many years *The Spotter* was a typewritten newsletter sent to the Dalmatian Club of America membership occasionally. An inquiry as to its schedule in 1953 brought back the response "It is published whenever the editor accumulates enough material to make it worth mailing." In 1967 when Esme was asked to become its co-editor she did it on the basis that it would be published quarterly. In 1971 it became a magazine, complete with articles, pictures, breed statistics and advertising.

In 1962 the American Kennel Club approved a revised standard which had been developed and under consideration for ten or fifteen years. Its publication clarified several points and increased the knowledge of both judges and breeders. Currently consideration is being given to further clarification of the standard. Whether or not the study results in any standard changes, the detailed examination of the breed requirements and discussion of ideas are providing more insights as to important characteristics of the breed. For some breeders and exhibitors this will create better goals. Perhaps it will enable the breed to establish a universal ideal type.

Considering the size of the United States of America it was natural that as the breed became more popular in given areas regional clubs developed which provided opportunities for discussion and learning. Such clubs also hold matches and engage in other activities to further the breed. Currently there are 25 of these clubs. Thirteen of them have been recognized by the American Kennel Club and are licensed to hold specialty shows at which championship points may be awarded. Four other local clubs have achieved eligibility to hold sanctioned matches under AKC rules. Another eight are in various stages of development. Two other clubs, one in Florida and the other in Hawaii, have fallen by the wayside. In most cases the club names in the list following tell us the part of the country in which they operate.

Licensed

Chicagoland Dalmatian Club
Dalmatian Club of Detroit
Dalmatian Club of Greater Atlanta
Dalmatian Club of Greater New York
Dalmatian Club of Greater St. Louis
Dalmatian Club of Northern California
Dalmatian Club of Southern California
Dalmatian Club of Southern New England
Dalmatian Organization of Houston
Davenport Dalmatian Club
Greater Pittsburgh Dalmatian Club
Puget Sound Dalmatian Club
Western Reserve Dalmatian Club (Ohio)

Sanctioned

Dalmatian Club of Greater Indianapolis
Dalmatian Club of Las Vegas
Greater Sacramento Dalmatian Club
Greater Washington Dalmatian Club (D. C.)

Developing

Aztalan Dalmatian Club (Wisconsin)
Dalmatian Club of Greater Phoenix
Dalmatian Club of Mount Hood (Oregon)
Dalmatian Club of San Diego
Dalmatian Club of the Finger Lakes (New York)
Dalmatian Club of the Greater Twin Cities
Delaware Valley Dalmatian Club
Piedmont Dalmatian Club (North Carolina)

6

The DCA AKC Dalmatian Standard

THE FUTURE OF ANY BREED depends upon many individual decisions by breeders and exhibitors as well as dog show judges. Their benchmark is the standard, once known as the standard of perfection. The dog fancy established the written standard as the basic description of the ideal dog in a breed. In the United States each standard is drafted by the parent club of the breed and approved by the American Kennel Club. A standard is intended to outline ideal goals for breeders, give judges a guide to select the best quality present in the show ring and assist potential buyers in deciding on the breed and then in selecting a satisfactory dog of their own.

1978 can be considered the centennial year for the Dalmatian standard. What is considered by many to be the "first detailed description of the breed" was published in 1878 in the third edition of *Dogs of the British Islands* by John Henry Walsh (Stonehenge). The British standard, made official in 1890, was used in America until after the formation of the Dalmatian Club of America in 1905.

The current standard in the United States was adopted by the Dalmatian Club of America on February 12, 1962 and approved by the American Kennel Club December 11, 1962. It became effective January 1, 1963. The standard follows this paragraph. Immediately after the standard is a glossary of terms with the accepted definitions as shown in AKC's *The Complete Dog Book*. Both are presented with the permission of the American Kennel Club.

POINTS OF THE DALMATIAN

Breed Standard of the Dalmatian

The Dalmatian should represent a strong, muscular, and active dog; poised and alert; free of shyness; intelligent in expression; symmetrical in outline; and free from coarseness and lumber. He should be capable of great endurance, combined with a fair amount of speed.

Head—Should be a fair length, the skull flat, proportionately broad between the ears, and moderately well defined at the temples, and not in one straight line from the nose to the occiput bone as required in a Bull Terrier. It should be entirely free from wrinkle. *Muzzle*—Should be long and powerful—the lips clean. The mouth should have a scissors bite. Never undershot or overshot. It is permissible to trim whiskers. *Eyes*—Should be set moderately well apart, and of medium size, round, bright, and sparkling, with an intelligent expression; their color greatly depending on the markings of the dog. In the black-spotted variety the eyes should be dark (black or brown or blue). In the liver-spotted variety they should be lighter than in the black-spotted variety (golden or light brown or blue). The rim around the eyes in the black-spotted variety should be black; in the liver-spotted variety, brown. Never flesh-colored in either. Lack of pigment a major fault.

Ears—Should be set rather high, of moderate size, rather wide at the base, and gradually tapering to a rounded point. They should be carried close to the head, be thin and fine in texture, and preferably spotted. *Nose*—In the black-spotted variety should always be black; in the liver-spotted variety, always brown. A butterfly or flesh-colored nose is a major fault.

Neck and Shoulders—The neck should be fairly long, nicely arched, light and tapering, and entirely free from throatiness. The shoulders should be oblique, clean, and muscular, denoting speed.

Body, Back, Chest and Loins—The chest should not be too wide, but very deep and capacious, ribs well sprung but never rounded like barrel hoops (which would indicate want of speed). Back powerful; loin strong, muscular and slightly arched.

Legs and Feet—Of great importance. The forelegs should be straight, strong, and heavy in bone; elbows close to the body; feet compact, well-arched toes, and tough, elastic pads. In the hind legs the muscles should be clean, though well defined; the hocks well let down. Dewclaws may be removed from legs. *Nails*—In the black-spotted variety, black or white; or a nail may be both black and white. In the liver-spotted variety, brown or white; or a nail may be both brown and white.

Gait—Length of stride should be in proportion to the size of the dog, steady in rhythm of 1, 2, 3, 4 as in the cadence count in military drill. Front legs should not paddle, nor should there be a straddling appearance. Hind legs should neither cross nor weave; judges should be able to see each leg move

63

SKELETON OF THE DALMATIAN

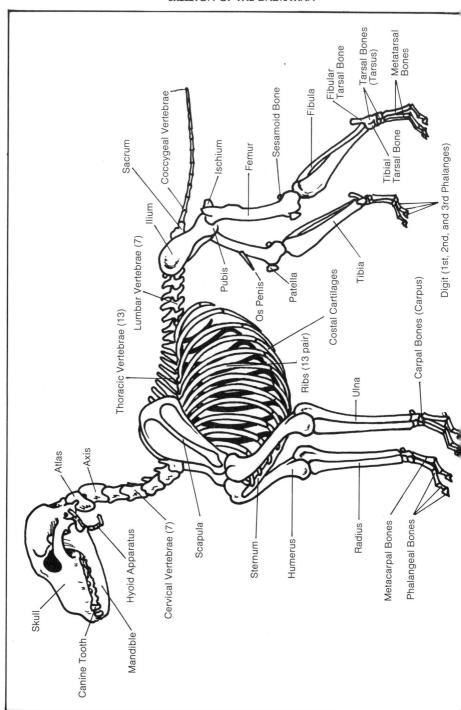

with no interference of another leg. Drive and reach are most desirable. Cowhocks are a major fault.

Tail—Should ideally reach the hock joint, strong at the insertion, and tapering toward the end, free from coarseness. It should not be inserted too low down, but carried with a slight curve upwards, and never curled.

Coat—Should be short, hard, dense, and fine, sleek and glossy in appearance, but neither woolly nor silky.

Color and Markings—Are most important points. The ground color in both varieties should be pure white, very decided, and not intermixed. The color of the spots in the black-spotted variety should be dense black; in the liver-spotted variety they should be liver brown. The spots should not intermingle, but be as round and well defined as possible, the more distinct the better. In size they should be from that of a dime to a half-dollar. The spots on the face, head, ears, legs, and tail to be smaller than those on the body. Patches, tri-colors, and any color markings other than black or liver constitute a disqualification. A true patch is a solid, sharply defined mass of black or liver that is appreciably larger than any of the markings on the dog. Several spots that are so adjacent that they actually touch one another at their edges do not constitute a patch.

Size—The desirable height of dogs and bitches is between 19 and 23 inches at the withers, and any dog or bitch over 24 inches at the withers is to be disqualified.

Major Faults

Butterfly or flesh-colored nose. Cowhocks. Flat feet. Lack of pigment in eye rims. Shyness. Trichiasis (abnormal position or direction of the eyelashes).

Faults

Ring or low-set tail. Undersize or oversize.

Scale of Points

Body, back, chest and loins	10
Coat	5
Color and markings	25
Ears	5
Gait	10
Head and eyes	10
Legs and feet	10
Neck and shoulders	10
Size, symmetry, etc.	10
Tail	5
Total	100

Headstudy of Ch. Colonsay's Olaf the Red.

Headstudy of Ch. Dal Haven's Oliver Twist.

Disqualifications

Any color markings other than black or liver.
Any size over 24 inches at the withers.
Patches.
Tri-colors.
Undershot or overshot bite.

Glossary of Terms

Barrel: Rounded rib section.

Bitch: A female dog.

Bite: The relative position of the upper and lower teeth when the mouth is closed. *See* level bite, Scissors bite, Overshot, Undershot.

Butterfly nose: A parti-colored nose; i.e., dark, spotted with flesh color.

Coat: The dog's hairy covering.

Cow-hocked: When the hocks turn toward each other.

Dewclaw: An extra claw or functionless digit on the inside of the leg; a rudimentary fifth toe.

Disqualification: A decision made by a judge or by a bench show committee following a determination that a dog has a condition that makes it ineligible for any further competition under the dog show rules or under the standard for its breed.

Dog: A male dog; also used collectively to designate both male and female.

Expression: The general appearance of all features of the head as viewed from the front and as typical of the breed.

Gait: The pattern of footsteps at various rates of speed, each pattern distinguished by a particular rhythm and footfall. The two gaits acceptable in the show ring are walk and trot.

Height: Vertical measurement from the withers to the ground; referred to usually as shoulder height. *See* Withers.

Hock: The tarsus or collection of bones of the hind leg forming the joint between the second thigh and the metatarsus; the dog's true heel.

Level Bite: When the front teeth (incisors) of the upper and lower jaws meet exactly edge to edge. Pincer bite.

Liver: A color; i.e., deep, reddish brown.

Loin: Region of the body on either side of the vertebral column between the last ribs and the hindquarters.

Lumber: Superfluous flesh.

Muzzle: The head in front of the eyes—nasal bone, nostrils, and jaws. Foreface. Also, a strap or wire cage attached to the foreface to prevent the dog from biting or from picking up food.

Nose: Organ of smell; also, the ability to detect by means of scent.

Occiput: Upper, back point of the skull.

Overshot: The front teeth (incisors) of the upper jaw overlap and do not touch the front teeth of the lower jaw when the mouth is closed.

Paddling: A compensating action, so named for its similarity to the swing and dip of a canoeist's paddle, Pinching in at the elbows and shoulder joints causes the front legs to swing forward on a stiff outward arc. Also referred to as ''tied at the elbows.''

Pads: Tough, shock-absorbing projections on the underside of the feet. Soles.

Ring tail: Carried up and around almost in a circle.

Scissors Bite: A bite in which the outer side of the lower incisors touches the inner side of the upper incisors.

Standard: A description of the ideal dog of each recognized breed, to serve as a word pattern by which dogs are judged at shows.

Throatiness: An excess of loose skin under the throat.

Tri-color: Three-color; white, black, and tan.

Undershot: The front teeth (incisors) of the lower jaw overlapping or projecting beyond the front teeth of the upper jaw when the mouth is closed.

Weaving: Unsound gaiting action which starts with twisting elbows and ends with crisscrossing and toeing out.

Whisker: Longer hairs on muzzle sides and underjaw.

Withers: The highest point of the shoulders, immediately behind the neck.

Wrinkle: Loose, folding skin on forehead and foreface.

In July of 1978 the British Dalmatian Club suggested the possibility of a World Congress on the welfare and future progress of Dalmatians with speakers from all parts of the globe. The plan is to hold it in England in April of 1980 with the club's championship show as one of the features. Meanwhile since size, acceptance of blue eyes and the disposition of undesirable features lack uniformity in the standards used in various parts of the world, one might hope these subjects will be high on the agenda of the Dalmatian World Congress. A comparison of differences in size and identification and treatment of undesirable features listed by governing bodies in various countries follows:

Country	Height Dog	Bitch	Faults	Disqualifying Faults
Canada	23 to 24	22 to 23	Partly flesh colored nose Cow hocks Flat feet Incompletely	Patches Tri-colors Any color other than liver and white or black

| | Height | | | Disqualifying |
Country	Dog	Bitch	Faults	Faults
			colored eye rims	and white
			Any eye color other than black, brown or amber	Undershot or more than .3175cm (⅛″)overshot bite
England and affiliated countries	23 to 24	22 to 23	Patches Black and liver spots on the same dog (tri-colours) Lemon spots Blue eyes Bronzing and other faults of pigmentation	
Mexico and other FCI* countries	21½ to 24	19½ to 23	Blue eyes Lemon spots Bronzing	
United States of America	19 to 23		Ring or lowset tail Undersize or oversize *Major Faults* Butterfly or flesh-colored nose Cow hocks Flat feet Lack of pigment in eye rims Shyness Trichiasis	Any color markings other than black or liver Any size over 24 inches at the withers Patches Tri-colors Undershot or overshot bite

*Federation Cynologique Internationale representing 46 member countries in Europe, Latin America and The Caribbean, Africa, Asia, Australia and New Zealand.

70

7

Judging the Dalmatian— The Standard Revisited

THIS CHAPTER might be called "What the Standard Means" or "Interpreting the Dalmatian Standard" or "Understanding the Dalmatian Standard." It is intended to give some background and insights that will be helpful in learning what a Dalmatian is supposed to be.

Breeding purebred dogs is working in an animate art form. Instead of using the traditional brushes and palette of the painter or the clay and modeling tools or the chisels and mallet of the sculptor, the breeder works with pedigrees, dominant and recessive genes and, after considerable observation, thought and study plans a breeding. Hopefully each breeding planned will create a better Dalmatian.

The breeder must work toward the picture in his mind of the perfect Dalmatian, the dog that has never been born. That mental picture is shaped by the standard, by his or her own feelings and perceptions for style and balance and the ability to project written words into visual concepts. That image is also shaped by the knowledge of the work the coach dog did. It is affected by what the breeder has seen of the judgments of numerous judges of varying degrees of knowledge and skill. It is not a picture made with a "by-the-numbers" paint kit or a computer operated with punch cards. If it could be done by formula there would be many more truly great dogs. It is a thing of beauty, a very personal creation which should agree in major concepts and vary in minor details with the picture in the minds of those who created the standard from the real dogs of their time. For some the picture is fuzzy. For others it is in sharp focus. But for all it should be better than the animals they are working with.

A standard is a compromise between the general and the specific, between the dream and reality, between the details and the total dog. In its simplest form it is described by William F. Stifel, AKC president, as "an elementary description of a breed, pointing out certain qualities that make the breed unique and indicating certain areas with respect to the standard (or sometimes with respect to general canine soundness), where judges should be alert for problems. A certain amount of detail may be necessary, but too much detail will, among other things, be confusing, will be difficult for judges to remember, and may put unexpected emphasis on some aspect where it is not wanted. The use of too much emphasis to correct a problem may create a problem of its own."

The first official standard of the Dalmatian Club founded in England in 1890 refers to two other breeds, Pointers and Bull Terriers. These were unfortunate bench-marks as the Dalmatian people had no control of later changes in these other breeds. In 1925 the comparison to Pointers was removed and by 1968 the Bull Terrier reference was gone. In the United States the phrase "as required in a Bull Terrier" remains as a misleading part of the American standard.

Aside from that the current Dalmatian standard is an excellent one. It needs, perhaps, clarification of the patch to give better understanding of this phenomenon for those people who are not yet breeders. And for those people who do not understand animal locomotion, perhaps an amendment giving a clear description of the Dalmatian gait would be of service. Those who do understand the science of movement and the sequence of foot falls can readily grasp what is wanted from the description in the present standard.

When a judge evaluates a dog in the ring he normally follows a regular procedure. A few years back AKC developed a guide for writing breed standards. One of its suggestions was to place the various sections in about the same sequence a judge would use in examining a dog. This seemed like a sensible approach for good understanding. Accordingly it seemed natural to follow that order in our comments. We have begun with general appearance and then the head, neck and body, forequarters, and hindquarters, followed by sections on color and markings, gait, size and temperament. Wording from the standard (printed in its official form and sequence in the preceding chapter) is in small type under each of the headings from AKC's guide, followed by our comments in the body type of the book.

Dog, of course, means dog or bitch; he, either he or she.

General Appearance:

The Dalmatian should represent a strong, muscular, and active dog; poised and alert; free of shyness; intelligent in expression; symmetrical in outline; and free from coarseness and lumber. He should be capable of great endurance, combined with a fair amount of speed.

Ideally the Dalmatian is an active medium-sized dog with a happy, alert and intelligent manner. His important characteristics are his colorful appearance, friendly manner and his ability to move well and with grace, yet displaying the potential stamina to keep up with horses for long periods of time. Ideally he is just under 23 inches at the withers and about as long (front of chest to back of rump). His coat is pure white with black or liver (brown) colored round spots from a dime to a half dollar in size, evenly distributed over his body, those on his extremities being slightly smaller than the ones on his body. His topline is level, his chest deep and his tuck-up moderate. His tail is long enough for the tip to reach his hock joint. It is carried straight back with a slight curve upwards. His shoulders slope moderately. His forelegs are strong and straight, his hindquarters well muscled and his hocks well let down. His feet are small and compact. He moves smoothly in a rhythmic fashion like 4/4 time in music and gives the impression he could continue all day.

Soundness and symmetry are important. Other than color and markings there are no features that are peculiar to this breed.

Head

Should be of a fair length, the skull flat, proportionately broad between the ears, and moderately well defined at the temples, and not in one straight line from the nose to the occiput bone as required in a Bull Terrier. It should be entirely free from wrinkle. *Muzzle*—Should be long and powerful—the lips clean. The mouth should have a scissors bite. Never undershot or overshot. It is permissible to trim whiskers.

In saying "of fair length" the standard means "beautiful to the eye; of pleasing form or appearance." The Dalmatian is not a "head-breed" but the *head* must be in proportion to the rest of the dog. It is a simple, clean looking head, smooth and free of wrinkle.

Viewed from above, the outline of the Dalmatian's head appears to be pear-shaped with the topskull and muzzle about the same length. The topskull is nearly as broad as it is long. The topskull is almost flat with a slight center groove starting at the occiput, coming down the stop between the eyes and extending onto the muzzle to the nose leather. The stop is not a pronounced feature, but a subtle rise where the muzzle blends into the upper head, further emphasized by the groove and by the position and shape of the arches over the eyes which should be well developed.

From the side, toplines of the skull and the muzzle appear approximately parallel.

Eyes

Should be set moderately well apart, and of medium size, round, bright, and sparkling, with an intelligent expression; their color greatly depending on the markings of the dog. In the black-spotted variety the eyes should be dark (black or brown or blue). In the liver-spotted

GOOD HEAD

TOO THROATY

SNIPEY MUZZLE

variety they should be lighter than in the black-spotted variety (golden or light brown or blue). The rim around the eyes in the black-spotted variety should be black; in the liver-spotted variety, brown. Never flesh-colored in either. Lack of pigment a major fault.

The standard is reasonably clear on eyes. One might miss the possibility that a Dal may have one brown and one blue eye. This happens occasionally. If it does not spoil the dog's expression, there is nothing wrong. There have been some famous beauties (human) with this characteristic. Previous to 1962 the standard had said, "Wall eyes are permissible." This raised the issue, "Is the blue eyed Dalmatian a second class dog?" The vote was "NO" and blue was accepted along with black and brown. In other countries, including Canada, England, Mexico and 46 FCI countries, blue eyes are considered a fault. Many do not agree. As far back as 1954 the foremost British authority, Dr. Eleanor Frankling, wrote: "It seems likely that the factor for blue eyes is fairly widely distributed among dogs of today. In most parti-coloured breeds such eyes are not considered a fault. They are not faulted in American Dalmatians, and although they are frowned on here, I personally think it is rather a pity, for a bright blue eye is by no means unattractive."

Nose

In the black-spotted variety should always be black; in the liver-spotted variety, always brown. A butterfly or flesh-colored nose is a major fault.

The nose is fully colored to match the spots as are the eye rims. Lack of pigment in eye rims and butterfly or flesh colored nose are both classified as major faults. Some breeders and breeder-judges consider it unforgivable to take a dog into the ring with either fault.

Ears

Should be set rather high, of moderate size, rather wide at the base, and gradually tapering to a rounded point. They should be carried close to the head, be thin and fine in texture, and preferably spotted.

It is really not necessary to comment on *ears* except to say that when alert their base is level with the topskull. Ear leather is thin and fine in texture. Fly-away ears are not typical or desirable. Ears must hang close to the sides of the head.

Are black ears considered patched? Not if broken—if white hair is visible to indicate overlapping spots.

Experimental breeding, most of it one hundred to one hundred and fifty years or more ago, left some unwanted recessive traits in many breeds. We see these reminders of other breeds occasionally in the heads of Dalmatians. A muzzle tilted so that the nose is slightly higher at the tip than where the muzzle joins the topskull says, "Pointer." A great depth from the point of the nose to the underjaw says, "Mastiff." A full square jaw says, "Great Dane." A head

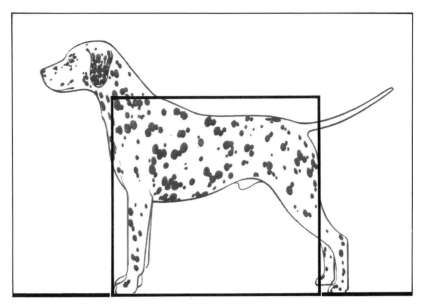

PROPORTION

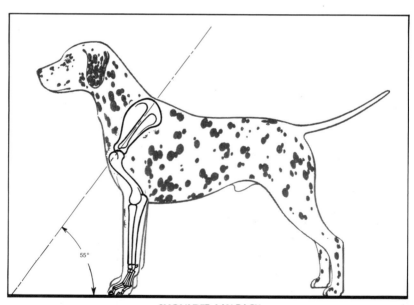

55°

SHOULDER LAY-BACK

tending to an oval or egg shape smacks of the Bull Terrier. Fortunately they are rarely seen. Hopefully, the specimens with these characteristics are not used in breeding. They rarely win in the ring under a knowledgeable judge.

Beyond that the standard is clear. The head is nicely balanced with a spacious skull and a powerful muzzle. The muzzle is never weak or pointed. The lips are clean and dry. There are no flews or dewlaps.

Neck and Shoulders

The neck should be fairly long, nicely arched, light and tapering, and entirely free from throatiness. The shoulders should be oblique, clean, and muscular, denoting speed.

The *neck* arches forward gracefully from the shoulders. If one were to extend a line along the front leg from the foot upward it would be well behind the head. While many Dalmatians have been trained to hold the head high in the ring, normally when running free, the head is thrust forward and is only slightly higher than the topline. A dog shown on a tight lead with the head pulled back so the neck is like a stovepipe rising from an old-fashioned baseburner is badly handled. The neck is moderately long and blends smoothly into the back and shoulders.

Perhaps a word about the anatomy of the *topline* is in order as a frame of reference. It is defined in the dog glossary of *Dog Standards Illustrated* (Howell Book House, 1976) as "Backline: profile of dog from top of skull to tail base." Its structural components are 1. seven cervical vertebrae (neck) 2. thirteen thoracic vertebrae (back), 3. seven lumbar vertebrae (loin), and 4. the sacrum which with the ilium forms the croup. The coccygeal vertebrae continue from the sacrum to form the tail.

Body, Back, Chest and Loins

The chest should not be too wide, but very deep and capacious, ribs well sprung but never rounded like barrel hoops (which would indicate want of speed). Back powerful; loin strong, muscular and slightly arched.

The *back* is relatively smooth and level but not necessarily flat. This is true whether one uses the dog glossary definition that identifies the back as "that part between withers and set-on of tail along the vertebrae" or the breeders' definition which limits the back to the area over the rib cage and adds the "coupling" (loin area) and the croup or rump to complete the horizontal portion of the topline. If the components are properly constructed and the muscles in good condition, the topline from the withers to the onset of the tail remains fairly level whether the dog is moving or standing.

The *chest* should be viewed from three vantage points. From head on one can see that it is deeper than it is wide and that it is well filled. From above we see it is wider at the shoulder than at the loin. From the side the forepart of the

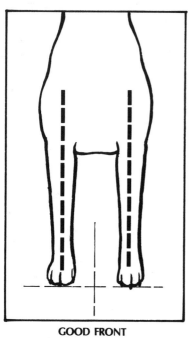

GOOD FRONT

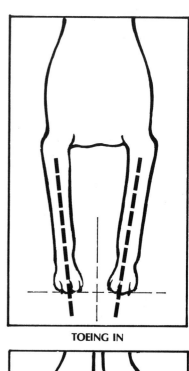

TOEING IN

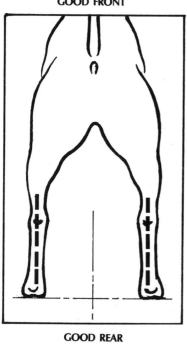

GOOD REAR

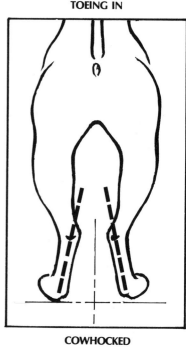

COWHOCKED

chest is only slightly visible in front of the forelegs but the lower portion of the chest (brisket) extends to or below the dog's elbow.

The bottom line slopes upward gradually from mid-chest to the end of the ribs. Only a moderate tuckup is required. The Dalmatian needs plenty of lung room. A "herring gut" bottom line which slopes up steeply from the front of the chest does not provide a large enough chest cavity for a Dal.

The degree of roundness of the *ribs* is not great enough to form a round or even an egg-shaped chest cross section. This would interfere with the set-on of the shoulders and would limit movement. It is a vertical oval tapering down to the brisket.

The *loin* is strong and, as it is in all breeds, slightly arched. Looking down at the dog's back we see that the sides through the loin area are not as far apart as on the chest or the croup. The *croup* is rounded.

Tail

Should ideally reach the hockjoint, strong at the insertion, and tapering toward the end, free from coarseness. It should not be inserted too low down, but carried with a slight curve upwards, and never curled.

The *tail* is important to the balanced picture of a Dalmatian. It extends naturally from the topline curving upward slightly. If the base of the tail is set lower or below the level of the topline it spoils the picture. So does a vertical tail or one carried over or curled over the back. The tail is strong and tapers gradually. It is not curled. Proper length can be determined by seeing if the tip will reach to the hock. When moving, the tip is never higher than the head.

Forequarters

Legs and Feet—Of great importance. The forelegs should be straight, strong, and heavy in bone; elbows close to the body; feet compact, well-arched toes, and tough, elastic pads. Dewclaws may be removed from legs. *Nails*—In the black-spotted variety, black or white; or a nail may be both black and white. In the liver-spotted variety, brown or white; or a nail may be both brown and white.

Good shoulders are important if the Dalmatian is to move efficiently. The angle of the scapula (shoulder blade) determines the extent of the reach. Visualize a line projected along the spline (ridge) of the shoulder blade to the ground. The sloping shoulder produces a greater range for movement than does the vertical one. Theoretically, since "oblique" means an angle not vertical to or horizontal to the plane of reference, in this case the surface on which the dog stands, the optimum or ideal angle could be 45 degrees from the horizontal. Actually the ideal has never been determined. Shoulders close to 90 degrees produce poor movement. The best moving dogs obviously will have shoulder blades which are less than 90 degrees from the horizontal, but how much less?

The optimum 45 degrees has been quoted by dog writers over a long period of time as producing proper movement. But this statement has not been made by an authority with standardized research data to support his or her conclusions. From observation in and out of the ring we are of the impression that shoulder lay-back on most good moving dogs is apt to be within the range of from 65 down to 50 degrees and that 45 degrees may be a worthy goal or a bit of dog fancy folklore.

Coming down the leg the upper arm (humerus) is normally joined to the shoulder blade at a 90 degree angle. Being slightly shorter than the shoulder blade it permits the lower leg to drop vertically so that the foot is directly under the center of the shoulder blade. Viewed head on, the legs are straight and parallel. From the side there may be a slight bend at the *pastern*. The Dalmatian's pasterns are flexible for a smooth gait and short for endurance.

The *feet* are tight and round, small and catlike for endurance. The Dalmatian does not need the additional leverage of long hare-like feet for a speedy start. This would waste energy. Large, spread-out feet would also be inefficient. The pads are tough and thick, should never be flat. Because more than half of the Dalmatian's weight is carried by the forequarters the front feet are larger than the hind feet. Feet point straight ahead.

Nails should be kept short. Long nails tend to make the feet splay. Long nails also cause dogs to develop weak pasterns and poor gait. The dog, avoiding stepping on the long nails, rocks his weight back to avoid this, and causes his feet to go down on the pasterns.

Hindquarters
In the hind legs the muscles should be clean, though well defined; the hocks well let down.

Since both drive and reach are essential to good movement the *hindquarters* must be in balance with the forequarters. While the standard is silent the *stifles* must be moderately well bent and the thighs well muscled for the Dalmatian to maintain his ability to move with the horses. The *hocks* are low (well let down) for endurance. Looking at the dog from the rear, the centerline of each leg is straight. Hocks which turn inward toward each other are a major fault.

Coat
Should be short, hard, dense, and fine, sleek and glossy in appearance, but neither woolly nor silky.

The coat should be of uniform texture as described with two possible exceptions. The hair on the ears is shorter, softer and more silky in texture than the rest of the coat. If the dog is patched the texture of the patch will match that of the ears.

The coat is a good indicator of a dog's health and condition. It should be clean and free from blemish. While there have been no scientific studies completed that would substantiate this, there seem to be some isolated genetic families and/or diet patterns which tend to produce more than the average amount of skin problems in a few dogs. Dalmatians should not be in the ring unless they are in good condition.

Color and Markings

Are most important points. The ground color in both varieties should be pure white, very decided, and not intermixed. The color of the spots in the black-spotted variety should be dense black; in the liver-spotted variety they should be liver brown. The spots should not intermingle, but be as round and well defined as possible, the more distinct the better. In size they should be from that of a dime to a half-dollar. The spots on the face, head, ears, legs, and tail to be smaller than those on the body. Patches, tri-colors, and any color markings other than black of liver constitute a disqualification. A true patch is a solid, sharply defined mass of black or liver that is appreciably larger than any of the markings on the dog. Several spots that are so adjacent that they actually touch one another at their edges do not constitute a patch.

The key to a nicely marked Dalmatian is even distribution of spots. There should not be too many places where spots overlap in large numbers. A confluence of spots is unsightly and might be mistaken for a patch by an unknowledgeable judge although patches are relatively easy to distinguish. Describing a patch so that someone not in the Dalmatian fancy can visualize one and instantly recognize the presence or absence of a patch isn't always the simplest of tasks. The description should create a picture in a person's mind which contrasts an unfortunately marked Dal with a patched one. Such pictures can be developed by comparing a handful of coins spilled on a counter top with the puddle created by a bottle of ink tipped over. Some of the coins may overlap. This does not create a patch. This is like a confluence of spots, each one at least partially discernible. The area covered usually includes some white hair. These white hairs define the edges of the overlapping spots to some degree.

Contrast this with the outline of the puddle or patch. This has no indication of spots or partial spots. There is an absence of white hair within the area covered. Typically the hair within the patch is shorter, finer and softer than the other hair on the animal being evaluated. With these features firmly in mind a judge from outside the Dal fancy is equipped to recognize the presence or absence of patches as quickly as a breeder. Without them he is lost. How does a breeder recognize a patch? It is present at birth and all too easily recognized, a black or brown blot on a pure white puppy.

Either too few or too many spots spoil the picture as do large blank areas which breeders sometimes refer to as white patching.

Coins illustrating range of spot sizes

Heap of coins touching yet separate entities as in a cluster of spots.

A patched Dalmatian

82

Gait

Length of stride should be in proportion to the size of the dog, steady in rhythm of 1, 2, 3, 4 as in the cadence count in military drill. Front legs should not paddle, nor should there be a straddling appearance. Hind legs should neither cross nor weave; judges should be able to see each leg move with no interference of another leg. Drive and reach are most desirable. Cowhocks are a major fault.

Gait is clearly outlined in the standard. It is best evaluated at a slow trot. It should be free from sidewinding. The dog's body should move in line with the direction he is going.

Gait in the ring is the judge's test of balance and soundness. Going away the judge should not see cowhocking or crossing over, nor should there be spraddling. Coming back the legs should be seen coming down straight with no paddling, weaving or out-at-the shoulders movement visible.

Size

The desirable height of dogs and bitches is between 19 and 23 inches at the withers, and any dog or bitch over 24 inches at the withers is to be disqualified.

The British Dalmatian Club standard's section on size starts: "Overall balance of prime importance, but the ideal height to be aimed at is . . . ." This certainly hints that height is not the only factor in the size of this symmetrical breed. Length of body, size of rib-cage, head and neck, bone and muscle all contribute to the impression of size. The Dal is a medium-sized dog. Bigger is not better. Once he ran beneath the whiffle-tree or the axle. There "big" could be "bad" with the vehicle beating or rubbing off his hide as they passed over irregular road surfaces. Maybe that is why some ran in front of, alongside, or behind the conveyances.

In the United States there was concern that the Dals were getting to be too big to be considered coach dogs. There were some too small, too. Accordingly in 1962 a fault was established for undersize or oversize dogs (Under 19 inches or Over 23 inches). Further, any size over 24 inches at the withers was considered a disqualification from the show ring. Other breeds have size disqualifications also. In the show ring if another exhibitor protests the size of a Dalmatian or if the judge believes a dog may be too tall, the judge sends for the AKC approved official measuring equipment called "The Wicket." This is then set for 24 inches. The handler puts his dog in a show pose and the judge brings the wicket forward over the back to the withers and lowers it. If both feet of the wicket rest on the ground or floor the judge marks his book "Measured in" and the dog is judged. If the wicket rests on the dog's withers but both ends do not touch the floor the dog is dismissed from the ring and the judge's book is marked "measured out—disqualified". Over 23 inches is a fault.

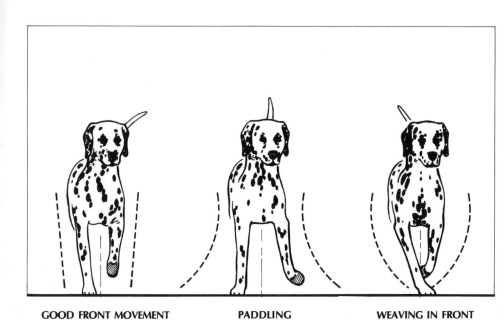

GOOD FRONT MOVEMENT   **PADDLING**   **WEAVING IN FRONT**

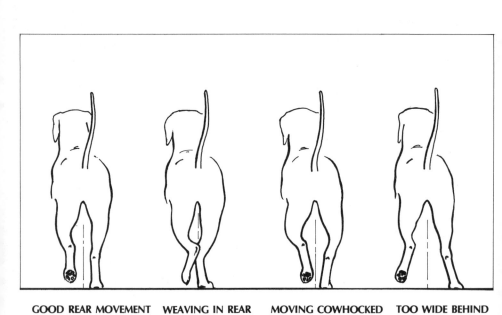

GOOD REAR MOVEMENT   **WEAVING IN REAR**   **MOVING COWHOCKED**   **TOO WIDE BEHIND**

84

Good front movement

Good going away

Good side movement

Horse and dog exhibit good reach

The galloping Dalmatian

It may be a shock to many to learn that at one time members of the Dalmatian Club of America voted to have any Dalmatian over 23 inches disqualified. The American Kennel Club asked DCA to reconsider this as at that time measurements of dogs could be so open to question. The Club then went on record as deploring the placing of oversized Dalmatians and urged judges to penalize any dog over 23 inches in height.

The influence of sex is not mentioned in the DCA/AKC standard. However, the standards used in Canada, England, Mexico and other FCI countries specify the ideal height of the bitch as one inch shorter than that of the dog. Some breeders, exhibitors and judges like bitches to be feminine. Others prefer "doggy" bitches. In the USA with a range of four inches in the desirable height and an additional fifth inch before disqualification, personal preference has full swing.

Temperament

While the standard does not develop it, a Dalmatian that is well-bred has a stable *temperament* that makes him a good companion. Aloof, yes. Shy, no. Eager, warm and friendly when his preliminary suspicions are satisfied, the Dalmatian for many years was bred to be a guard dog. He ran with the coach or carriage to ward off the wolves and highwaymen. He protected his master's belongings from thieves while his master was dining at the inn. He still fancies himself the guard dog when a stranger appears at the door, but when a member of the family makes the caller welcome, he does too.

A Dal should be neither shy nor aggressive. Respected breeders breed for stability. The American Kennel Club expects a judge to dismiss forthwith from the ring any dog in any breed that shows any signs of viciousness. This is a rare problem in Dals.

Dogs exhibiting a streak of viciousness are eliminated from breeding programs so that only puppies of sound temperament are produced. These are usually socialized individually during their first seven to ten weeks of life to enhance their ability to accept human as well as canine friends. A well-bred Dalmatian's behaviour should make him trustworthy around unattended young children. He is intelligent and perceptive.

Breeders and judges need to pay serious attention to temperament. At home the Dalmatian should be the careful guard, the sensible, friendly companion. In public places he walks calmly at at his master's side, accepts whatever praise or interest is expressed in his colorful appearance with wagging tail. In the ring a Dalmatian should exhibit stability and poise. He should be trained to show. He should be calm and alert. A judge will do well to pass over an excessively exuberant dog or a shy one.

Major Faults

Butterfly or flesh-colored nose. Cowhocks, Flat feet. Lack of pigment in eye rims. Shyness. Trichiasis (abnormal position or direction of the eyelashes).

Faults

Ring or low-set tail. Undersize or oversize.

Scale of points

Body, back, chest and loins	10
Coat	5
Color and markings	25
Ears	5
Gait	10
Head and eyes	10
Legs and feet	10
Neck and shoulders	10
Size, symmetry, etc.	10
Tail	5
TOTAL	100

Disqualifications

Any color markings other than black or liver.
Any size over 24 inches at the withers.
Patches.
Tri-colors.
Undershot or overshot bite.

Faults mentioned in the standard are genetically undesirable in breeding.

The most serious faults in Dalmatians are patches, height over 24 inches at the withers (less serious is over 23 inches), tricolor (both black and liver spots), undershot or overshot bite, and any color other than black or liver. These are considered so serious that a dog with even one of the characteristics is dismissed from the show ring as "disqualified."

Other faults serious enough to be mentioned in the standard include size over 23 inches and under 19 inches at the withers, cow hocks, eye rims without pigment, shyness, flesh-colored or butterfly nose, flat feet, trichiasis, ring tail or low-set tail.

There are other faults which require disqualification in all breeds under AKC rules. These are not listed in each standard. A dog which is blind, deaf, castrated, spayed or which has been changed in appearance by artificial means except as specified in the standard for its breed, or a male which does not have two normal testicles normally located in the scrotum will be disqualified.

Certainly a judge penalizes for faults but he does not judge by them. He looks for quality. The serious breeder breeds for quality and avoids a breeding which would involve using two dogs with the same fault.

Personally we like the definition of quality found in Howell's *Dog Standards Illustrated*:

"QUALITY——an air of excellence, combining breed characteristics and including soundness and harmony, making the animal an outstanding specimen of the breed, both standing and in motion."

8

Living With a Dal

Anyone contemplating buying a Dalmatian puppy should be aware of a number of things concerning these dogs. It is always a good idea to learn as much as possible about any breed before acquiring a puppy.

A good Dal puppy will grow to a sturdy, well muscled dog, one that is able to keep going on the road or in the field for hours on end. The dog will have a trusting attitude toward you, his master, and will present a reserved manner toward strangers. After he has been introduced to the stranger he will be friendly and loving. Some Dalmatians smile. It is necessary to determine that the dog is smiling and not snarling. The entire attitude of the smiling Dalmatian is quite different from that of a dog who is daring you to approach one step nearer. The uninitiated person may be unable to tell the difference and thus will fear your dog. The Dalmatian has great ability to guard and protect his own property. He was bred to guard. He is willing to learn if you don't push him. Pushed, he can seem quite stupid. He will become a member of your family so it behooves anyone acquiring a puppy to train him properly. He cannot know what you want him to do unless you teach him.

Training a Dalmatian for obedience work is a little more strenuous than training him to be a good house dog. Many areas offer puppy kindergarten classes which will introduce your dog to other dogs, to simple behavior patterns all of which are useful in the home.

Training in obedience will require a good deal more time and effort but can be extremely rewarding. After you have trained your dog in obedience you may want to enter obedience trials. If you have purchased a ''show

Breakfast with Brewster.

A family portrait. The Robert Migatz daughters and their Dalmatians.

prospect'' Dalmatian you should attend conformation classes as well as obedience classes. Some training clubs use the conformation showing as another obedience exercise, changing collars and teaching the owner how to present his dog in the breed ring. Other clubs offer one or the other, breed or obedience showing, requiring you to go to two different classes. In either case you will have a great deal of fun showing your Dal in obedience and/or conformation. Rules governing the sport of showing and regulations covering obedience trials can be obtained at no cost by writing to the American Kennel Club, 51 Madison Avenue, New York, NY 10010. The instructors at the classes you attend can advise you about where and how to enter your dog. The sport of showing dogs can become a great family hobby, one in which every member of the family is involved. It is an activity which affords a great deal of friendship with many people from different parts of the country and which can become a lifelong hobby.

When you acquire your puppy you will want to establish certain patterns in his life. Start as soon as possible to make a habit of these things so that as your dog grows he will expect them.

Grooming a Dalmatian is the simplest thing in the world. If you have a pet Dalmatian the important thing is to keep him brushed. Dalmatians shed. No one understands why only the white hairs are shed, never the black or liver, but it seems to be true. Actually, this is simply myth. The shed hair just seems to be all white because the darker hairs rarely show on clothing, furniture, etc. A jokester once quipped that ''Dalmatians shed only twice a year, every morning and every night!'' Brushing will keep the shedding down.

If you are preparing the dog for the show ring you will want to trim his whiskers and to trim his ''pants'' and tuck-up. The entire idea is to give him a smooth outline. The dog should look smooth in the ring and scraggly hairs left on the outline of the rear legs, the tuck-up, and some ''moles,'' those funny little growths found on all dogs, spoil the appearance.

Toenails should be cut on a regular basis whether the dog is a pet or a show prospect. If the nails are allowed to grow the feet can splay. A tight, cat-like foot is most desirable and long nails will prevent this type of foot development. Running a dog on concrete at all times will also spoil the development of a foot. A good type of kennel run surface is pea gravel. This seems to make the foot arch well and stay tightly knit. The only danger of using pea gravel is that some dogs will eat it.

In cutting toenails, if you start the process at an early age and do it regularly you will not have problems. Putting the dog up on a grooming table or something higher than he is used to will help in making him behave for the cutting process. The quick is retractable and keeps moving back when the nails are properly cared for. Have a container of ferric subsulphate powder

Dalmatian puppies at 8 weeks. Left, Ch. Deltalyn Decoupage. Right, Ch. Deltalyn Mystic Brandy. Owned by Robert and Judy Rivard.

The Dyker children and pups, 1968.

handy to stop bleeding if you cut too deep. To smooth the nails some people use a sandpaper disk on the end of a power hair clipper. Some people have found that a wood rasp makes a good file.

Other than giving your dog a bath from time to time with a quality dog shampoo, brushing him well, and keeping him in good health so that he is not plagued by skin problems which canine flesh is heir to, there is very little more to do than to train him to show well.

In training your dog as you move him around on a loose leash and stop him, at least one foot will be in the correct position. With much effort and practice you should be able to walk him into a show pose and with the use of a little liver for bait, keep him showing well. Wag your hand in front of him and say, "Wag your tail." It won't take too long a time before a wag of your hand will produce a wag of his tail. Dals look better with the tail moving than just hanging at half mast.

Exercise is important. If it is at all possible to move your dog for a mile or so each day at a given pace, do it. Determine which speed shows your dog's movement to best advantage by having someone else move the dog for you at various speeds. Then work at that pace each day. Too fast for you to keep up? Try using a bicycle.

Swimming is good for the Dal but you have to be careful not to overdo this form of exercise. Loaded shoulders can be the result. There are many ailments which can befall all dogs including the Dalmatian. The Dal is subject to skin troubles which crop up from time to time. Much of the pinking which occurs on Dals is diagnosed as skin allergy. Many people refer to "grass allergy." Whatever causes the rash or pinking probably has more to do with the general metabolism of the dog than with grass.

When you notice this sort of rash occurring on your Dal, get a fungicide lotion from your veterinarian to put on it. The reason for this is that scratching the lesions, and surely the dog is going to scratch an itch, can cause a fungus to start in the skin and this will then spread over the dog's body and make the skin condition much more difficult to control.

Also check your dog's diet. Mr. John Lowery of the Dalmatian Research Foundation developed a rice diet which is very good for those dogs who tend to have skin problems. This diet is not difficult to prepare and the dogs seem to love it. A recipe and instructions can be obtained by writing to Mr. Lowery at the Dalmatian Research Foundation, 720 Woodberry Road, York, PA 17403.

The Dalmatian has a urinary system rare in canines. The Dal is the only breed of dog whose urine, even as yours and mine, stops short of forming urea or allantoin and produces, instead, uric acid. This peculiarity is thought to be one of the causes of bladder and kidney stones in Dalmatians. Too many dogs are lost to this condition. Sometimes a stone will be lodged in the urethra and will cause great pain. Other times "gravel" will be passed in the urine. Sometimes, in acute cases, the stones will pile up and completely block the passage from the bladder and this situation will require surgical removal of the stones.

Again, the rice diet is of help in maintaining a healthy animal. Massive doses of Vitamin A are frequently prescribed to keep the epithelial tissues healthy. The bladder is lined with these tissues. Use of Allopurinal in treatment of dogs subject to stones has had some success.

Much research is being done in these areas and it is to be hoped that a cure will be found in the near future.

9

Breeders' Practices

THERE ARE CERTAIN PRACTICES common to all breeds of dogs among the ethical breeders. These cover breeding, selling and showing, and have been developed as unwritten laws to protect both buyer and seller.

A bitch should not be bred before the age of one year or after the age of eight years. A male should not be used at stud under the age of nine months. A registration application showing the age of the stud to be less than this will probably be questioned by the American Kennel Club. The bitch should not be bred more than two out of three seasons and, preferably, only every other season.

Before going into the breeding aspects of the sport of dogs it would be well for the breeder to become familiar with the breed standard and understand what he is doing. Breeding pet stock is not in the best interests of any breed. Pet buyers should be encouraged to have their puppies neutered. The breeder should explain to the puppy buyer the faults of the animal and why it should not be used in a breeding program. Anyone who intends to breed should buy top quality "show stock," study pedigrees, compare his own dog to the dog he plans to use in the breeding, avoid common faults, and be prepared to cull when the puppies arrive.

It is considered proper for the bitch to "visit" the stud dog. Two breedings about 24 to 48 hours apart are the custom. Some stud owners prefer one breeding and feel that is sufficient. It is the custom, too, to offer a repeat breeding for no cost if the bitch fails to have a litter. One puppy constitutes a litter. However, most stud dog owners will allow a repeat breeding in the case of a single puppy in the litter. Many stud dog owners will allow a repeat breeding if the bitch is so unfortunate as to lose a litter after it has been whelped. The stud fee pays for the stud service only. It does not guarantee puppies. The proven male covers the bitch. If the bitch is a proven bitch there should be puppies.

Before selling puppies, the breeder should have had them checked for worms, wormed them if necessary, and given either temporary or permanent DHL inoculations depending upon the advice of the veterinarian. Puppies should not be sold under seven weeks of age. According to dog behaviorists the 49th day is the ideal time for a puppy to move into its new home. Earlier than that the puppy is still in need of its dam and litter mates.

Every Dalmatian breeder should make sure that the homes to which his puppies are moving are suitable. Small children can be cruel to dogs without meaning to be and parents must be aware that the dog should have some protection from them. A fenced yard is a plus but an unfenced yard is not necessarily an insurmountable drawback if the new owners are responsible people and are prepared to take on the care, walking on leash, etc., and training of the pup.

The buyer should be given a return privilege written into the sales agreement. A limited amount of time should be specified so that the new owner may have the puppy inspected by his own veterinarian. This practice should be encouraged. And there should be a written bill of sale signed by the breeder and the buyer. This should contain the name of the sire and the dam, their AKC registration numbers, date of whelping, color of puppy, and any other pertinent information either party specifies and both agree to. If the litter has been registered a registration application should be given the buyer along with the bill of sale. If the dog has been individually registered, the registration certificate, duly signed is given along with at least a three generation pedigree of the pup.

Dalmatian puppies which are born "patched" should not be sold. However, if one is sold it should be without registration papers and with agreement to neuter the animal. The new owner should receive a bill of sale with these facts stated in writing, which both buyer and seller should sign.

A patched Dalmatian has its patch at birth. This is a large area of solid color, black or liver, which can be seen while the puppy is still wet and which does not disappear when the coat dries. The pigment remains. Tiny touches of color on the ear, toes, nose, etc., are not to be confused with a patch. The color in a patch is intense and uniform. And the texture is quite velvety in the adult dog as the patch, soft and silky like the rest of the puppy coat, does not change when the puppy matures. Sometimes spots will form and run together. These can be distinguished from patches because of the white hairs which intermingle with the black or liver spots which have run together.

Ch. Melody Up Up and Away CD, Pooka, producer of
11 champions. Owned by David and Susan MacMillan.

Three week old puppy - "pick of litter!"

Litter of British puppies.

Perhaps the most discouraging thing is to find a deaf puppy in the litter. Fate seems to enjoy making the very best puppy in the litter, the one with the best markings, the best movement, etc., the deaf pup. It is heartbreaking as there is nothing which can be done for this pup. The best course is to have the veterinarian put the puppy down.

There is a deaf gene in Dalmatians. Deafness can be tested in the puppies at about four weeks of age. The test should be repeated at five and again at six weeks to be sure. Generally, if a puppy is deaf the evidence will appear by this time. Occasionally a puppy will lose its hearing at a later time but this is not usual. Of course, a deaf puppy cannot be sold. Most people euthanize them. However, you may prefer to contact the Dalmatian Research Foundation or the Kellogg Institute at the University of Michigan, Ann Arbor, concerning any deaf puppies. Many research studies are being done on the problem of deafness and the puppy may make a contribution to one of them.

A puppy sold as a "show" prospect offers another situation which both the buyer and seller must consider. When the dog has reached maturity, if it has developed any disqualifying faults, the buyer should receive as rebate a portion of the purchase price bringing the cost of the puppy to the level of the pet prospect. This, of course, is an item to be included in the sales agreement. Generally the buyer does not wish to give up a dog he has had for a year or more but since the dog did not live up to its promise as a show prospect, he should not have more than a pet price invested.

Too often we hear of a breeder who advertises extensively and who represents every puppy sold as a "Show Dog." This is rationalized on the basis that the only requirement for a dog to be classified as a "show dog" is eligibility to be registered with AKC as purebred and having no disqualifying faults. It may still lack quality.

Unfortunately, there have been cases where inferior dogs have been campaigned to their championship even though originally these dogs were sold as pet quality by knowedgeable breeders who believed them not worthy of competing for a title. All too frequently because of advertising and other promotion such dogs have sired many litters and left their less-than-desirable mark on the breed.

Most dog fanciers are in the sport as a hobby and few, if any, actually make or attempt to make any money from their dogs. And most dog fanciers who have been in the sport for a number of years are willing to help novices with advice and physical aid if the novice will accept it. Too often the novice after obtaining his show dog, breeding one litter, sounds as if he "wrote the book." This attitude causes old timers to resent the newcomer. Those novices who listen and ask questions will learn a great deal from those with more experience. There are no stupid questions.

98

Puppies at play. Owned by Jane Helms Venes. The leader was Ch. Spattered Sunshine Teddy Bear.

Puppies at age 3 weeks owned by John Yama. Sired by Ch. Coachman's Chuck-a-Luck ex Ch. Lancer's Cinnamon Snow.

The Williamsburg Village in Virginia was restored to its original pre-Revolutionary condition "that the future may learn from the past." Besides asking old timers, newcomers can also read and study. The following suggesting basic reading guide offers much useful knowledge

American Kennel Club, an Official Publication, *The Complete Dog Book*

Brown, Curtis and Thelma, *The Art and Science of Judging Dogs*

Dangerfield, Stanley, and Howell, Elsworth, eds., *International Encyclopedia of Dogs*

Fiennes, Richard and Alice, *The Natural History of Dogs*

Frankling, Eleanor, *Practical Dog Breeding and Genetics*

Gaines Dog Research Center, *Basic Guide to Canine Nutrition*

Lyon, McDowell, *The Dog in Action*

Nichols, Virginia Tuck, *How to Show Your Own Dog*

Onstott, Kyle, *The New Art of Breeding Better Dogs*

Pearsall, Milo, and Leedham, Charles G., *Dog Obedience Training*

Pfaffenberger, Clarence, *The New Knowledge of Dog Behavior*

Riddle, Maxwell, *Your Show Dog*

Saunders, Blanche, *Training You to Train Your Dog*

Whitney, Leon F., *How to Breed Dogs*

10

Background For Breeders

REGISTRATION wasn't nearly as important in the early part of this century as it is today. Until the early 50's it was possible to register dogs solely by virtue of their wins. Early on the requirement was 10 championship points acquired. These would allow a dog or bitch to be entered in the stud book. Later this was changed to 15 championship points, or a championship.

One of the most prominent lines in the breed came from some of this unregistered type stock, Reigate. Ch. Reigate's Lady Culpepper and Ch. Reigate's Lady Fauquier were litter sisters out of an unregistered bitch named Jo and sired by Freckles who was also unregistered. Freckles' dam and Jo's dam were the same, Betty, an unregistered bitch. Freckles' sire was Cress Brook Pepper owned by George W. Cutting and bred by A. E. Bonner of Coopersville, MI. Jo's sire was Skipper, unregistered as were his parents, Tom and Star. Betty's sire was Nip, an unregistered dog but her dam was Borodale Witch, bred and owned by Mrs. John R. Gladding, Providence, RI.

Ch. Reigate's Lady Culpepper's claim to fame is, of course, the fact that she is the dam of Ch. Reigate's Bold Venture. This great dog is in the pedigree of many of the leading dogs of today. He had one blue eye, perfectly acceptable even in those days.

Until 1963 there wasn't a single word in the Dalmatian Standard concerning the dog's bite. We have watched the judging at many specialties and many other Dalmatian classes where the judges never looked at the mouths. The first judge we saw do so was Derek Rayne back in the late 50's. When asked why he checked bites since the standard didn't cover it, he replied that a dog with a bad bite was an unsound dog and he wouldn't put it up. Since 1963 a bad bite is a disqualification. From time to time puppies will be born with a bad bite and the breeders are hard put to tell where this is coming from. Those of us who have Bold Venture in the background of our pedigrees can stop wondering. His dam, Lady Culpepper, was badly undershot! This information comes from correspondence with Mrs. Close who showed the bitch to championship for her in-laws, George and Mary Leigh Lane, owners of Reigate Kennels. Correspondence with Mrs. Close supplied by a friend of the breed has revealed much of what is in the past of many of the great ones, and what many people thought of some of the greats and near-greats in the breed. Comments on judging, breeding, and showing were most interesting. It is unfortunate that we cannot publish the letters for the edification of all.

Of course, Lady Culpepper was not the only Dalmatian to have a bad bite but since her son was a great sire and appears in so many extended pedigrees she has been singled out as a culprit.

Importing stock can be a risky business. It can improve a breeding program or wreck it with new problems. A breeder should have a reason. The import should be able to make a contribution to his breeding program. The breeder had better definitely know what he is looking for in an import. Just because a dog comes from overseas does not necessarily make him a great sire or dam. One must take into consideration the genetical background of the dog, his good points and his faults, the good points and the faults of the bitch or bitches to be bred to him, and make sure that the breeding would be a good one. A careful breeder will take all these things into consideration when breeding to a domestic dog. To import or not to import can be a puzzler. Naturally at one time it was a necessity. Now, it probably isn't as necessary. Get from most of the good English bloodlines can be found in the U.S.

One additional important thing to remember when importing from England is that there is no size disqualification there. The English dogs tend to be larger. The spotting patterns, however, seem to be better.

Early imports which had a great deal of influence on the breed (early after World War II) include the dogs which Leo Meeker brought over. He had a number from the famous Cabaret Kennels of Miss Monkhouse. A few years later Dr. Jackson of Fort Worth, TX, imported Cabaret Courtcard who became an American champion. Courtcard would probably be measured out today. Ch. Nigel of Welfield and Stock-Dal is another import which can be found in many pedigrees. Sidney Stockdale imported this dog as well as Ch. Welfield Guardsman and Ch. Jason Widdington. Nigel, of course, was the greatest of these three.

Ch. Astwood Qui Vive was imported by Hugh Chisholm of Strathglass Kennels. He also imported Mesra Dilema and Ch. Moonmageic of Chasfield.

All of these can be found in old pedigrees behind the dogs of today. Long Last Kennels of Lorraine Donahue did some important importing. The great Am. & Eng. Ch. Colonsay Blacksmith who did much for the breed in England as well as in the U.S. was one of the dogs Mrs. Donohue imported. She also imported Washakie Bolehills Barbara and Am. Ch. An English Rose of Colonsay.

The great liver dog imported from England was Am. & Eng. Ch. Colonsay Storm. Storm came to this country via Mexico. His first owner on this continent was Dalmex Kennels of Mexico but he was later purchased by Dr. Josiah Harbinson of Ard Aven Kennels. He was a magnificently balanced dog, well marked with very dark liver spots, moved well, and had a commanding appearance in the ring. He was a true coach dog.

The Prescotts of Tandem Acres and the Garrets of Garrett's Ice Cream Dals were also among those who imported some English stock. The Hayes of Coachmaster Kennels also imported from England, and Little Slam Kennels of Lita and Bill Weeks, formerly in California, now in Arizona, imported three Ascotheath dogs from the kennels of Mr. and Mrs. C. D. Cudd.

The year before she died Mrs. Bonney imported Ch. Duxfordham Yessam Marquis. He appeared at the DCA specialty in Chicago in 1966.

The foundation dog of the great Williamsdale Kennels was Am. Can. Ch. Elmcroft Coacher who was imported in dam. This dog sired 27 champions and had great influence on the breed. In addition to all the good things he did for Dalmatians, he also left a very straight left stifle in many of his descendants. Williamsdale imported a number of other dogs including Am. Ch. Colonsay Tantivey Claudia, Am. Ch. Penny Parade of Williamsdale, and the famous Igor of Key of Williamsdale, also an American champion. This latter dog was to be a great sire as Coacher had been before him. He sired many champions but his prepotency as a stud did not measure up to that of Coacher.

Igor produced many champions. However Igor did not help the breed as the greatest contribution to his get was made in the area of his less desirable features. Coacher, on the other hand, did make a great contribution. He marked his progeny with good shoulders, heads, fronts, and excellent movement, and his good points are to be found even into the third and fourth generation. His poor angulation, however, unfortunately also has come through the ages.

There have been other dogs who, in themselves, have been great dogs and who have sired a number of champions but have not contributed to the improvement of the breed. Generally, these were not the result of planned line breeding.

At the present time there is a great deal of exporting of dogs going on from the United States. Some unethical people feel this is an opportunity to get rid of the culls. Others realizing that people overseas are trying to better their stock are willing to ship good specimens of their breed. Dog shows are such a new popular activity in so many countries it behooves us to send only the very best. The name of the breeder remains on the dog forever and regardless of the language involved, the name can be read in the catalogs.

Judges from the United States are invited to judge everywhere. If you sell a poor specimen overseas and it is shown in the country where it was sent, your name as breeder will be seen in the catalog and your reputation as a breeder will be diminished in the eyes of the U.S. judges who see it. If, on the other hand, you ship a good dog to a foreign country your name as breeder will be enhanced because of this dog. Fortunately the Dalmatian breeders seem to be exporting good dogs. Some of the dogs return to the U.S. to be campaigned and it is good to know we helped the breed in another country.

Many dogs have been imported from Canada. One Canadian kennel, now no longer active, can account for the foundation stock of several very successful breeders in the States. The kennel was Kay Robinson's Willowmount. Looking into some fairly recent pedigrees we find many references to the Willowmount prefix.

When the standard was changed in January 1963 it carried a requirement on size. The ideal Dalmatian is from 19 to 23 inches at the withers. A Dal standing over 24 inches is disqualified. At the Wisconsin Kennel Club show in January 1963 the judge, Mr. William Kendrick, called for a measurement in the ring on the first Dalmatian to be questioned on size. According to the measuring committee the dog was under 24 inches and was allowed to remain in the ring. Mr. Kendrick did not put the dog up as it was, he said, too tall for his taste. Many of the spectators were surprised that the dog was not measured out. It was never shown again. Mr. Kendrick later commented that he would never measure another Dalmatian. We have not discussed this position with him since the wicket system has been in use in the United States.

When breeding Dals it is difficult to know what to expect in the way of numbers in the litter. There are litters of one puppy on record and also litters of over 20. Most litters run to about 8 dogs, on the average.

Choosing the show puppies from the litter is a difficult task. Check the litter at 5 weeks and again at 8 weeks. Old time breeders have taught us that at those ages the puppies are most nearly like they will be at maturity. After 8 weeks do not look at the puppies except as pets until they are almost a year old. During those months some parts of the pups grow in peculiar fashion. Sometimes they are too high in the rear; other times you can begin to wonder what happened to their hind legs. And heads!—ugh! As the bones grow, and they grow at different rates of speed, the dogs can look dish-faced, roman nosed, too broad in skull, too narrow in skull, you name it. . . . but if the head was okay at eight weeks it will probably be a good head at maturity.

Pigment is another worry for the Dal breeder. A good rule of thumb is the outside-inside theory. Eye rims which are not filled will probably fill by maturity if the color starts in the corners. Noses which have color on the edges will probably fill. Noses which have pink corners probably will not. There is no hard and fast rule to cover this but experience has taught us that the probabilities are as stated.

Patched puppies should be put down. Mrs. Bonney, the true Mrs. Dalmatian of the United States, did not put down patched puppies which were otherwise sound. She gave them to people without papers. She said that people who received a dog as a gift hardly ever asked to have the registration on the dogs. She also made it quite clear that the patched puppies were not to be used for breeding.

Dalmatians have certain characteristics which are quite different from most other breeds. The puppies, for instance, are born white. The spots appear at about the time the eyes open. Shadows of the spots can be seen on the skin while the whelp is still wet and as the days pass the shadows become more pronounced until they are truly spots. Some of the dogs continue to spot out for a year or so. Others get all of their spots at one time. Frequently these latter seem to be too heavily marked for the show ring but as the puppy grows, it grows into its spots. Other dogs will start to "tick out" when they reach about five years of age. This, of course, is undesirable. But it happens.

There are many tales told of uninformed first-time breeders destroying whole litters of puppies because they were all white at birth, feeling that the bitch must have been bred by some unknown dog and the puppies were all mongrels. Alas, too many of these tales are true.

Occasionally a puppy will be born with a slight touch of color on an ear, a toe, across an eye or perhaps a tiny spot on the nose. These, to the experienced breeder, are the sign of good pigment.

At one time, in England, the Dalmatian was interbred with the white Bull Terrier, supposedly to help broaden the chest and deepen the brisket of the latter breed. Many people and they are knowledgeable people, say that the deaf gene in the Dalmatian came from this mixing of the breeds. The Bull Terrier people bemoan the fact that some of their choice specimens carry some spots. These are not permitted in the show ring if they occur behind the neck. Stand behind a group of Bull Terriers sometime. You can see the shadow of spots on their skin showing through the fur when the light is right.

In the 1850's a James Hinks of Birmingham, England, decided to work with crosses between the Bull Terrier and the White English terrier to produce a true bull terrier. Before his experiments there was no true bull terrier. As the name suggests he is descended from the Bulldog but not the type of Bulldog seen today. The early Bulldogs were long tailed and resembled the present day Boxers more than any other breed and they were used for the cruel sport of

Dinner time!

Part of a Pryor Creek litter. Puppy on far right grew up to be Ch. Coachman's Courbette, a group winner.

bullbaiting. The dog frequently suffered from goring by the bull. Trying to get more determination into the breed various terriers were introduced to the bulldog breeding in an attempt to obtain a more intelligent and more agile dog. The results were called the Bull and Terrier. But about then the sport of bullbaiting was outlawed. The dogs were then put in the "pits" for dog fighting. Over a period of time the dogs developed their own type similar in appearance to the Staffordshire Bull Terrier.

Then Mr. Hinks started his work. The white English terrier he used is now extinct. These dogs were said to be similar in appearance to the modern Manchester but were, of course, white. Mr. Hinks used Dalmatians in his experiments and eventually produced an all-white strain which he named Bull Terriers. At first his dogs were not accepted by the fighting fraternity as there was a feeling that they wouldn't have the aggressive ability of the old Bull and Terrier. A fight was arranged and Mr. Hink's bitch demolished a well-known old type fighter and was so little marked she was able to compete at a show the next day. Thus the Bull Terrier was accepted.

Since a deaf gene can be a color-linked gene with white animals it is felt by some that the deafness in Dalmatians came from this experiment.

We do know that many white Bull Terriers have been left with latent spots on the skin and sometimes the spots develop on the body, thus making it impossible for them to be shown. Color on the head of a Bull Terrier is allowed. This entire experiment dealt with white Bull Terriers. The colored one came later.

The deafness found is characterized by the deterioration in the organs of Corti, that membrane stretched across the ear drum of the dog and named for the scientist who discovered it.

Among the studies which have been made concerning congenital deafness in Dalmatians is one by M. H. Lurie, M.D., Boston, MA, found in *The Laryngoscope,* Vol. LVIII, No. 4, April 1948. Another was made by Cezar Fernandez, M.D., at the University of Chicago. W. R. Hudson, M.D., Durham, NC and R. J. Ruben, M.D., Baltimore, MD, reported on *Hereditary Deafness in the Dalmatian Dog* in *Archives of Otolaryngology,* Vol. 75, March 1962, and a group of Swedish scientists reported on *Genetic Hearing Impairment in the Dalmatian Dog* for the Royal Veterinary College and King Gustaf V Research Institute, Stockholm.

In any event there is deafness in Dalmatians. Some unscrupulous people try to sweep this fact under the rug. We have heard people say, "I have never had a deaf puppy in my kennel." To us this means they have disposed of the puppy as soon as they found it was deaf. When someone says they have never bred a deaf puppy our eyebrows are raised. Either these people have not bred any Dalmatians or have had no more than one or two litters. Deafness occurs. It is in the breed. It would be better to admit the deficiency and keep good records on it and see if it can be stamped out by selective breeding. This is a difficult project, of course, but it could be done. The Alaskan Malamute fanciers are hard at work getting rid of dwarfism. All studs are test bred before being used as breeding stock. We could probably devise some way to do this with deaf dogs. Surely the scientists are working on the problem.

A study made at the University of Chicago in the late 50's indicated that the histology of deafness in Dalmatians is the same as that found in a child born of a mother who experienced German measles during the first trimester of her pregnancy. Other studies show that the organ of Corti is missing in deaf Dalmatians. Some Dalmatians lack an eardrum altogether and, of course, cannot hear.

All Dalmatian puppies should be tested for deafness. At about four weeks, after the ears have opened, the puppies should be observed and tested for this sense. There are various ways of doing the test and consultation with other breeders, your veterinarian, and possibly an ear, nose and throat physician, will explain how to do it. Stamping on the floor, clapping your hands, blowing a whistle, are all useless activities. The puppies who are deaf compensate for the lack of hearing to the extent that it is sometimes almost impossible to detect. However, the puppy who continues to sleep when the food pan arrives and doesn't stir until all the other puppies are scrambling for the goodies is the one to watch. The yelper is another. There are times when a deaf puppy will sit and howl at the world. The rest of the litter is quietly sleeping. The "yelper" is giving vent to his frustrations. Watch him. He may be deaf. All of these points are possibilities. None is definite proof.

Testing at four weeks, again at five, and then again at six weeks should determine which puppies are hearing puppies and which are not. Reports have been made, however, that sometimes a pup which can hear at six weeks suddenly goes deaf at three months. We have never experienced this phenomenon but others have reported that it has happened.

Quite recently someone in Michigan reported that a puppy which tested as deaf at six weeks, who lacked the proper ear membranes at six weeks, could hear at the age of four months and at that age had developed the membranes. This is a startling development and one to be followed up on.

Another unfortunate characteristic of the Dalmatian is the shedding. Contrary to popular belief all shorthaired dogs are harder to clean after than the longhaired varieties. The hair of a Dalmatian (and of Labrador Retrievers, Boxers, and other shorthaired breeds) seems to have a barb on its end. It sticks into furniture, clothing, and even your skin! And the white hair shows up on all dark materials. Brushing your dog's coat each day helps but does not entirely clear up the problem. If you are squeamish about seeing dog hair around your home, do not get a Dalmatian. If you are willing to excuse this problem, you will have a great dog as your pet.

Dalmatians seem to have a sixth sense somewhere in their make-up. We know of a Dalmatian which was purchased by a family to be a companion to their children, four active, rambunctious boys. The fourth child was a cerebral palsied child who had difficulty walking and talking but who wanted to romp and play with his older brothers. The Dalmatian was seven weeks old when he went to live with this family. He grew up being the center of attention, playing football, baseball, racing up and down next to bicycles, and enjoying all the normal activity of small boys. However, when the handicapped child touched his collar he stood very still, walked very slowly with the boy, was as gentle as he could possibly be. When the boy released his collar, the dog was off and running with the gang, so to speak. The parents of these children were both physicians and were both delighted to know that the dog was aware of their child's problem and could adapt to it.

The occasional bad bite in Dalmatians is always shocking to the breeder because, of course, the careful breeder would not have used an animal with a bad bite in his breeding program. Since it is found so rarely it is almost certain to be a recessive characteristic which pops up in an occasional specimen and shocks the breeder. We have found bad bites on both coasts and in between. As we now know some of the "greats" of the past carried bad bites and are probably responsible for the inheritance. All of this points to knowing more than the names on the pedigree and the show records when we are planning a breeding.

Because color in animals is not always constant there are two things which happen which breeders and exhibitors should be aware of. One is bronzing and the other is blackening. Bronzing starts in the shedding of the coat and means that the black or liver hairs lose their color somewhat, so the spots become rust brown in tone, darker in the black, lighter in the liver. How bad the bronzing can be is difficult to determine and many times it can be almost impossible to decide whether the bad color is bronzing or faulty pigmentation in that particular dog. Should the change of color completely disappear after the shedding and the spots become clear black or clear liver, it was only a question of bronzing.

Blackening is another problem in color Dal breeders have to face. Blackening is the opposite of bronzing and occurs only in the liver variety. The liver color darkens, particularly on the back, so much so that the dog, at a quick glance, appears to be marked with both black and liver spots, a tri-color. In the show ring it is sometimes difficult for judges to determine whether or not this process is taking place. Dogs have been disqualified for being tri-colors because the blackening in the spots has given an appearance of black on the back and light liver on the head, sides, and extremities. An informed owner will wait until the dog has completed his shedding and the colors have cleared before applying for reinstatement.

A kitten can be handled as gently as a puppy. Lady, formal name, Ch. Crown Jewel's Flawless Emerald, received widespread newspaper publicity for mothering a 10 day old kitten. Owned by Jane Schenn.

Ch. Pryor Creek's Tuxedo Satin with day-old litter. "You think you've got problems!"

While discussing color it might be well to explain the genetic combinations which occur in the breeding of Dalmatians. The black color is dominant, the liver color is recessive.

The letters BB represent pure for black. Letters Bb represent a black dog carrying the liver gene. And liver is shown with bb. According to some geneticists a dog that is BB can NEVER produce a liver puppy even if mated to a liver. A dog which is Bb can produce either black or liver offspring. A dog which is bb is always liver. However, genetically *anything is possible*.

The usual rule of thumb in breeding shows that a BB dog mated to a BB bitch will produce only black puppies. A BB dog bred to a Bb bitch will produce only black puppies but 50% of the litter will carry the liver gene. A Bb dog and a Bb bitch will have a litter with 25% of the litter BB, 25% bb, and 50% Bb. The genetics' rule also says that a bb dog bred to a bb bitch will always produce liver offspring. There are cases on record, however, where two livers have produced black offspring. This is exceedingly rare. When breeding a Bb dog to a bb bitch 50% of the litter will be liver factored blacks and 50% will be liver. Because these are percentages and the litters are not always divisible in this way, it really takes a large number of dogs and a large number of litters to determine the accuracy of this formula.

According to Dr. Robert H. Schaible, geneticist, University of Indiana, the so-called tri-color is actually a bi-color as there are only two different colors involved, usually black and tan. The white part of the pattern in the Dalmatian results from an absence of color rather than to the presence of a third color. Pigment cells are absent from the white regions of the Dalmatian and the tri-color Sheltie as determined by electron microscopy. Dr. Schaible says, "The absence of pigment cells in the white regions of both breeds is due to one of the mutant genes at the piebald locus. The occurrence of tan spots on the muzzle, feet, which is objectionable in Dalmatians, is due to the effect of the bi-color gene."

Dr. Schaible classifies the color pattern of a Dalmatian showing both black spots and liver spots in two different ways because he feels there are probably two different genetic mechanisms involved. One of these patterns he calls a "mosaic pattern," a black spotted dog showing one or more liver-colored spots. The other is called the "variegated pattern," a liver spotted dog showing one or more black spots. The mosaic pattern is the most common. Explaining it, Dr. Schaible reports "The genetic locus for brown (liver) may be located near the end of one pair of chromosomes. The terminal portion of the chromosome bearing the allelic gene responsible for normal (black) pigmentation is deleted (broken off and lost). The recessive gene for brown which remains on the intact chromosome is then free to be expressed in all pigment cells that descend from the cell in which the loss of chromosome tip occurred. The descendant cells could form a brown spot."

Dr. Schaible has reported that studies of cases of mosaicism in mammals have offered no evidence that mosaicism or variegation is genetically transmitted. In other words, this type of marking is not passed on from one generation to the other. Early prints of Dalmatians show a definite tan marking on the cheek.

Another color variation found in the Dalmatian is in the eye. Many people object to the occasional blue eye. In fact, in many countries the blue eye is frowned upon. Since it is in the genetic make-up of the dog it would take centuries of selective breeding to breed it out. Most geneticists do not know how it is inherited. No experiments have been carried out to breed single blue eyed dogs to double brown eyed dogs and find the ratio of blue to brown in the offspring. What does a double blue eye bred to a double blue eye produce in pups in eye color? Is the blue eye color dominant or recessive to the brown or is it a multiple allele? We need answers to these questions before doing anything to outlaw the blue eye. To date, there is not a shred of evidence that blue eyed Dalmatians produce more deaf puppies or tend to be deaf themselves. It is true in other mammals that blue eyes and deafness are paired, but in the canine this fact has yet to be established. The old wives tale keeps fluttering about: the blue eye and deafness in the Dal are connected. There are absolutely no scientific facts on which to base this claim.

In 1978 the Dalmatian Club of America initiated a study on deafness. Questionnaires were sent to the membership asking for statistics on the correlation of deafness with variables of pigmentation in Dalmatian dogs. The membership is anxiously awaiting the results of this study.

11

Showing The Dalmatian

Now that you are ready to show your Dalmatian you will want to groom him properly.

Usually the whiskers are clipped and any scraggly areas around the tuck-up, the "pants," and cowlicks are trimmed away. The idea is to present as smooth an outline as possible. If you have not trimmed your dog, don't worry so long as he is clean. Many Dals are shown untrimmed and unclipped in the rough area. But there are few more unpleasant sights than a dirty Dalmatian in the show ring.

It is a good idea to carry a tote bag equipped with a damp sponge and a towel, among other things, so that you can clean off any extraneous dirt from travel or exercise pens. The short coat will respond to a quick sponging and toweling. This is one of the plus values of the Dal as a show dog. And be sure the visit to the exercise area has produced results. The dog will show better and will not embarrass you in the ring. You should be at the show approximately an hour before your scheduled judging time so that you can observe the judge in the ring, his movement pattern, and how he goes about examining the dog; and so that you may check in with the ring steward and get your armband. Of course, if you are the first dog in the ring the first thing in the morning, the judge will explain what he wants you to do. Be sure to carry out all the judge's instructions to the best of your ability.

If your dog is absent, (has been "pulled" or is just not be shown that day) report this to the ring steward so that poor soul is not searching all around the ringside for the missing dog. And watch the ring steward so you will be on hand when your class is called. There is nothing so annoying to a ring steward as the exhibitor who has picked up his arm-band, stands ring side in conversation with other exhibitors, and ignores the time to enter the ring. It happens at every show and in almost every breed. The ring stewards are exhausted by the end of the day because of non-heeding exhibitors.

When you enter the ring take your dog to the position the steward points out to you. It may be the other side of the ring, or it may be just inside the gate. The judge will have instructed the steward where he wants his dogs set up. Set up your dog and wait for further instructions from the judge. If you are first in line and the judge asks you to lead the class around the ring (and this is done counter-clockwise) make sure all of the handlers in the ring are ready to take off when you do. It is bad manners and looks silly for a single entry to whip about the ring when the rest of the class is just preparing to do so.

After the dogs have been moved together, the judge will examine each entry and move it individually. Be sure to move your dog on a loose lead. Practice at home before the show so that your dog will move with you at a good pace, a pace you have determined in practice shows off your dog's movement to best advantage. And practice having your dog walk into a show pose so that when you return to the judge after your individual gaiting your dog will show himself to be the winner you know he is. If you are in the line, remember to allow space in front of you so that you are not running up on the dog in front of yours. Remember, you are the only one who can determine this space, the dog in front cannot. And when you move your dog in the ring do not give the command "Heel!." This is an obedience command. When you move your dog in the show ring he is not heeling. In fact, a dog which moved in the obedience ring the way dogs are moved in the show ring, would fail the heeling exercise. Find another word such as "Show!" or "Gait!" or just "Let's Go!." Remember there are some breed judges who have little or no interest in obedience and when they hear an obedience command they are turned off. This shouldn't be true, but unfortunately it is.

Most people prefer a show lead. It isn't necessary, however, to use one. Some people use the simple choke chain, the one with tiny links, and others use a martingale type lead, one which gives a little more control of the dog than the plain nylon show lead. Make sure it fits well up about the ears from around the neck. In any event, practice with all of these leads and find the one with which you and your Dal are the most comfortable. Do not "string up" your dog on any lead. Showing in a relaxed fashion will put your dog at ease and he will show naturally.

The subject of dress is also of importance. Do not wear anything which will flap, such as a loose jacket, vest, or coat. Any clothing flapping at the dog as you move detracts from the dog. Women should never enter the ring in high heels, which are dangerous and noisy on hard surfaces at indoor shows.

Flat heeled shoes with rubber soles are best for either sex. And choose your color with care. A checked skirt or pants will not give your dog a good background. Solid colors of red, blue, green, or even black, are much better. If you are showing a liver Dalmatian you may choose green or brown as they probably show off the dog to best advantage. Some people use colored show leads to emphasize the color of the dog. A red lead on a black spotted dog is very pretty. A green or brown show lead on the liver spotted variety is most attractive. A white lead is always in good taste.

When people start becoming involved with Dalmatians there is a tendency to have every accessory a spotted one. Some have worn polka dotted dresses to show their dogs. This is a poor idea as the spots on the dress detract from the dog. We must remember that we are showing the dog not the handler. Some enthusiastic people have had their automobiles painted white with black spots. A newspaper photo of a young man in a convertible with his Dal in Rhode Island during the 50's attracted a great deal of attention all over the U.S. as it made the wire services. At the present time some have spotted their station wagons and one enthusiast went so far as to paint his house white with black spots.

When the late Harland Meistrell and Mrs. Meistrell were living in Great Neck, L.I. and were doing a great deal of training of Dals, they painted their fence on the inside of the yard to match the dogs. It was a *trompe d'oeil* sort of thing and it was difficult to distinguish the dogs from the fence. Photos of a dog going over the broad jump against the fence also made the wire services and caused interest and amusement all over the nation.

But we must remember when showing that the dog is the spotted wonder, not the handler, and do nothing in the ring to detract from the dog. Even a dangling leash can be annoying to the judge. As you move with your dog the movement of the end of the leash can catch the eye of the judge and so move his attention away from your dog momentarily.

If you are so fortunate as to be placed in a class, any place, do say something to let the judge know you understood his placement. Signal with a nod, a wave, or a "thank you". And then move to the proper ring number immediately. Stand so that the judge can see your armband and can mark his book properly.

Ring manners are important. They are nothing more than good manners in any given situation. Remember that showing dogs is a sport and good sportsmanship should prevail.

12

Obedience

THE TOP WORKING DALMATIAN is a joy to behold in the obedience ring. Many people feel that the Dalmatian is a difficult dog to train. The true problem is not with the dog but with the handlers. You must be smarter than your dog to do well in obedience. The Dalmatian is as easily trained as a Poodle or a Golden Retriever if the handler will take the time to study his dog and learn its own particular idiom. This is platitudinous in itself as most dogs have their own set way of doing things and you have to learn what these are.

Once you and your Dal click, there will be few problems in his training. He is quick to learn and retains his lessons well. As with most dogs, doing something twice the same way is a habit. If, in training the handler will take the time to make sure the dog can NOT make a mistake, a la the Pearsall method of training using gadgets to help, the dog will work well and without goofs.

When the sport of obedience was introduced into this country in 1933 by Mrs. Whitehouse Walker, former owner of Carillon Kennels, Standard Poodle breeders, many people became interested in it.

Before this time obedience training had long been known and practiced in Europe. Dogs were used in police work and the armies had also made use of canines as guard and sentry dogs.

The American Kennel Club adopted obedience in 1937 and almost immediately the Dal people jumped into this phase of the sport. The first UDT dog was Io, owned by Harland and Lois Meistrell who trained and worked

116

Dals in obedience from the inception of this side of the sport, winning frequently. The first Ch. UDT Dal came from the Cleveland area and was named Ch. The Duke of Gervais.

The interesting thing about these early UDT dogs in this country is that they were both 10 years old at the time their training was started. Who says you can't teach an old dog new tricks?

Of course the exercises were different in those days, and so was the scoring. In those days a tracking test was required in order to obtain the coveted UD. Now a successful tracking dog can earn a Tracking title without any other obedience degree. At the present time we have a number of UDT Dalmatians and a number of Ch. UD Dals.

Another exercise which has since disappeared was the "speak" on command. On signal from the handler the dog was required to bark and continue to do so as often as the handler gave the signal, the judge determining when to stop the "speaking."

The DCA added obedience classes to its specialities almost as soon as AKC added obedience to its jurisdiction. Among the early exhibitors were the Meistrells. They seemed to win at the DCA shows with embarrassing regularity as did Kenneth Naumer with his Dal, Checkers, who became a UDT dog.

Among the early afficionados of both sides of the sport, obedience and conformation, were Mrs. Wilbur Dewell, Mrs. Lee Ramsey, Mrs. Paul Moore and Mrs. Mary Munro Smith.

Perhaps there is something in the physical and mental make-up of the Dalmatian which makes them eager to work at an older age. In March 1977 an eight year old Dalmatian bitch competed in the Los Angeles Schutzhund Club trial and was awarded NASA A.D., or endurance test. Her name is Der Heidelberg of Linfield, CDX, PGE, AD, and she is owned by Harry Lockhard. The test required the dog to go 12½ miles in 2 hours and still be able to do some obedience work, including jumping a 40 inch jump. Heidi is the first Dal to earn this degree in either the U.S. or Canada.

Other well known obedience dogs in the early years of this side of dog showing were Ch. Whiteside Sioux Oros UD and Tihera UDT, an unregistered Dal from English breeding. These dogs were trained by the Meistrells.

When the war broke out a number of dogs were needed for dogs for defense. The Long Island Kennel Club was active in this effort and in cooperation with the Long Island Dog Training Club and some other training groups they organized a group of amateur trainers to train guard dogs. Lois Meistrell was among those trainers.

Although many of the clubs continued to hold their shows annually, much of the dog activity was slowed down because of the war effort. When the K-9 Corps was formed by the armed services the late Harland Meistrell was tapped to assist in this project and Dogs for Defense became a supplier of suitable dogs to the Corps.

Mrs. Bonney of Tally Ho Kennels gave a Dalmatian called Hector. The Meistrells trained this dog for the Corps and he was so quick to learn and so intelligent that he acquired two legs on his CD and 7 points toward his championship before going on active duty as a guard dog for the Army. He spent the war patrolling an oil refinery in New Jersey.

When he returned to Mrs. Bonney after the war he was still an affectionate dog. All thought of his finishing his championship had to be discarded as his shoulders were completely "loaded" with muscle. He did, however, manage to get his third leg on his CD. He did not have much difficulty in returning to civilian life except that he objected to anyone holding any object in hand. All gardeners and staff members at Tally Ho had to be warned to drop rakes and hoes until Hector had passed by. Newcomers were always treated as enemies by Hector until they were introduced to the dog and he was convinced that they were acceptable.

At one time Quaker's Acre, Mary Munro Smith's famous kennel in Florida, held the record for the most champions with obedience titles in the U.S.

Ch. Quaker's Acre Ditto, CDX, a Velvet Frank son out of Quaker Oats Pirette was Mrs. Smith's first obedience dog. He qualified for his CD in three consecutive shows, earning an HIT in two of them and a second high in the third. At the same time he was being shown in conformation. He earned his CDX in three consecutive shows with all scores above 195. And at one show he was HIT and Group I, quite an accomplishment.

Mrs. Smith had so many obedience dogs and so many champions it is impossible to name them all. She had 80 champions to her credit when she moved from the Miami-Fort Lauderdale area to North Carolina. (She has since moved to Canada). At the same time she was also involved in breeding Morgan horses, served as secretary for the Miami Dog Club, as president of the Dog Training Club of Hollywood and Fort Lauderdale, as secretary of that group for a number of years, show chairman, trophy chairman, and as a trainer.

One wonderful story Mrs. Smith tells concerns a dog she had sold to some people in New York City who took him to obedience training classes held in the basement of a church near where they lived. After he was trained and could be trusted (they thought) they took him for a walk one night, off lead, passing the church where he went for training. The door was open so the dog trotted off into the church and up on the platform where Alcoholics Anonymous was holding a meeting. Mrs. Smith says she wonders what the AA people thought when they saw so many spots before their eyes instead of pink elephants.

118

ois Meistrell with Ch. Whiteside Sioux
ros UD and Tihera UDT, an unregis-
red Dal from English breeding. The
ame of the Dachshund is unknown.

Lorraine Donahue's Spur of Victory
UDT with friend, Ch. Perro Bruno.

A bevy of Quaker's Acre's dogs, all with obedience titles and some with championships. Ch. QA Dalrymple CD, Ch. QA Gay Lady CDX and Ch. QA Abercrombie, CD are in the second row.

119

Ch. Dal Down's Dicie of Shadodal UDT, pictured going over high jump. Her title makes her the first champion UDT bitch in the history of the breed. Owned by Robert and Marge Sullivan. The puppy pictured seated with Mrs. Sullivan is Labyrinth Obviously.

In quite a different section of the country we find the Sullivans pioneering in the field of obedience. They also show in the breed ring. Again the connection with horses is quite plain. Bob Sullivan was a trainer at the Aksarben Stables in Omaha in the years before World War II. The stable dogs there were two liver Dals named Whiskey and Soda, and Bob admired them very much. During the years of the war Bob was in service and while stationed at Fort Knox the Sullivans purchased their first Dalmatian, Maggie. She was an unregistered bitch. After the war the Sullivans moved to Tulsa and purchased Duchess of Dal Downs. This was the foundation of Dal Downs Kennels. Duchess came from the Surbers in Ohio. Bob trained her through her CDX.

In those years it was difficult to find obedience trials in the area but the Sullivans kept trying. They bought a bitch, Pamela of Dal Downs from Mrs. Kane's Dal Dale Kennels in Illinois. Pam was trained and made it through to UD. She was the first UD dog of any breed in the state of Oklahoma. It was difficult to obtain the UD for Pam because very few trials had the required 3 dogs competing in the Utility class.

Cyde Beebe, owner of Ch. Rovingdale's Impudent Ingenue, after winning two Best in Shows with her, allowed the Sullivans to have her. Imp received her CD in 1957. The Sullivans have earned innumerable CD's and CDX's on Dalmatians. In the early 60's they established Sandstone German Shepherds and have accumulated nine CD's, three CDX's, and one UD, plus two tracking titles in German Shepherds.

But the Dalmatians came back to their rightful place with the Sullivans. In 1972 they bought Dal Downs Dicie of Shadodal. Shadodal is the kennel operated by the Whites in Joplin, Mo. Bob completed her obedience titles and Marge finished her championship. She is the first bitch to be a Ch. UDT in the history of Dalmatians in the U.S.

When the Theissens of Brain Tree became interested in the obedience field they spent a great deal of time working their liver Dals to become UD dogs. And Mrs. T. was deeply involved in tracking. Their first Dal was Roadcoach Tess UDT, purchased in 1946 from Roadcoach Kennels. Subsequently their Ch. Green Starr's Antoinette earned her CD but as Dolly writes, "that was the end of my obedience training. After losing Tess, my heart wasn't in it". Her interest in tracking continued, however.

The Theissens were the breeders of Ch. Ginger Gem of Brain Dals and Ch. Didymus of Brain Dals in the 50's. "We bred the sires or dams of quite a few of the puppies we purchased and put them through to their championships," Mrs. Theissen reports.

People ask what makes a good obedience dog? Actually, if you will take time to think about this, the qualities needed to succeed in the obedience ring are exactly the same as those needed in the show ring. You need a dog properly constructed if you are planning to have him jump, run and retrieve. A dog with straight shoulders is going to resent jumping after a short time. Landing on straight shoulders will pound his back teeth and he will begin to resist the commands to jump. A dog with good shoulder lay-back is built to receive the landing; the construction of his fore-arm, upper-arm, and shoulder will cushion the landing and prevent pounding. His rear should be a good one, too, to give him the proper spring needed for a jump.

Of course, not all dogs in obedience trials are worthy of the conformation ring but it would be better if they were.

Notice the number of dogs which are competing in both rings. And a dog that is properly trained for obedience is easier to handle in the show ring. Don't walk into the show ring with your dog after one or two lessons in an obedience class and wonder why the dog sits. It is too soon to show in the breed ring after starting an obedience program. And don't tell your dog to heel in the breed ring. The movement required in judging conformation is not heeling. If a dog were to do the heeling exercise in obedience moving as he does in conformation he would probably fail.

After a few weeks your dog should and most probably will recognize the difference in collars and leashes. These are intelligent animals. They know.

The interest in obedience competition is so keen today that the American Kennel Club has now introduced an OTCH title. In order to win this title a dog must have won 100 points in competition towards it. The number of points available depends upon the number of dogs competing as in the conformation point system. The dog must have been awarded a Utility title before he starts accumulating obedience championship points.

In addition to the 100 points the dog must have won a first place in Utility (or Utility B, if divided) with a minimum of three dogs competing; and must win a first place in Open B with at least six dogs in competition; and a third first place must be won under the conditions of the first two; and there must have been three different judges officiating over the wins.

After winning an OTCH title the dog may continue to accumulate points and the dog having the highest number of points at the end of the year will receive recognition from the American Kennel Club by being published in the *Gazette*. The dog will also receive an award from the Quaker Oats Company which is presented at the obedience cocktail party sponsored by the Association of Obedience Clubs and Judges, at the time of Westminster in New York. To date there are no OTCH Dalmatians but there are several on their way.

In addition to the competition in AKC events the Gaines Dog Food Company has, for several years, sponsored the Obedience Classic. Dogs are required to have accumulated scores above a certain level to be eligible. Three shows are held in two days, a red, white, and blue show. The scores are tallied and averaged and the top dog becomes just that, TOP DOG, for the year.

Regionals are held in various sections of the U.S. in preparation for the Classic itself.

Earning a UDT title is something to be proud of and earning a UDT and a championship is even more of an accomplishment. To date, four Dals have acquired the dual titles. Three of them are still living so it will be interesting to see if any of them can acquire an OTCH.

The four Dalmatians with Ch. UDT are Ch. Duke of Gervais, owned and trained by Maurice Gervais in 1946; Ch. Dal Down's Dicie of Shadodal, owned and trained by Bob and Marge Sullivan in 1976; Ch. Cal-Dal Chocolate Chip, owned by Jon and Karen Mett; and Ch. Spotted Dapper Dan, the most recent to join these special ranks, owned by Edward J. and Mary Ann Murphy. He received the final title, UDT, in 1979.

Obedience buffs will tell you that getting a 200 score is almost an impossibility and a dog which has earned a 200 is always looked upon with awe. In California Jere Bates showed a dog named Monti's Mister Mickey UD. Mister Mickey not only scored 200 in Utility but he acquired a total of nine—count 'em—nine 200's. This was accomplished during the 60's and covered virtually the same exercises that are in use today.

Sandra Hodson and her Freckles (Belle Monti's Little Freckles UD) was also a combination to contend with in the obedience rings on the West Coast. This dog, too, compiled a record which is the envy of many. In 1966 she was the top obedience Dal in the nation.

After Mr. Meistrell's death, Mrs. Meistrell established a memorial award offered through the Dalmatian Club of America for a number of years. The Harland Meistrell Memorial Trophy winners include Princess Cinder Babe CDX owned by Irene Brink; Belle Monti's Little Freckle UD, Sandra Hodson; Cinders Chief, owned by R. F. Noonan; and Belle Monti's Mr. Mickey, Jere Bates. The only records on the Harland Meistrell Memorial Trophy winners show that three of the four dogs were from California.

The first Dal to score a perfect 200 points was Lady Jane, owned by Naomi Radler, winning Novice B at Garden City, NY. The next day, Monty, owned by Mr. and Mrs. Melvin Lord, scored 200 at a trial in Oakland, CA.

Ch. Tally Ho Black Eyed Susan CDX was the first Dal champion to attain an obedience degree. Susan was owned by Mrs. Bonney who turned her over to the Meistrells for training. When war broke out the bitch was returned to Tally Ho as the Meistrells were deep in training dogs for wartime duties.

Obedience continues to claim the attention of a great many Dal breeders and exhibitors. More and more of the regional Dalmatian clubs have qualified for obedience classes at their shows. The entry may not be large to start, but it will build. And despite the fact that many all-breed trainers are of the opinion that Dalmatians are difficult to train, many of these in obedience competition are winning and winning well. Dals have an idiom all their own. They are probably showing their English heritage as they resent being told to do something. Ask them nicely and they will comply. This seems to be the difference in the training in this country and in the United Kingdom. Most of our training started with German immigrants who came to this country after the First World War where they had served in the German Army. A bit of Achtung! crept into their training methods. But in England the gentle approach has always been the rule and, in the end, their dogs seem to be better trained than ours. It may take a lttle longer to perfect the training but it is a better training. And the really successful Dalmatian trainers in this country use the gentle touch.

All dogs deserve obedience training whether for home or for competition. The Dalmatian is no exception. And most of the Dals love to do the exercises. On the fun side, many of our dogs are allowed the privilege of serving in a team for the scent hurdle races. This is strictly fun, the dogs and the handlers enjoy it, and the audiences from coast to coast go wild with enthusiasm.

In 1970 obedience had a fair entry at the National Specialty held in Kentucky. Interest had fallen off at specialty shows on the West Coast and in the East. Specialties in the Middle West would draw a fair entry but overall things were not startlingly well supported. Because of this lack of interest obedience classes were not offered at the eastern specialty shows.

Following the 1971 specialty show held in New England, the Board of Governors of the Dalmatian Club of America decided that obedience was an important part of the dog picture and so decreed that all future DCA specialty shows would offer obedience classes. Apparently this was a wise step. The entries have continued to climb and at the 1971 national specialty the obedience entry was sufficiently large to require a second obedience judge.

The idea of teams in Dalmatian obedience work is not new although many will be surprised to learn this. In the early years of obedience, in the early forties, there was a team in the New England area composed of Lois Meistrell, Virginia Lindsay (later Prescott) and Wendell Sammett.

On the West Coast the Coach 'n Four Dalmatian obedience club was founded in 1953 by a group of breeders from the San Fernando Valley. At first it was called the Dalmatian Forum and proposed to study genetic and obedience problems. In January 1955 the members applied to AKC for recognition as an obedience club. From this group they formed a drill team which performed at many places in the southern California area. The initial performance was at the DCSC's futurity match. It is too bad that this club has dropped from the Dalmatian picture.

In the early fifties three young teenagers developed a complete act with their Dalmatians in the Northern California area. They were Mary and Nancy Harbison and Trudy Caddel. Only one of the Dals had had obedience training

Four generations of obedience titled Dals plus the silver poodle, a UD, make up this family portrait in 1962. They are Lightning Spark UD, Princess Lilian CD, Ch. Princess Lois of Loki UD, and Ch. Charcoal Chips UD. Owned by the Kenneth Naglers.

Coachman's Capricorn CD takes the broad jump. Owned by Dr. and Mrs. Chris Fetner, Dallas.

Dalmatian Drill Team at Greenfield Village, Detroit. Members of the Detroit Dalmatian Club.

and one of them was past six years of age before the vaudeville type training was started. These young ladies trained their dogs to roll barrels separately and together, climb ladders, walk tight ropes, stand on broom handles elevated at least four feet from the ground, and a variety of other entertaining feats.

Dalmatians were used frequently in circuses because of their colorful appearance and their ability to perform circus type exercises. In recent years throughout the midwest we have been entertained by Willy Necker and his troupe of Dalmatians. They appear at sports shows, as added attractions at dog shows, at charity events, etc. Mr. Necker is a well-known trainer in the Chicago area. His ''Joker'' (and there is always a Joker in the group) is always a guarantee of laughs from the children in the audience as the dog misbehaves and disobeys, all, of course, a part of the act.

A plus for obedience competition among Dal fanciers has been the publishing of a bimonthly newsletter named THE DOTTED LINE. It was started in 1976 by Marilyn Suthergreen with the help of Mike Pumilia. This little magazine has served as a communication between Dalmatian owners who are also involved in obedience training. It covers all titles earned by Dalmatians, gives profiles of Dal obedience competitors, gives the history of some of the dogs of the past which have had fine obedience records, and much general chit-chat concerning obedience work, training hints, etc.

At the present time obedience among Dalmatian fanciers is at its very healthiest, competition being keen and exhibitors having fun. At the 1977 National specialty show, the Chicagoland Dal Club's show and the Steel City all-breed show—a three-day weekend—exhibitors, spectators and judges alike were all dazzled by the performance of a seven-month old pup in the Novice ring. Dominque's Rusty Nail, owned by Elaine Newman from the Atlanta area, earned himself a Dog World Award for his performances those three days. He racked up scores of 195, 198, and 197 to earn his CD title and the Dog World Award.

Rarely does one find so young a dog, so willing and such a happy, eager worker. This dog completed his UD work in October, 1978. We expect he will qualify easily for the OTCH title.

Currently exhibitors in the obedience ring who are working hard to keep the Dalmatian among the top working obedience dogs are Cathy Murphy of Ohio, Kitty Braund, Missouri, Judy Zlatarich, Michigan, Sue MacMillan and Jan Nelson of Minnesota, Sandi Long, the Garvins of Ohio, Marilyn Suthergreen, Washington, the Pumilias, California, Marleen Chittum, West Virginia, Brenda Anderson of New Jersey, the Brinks in Southern California, the Gates, the Murphys in the New England area, the Naglers in the national capital area, and many, many more. We have just named a few. Many people who have never been interested in obedience have suddenly discovered what

126

fun it is to work their dogs and so we expect to find larger and larger entries of Dalmatians at the all-breed trials and at the specialty shows.

UDT Dalmatians

1941	Io	Harland and Lois Meistrell
1942	Kotor	Harland and Lois Meistrell
1944	Checkers	Kenneth Naumer
1946	Ch. Duke of Gervais	Maurice Gervais
1947	Spur of Victory	L. Levin
1955	Roadcoach Tess	Mrs. Charles Thiessen
1955	Dickies Candy	Richard D'Ambrisi
1960	Rickway Dice	Thomas Darden
1975	Domino's Winter Midnight	Michael and Catherine Pumilia
1976	Ch. Dal Down's Dicie of Shadodal	Robert and Marge Sullivan
1976	Cassandra of Camelot	Irene Potocki and Julia Kubat
1976	Beautysweet Cindi	Marilynn Suthergreen
1976	Labyrinth Obviously	Robert and Marge Sullivan
1977	Ch. Cal-Dal Chocolate Chip	Jon & Karen Mett
1977	Sa-Mi's Buggy Whip	Michael and Catherine Pumilia
1979	Ch. Spotted Dapper Dan	Edward J. and Mary Ann Murphy

Dalmatians were used as war dogs during World War II.

Walter Back and his Dalmatians after a day's hunting.

Rough Rider Dakotah CD, the flushing Dalmatian with
his trainer, the late Jack Godsil. *Photo Mike Godsil*

13

The Hunting Dalmatian

ALMOST EVERYONE who has been around Dals has noticed the manner in which they stop and hold up one front foot. This is undoubtedly a carry-over from their Pointer forebears. And Dals will point in the field.

Most of the dogs known to us used in hunting, however, have been trained and used as retrievers. Walter Back of Zion, Il., has been using his Dalmatians for more than 20 years as retrievers when hunting pheasant. Almost all of Walter's dogs have their championships and their UD titles as well. He trains them himself and has found the activity a pleasurable one.

So many people feel that it is difficult to train a Dalmatian to do anything. In each case where we hear a tale of woe we are usually able to pinpoint the fact that the trainer has spoiled the dog, has not been firm with the dog, has expected the dog to catch on without getting through to him what is wanted.

Dalmatians are easily trained. And it isn't necessary to train them at an early age. As we have reported, the first Champion UD Dalmatian in the United States was 10 years old before his owner started training him in obedience.

Walter Back has been hunting with Dals since 1950. He purchased a puppy which learned how to hunt very quickly. Unfortunately the dog was hit by a car and killed. Then Walter bought an older Dal, a two and one-half year old bitch. To his surprise, she turned out to be gun shy.

Slowly but carefully, Walter trained her. This bitch was to become Ch. Little Miss Lucy, UD, the foundation bitch of the Dal Haven breeding. After all the careful training Walter gave her it is great to report that she became a terrific field dog. Lucy's half sister, Miss Pepper of Pistakee, and Lucy's daughter, Dal Haven's Debutante, were also used in the field each fall on Walter's hunting expeditions. Both of these bitches were also shown in the breed ring, obtained their championships, and were trained for obedience where they both earned their UD titles.

Walter will tell you that he finds the Dalmatian an ideal hunting breed. "They are intelligent dogs, have great stamina, common sense, are alert, have good noses and are aggressive enough to make good field dogs."

Walter also points out the advantages of the Dalmatian coat in the field. Being short, the burrs and stickers do not adhere to it and if the dog gets wet, the coat dries out quickly.

Walter counsels that it usually takes two to three years to develop a good hunting Dal. (Field trial enthusiasts will tell you that it takes two to three years to develop *any* field dog).

In choosing a Dal for hunting you must pick one that is interested in hunting. Some Dals have little or no interest in birds or game, varmints or whatever. A Dal that is interested in hunting birds can be trained. But the Dal MUST be trained.

Dalmatians are generally flushers rather than pointers although they do fancy themselves pointers. It is easier to train them as a flushing dog than as a pointer.

A jeweler, Mr. Paul Shallow, West Allis, WI, has a Dalmatian bitch which he used as a pointer. Her muscles are rock hard from all the field work she has done. After she had been used as a pointer for about three years she was somewhat "loaded" in shoulders. Her name is Shallow's Flee-go Patrick. She is now twelve years old and just last fall Mr. Shallow took her out hunting. She was always an eager hunter and her age didn't deter her. Mr. Shallow reported that she out-hunted a three year old Labrador Retriever.

"When I first started using Flee-go as a hunting dog other hunters would split their sides laughing at me. Each time I arrived at a hunting area other hunters would yell, 'What are you going to do with that ridiculous dog?' After awhile, when they saw how well Flee-go would hunt, they'd put their own dogs up and ask to hunt over my Dalmatian. Her hunting in the last few years has been slow and deliberate but she always gets the birds."

Mr. Shallow says that Flee-go would also flush. "If a bird ran on the ground, she would flush it . . why, she even caught her own birds!" Mr. Shallow feels that the Dalmatian is too fast for the hunter to make a really good flushing dog, but he swears by them as pointers.

On the other hand, Koda is known as the flushing Dalmatian. Kathryn Braund, well-known dog writer and obedience trainer, has two hunting Dals. One of them is Kamper of Big Sky which she trained herself, and the other is

130

"Koda" springs for the bird. *Mike Godsil*

Koda whirls to catch the falling bird. *Photo Arnst*

131

Success on the wing. *Arnst*

Attention! *Arnst*

Koda, Roughrider Dacotah, CDX, who was trained as a flushing Dalmatian by the late Jack Godsil at his training grounds in Illinois. Mr. Godsil's methods of training this Dalmatian have been described in numerous hunting publications step by step. *Hunting Dog* magazine carried the information on training this Dalmatian in the fall of 1977. An article written by Mrs. Braund was also published in *The Spotter,* the quarterly publication of the Dalmatian Club of America.

The success of Koda's training lies in his ability to hunt and both Mrs. Braund and her husband, Buzz, are more than pleased with his performance in the field.

Surely there are other hunting Dalmatians. All of the dogs at Pryor Creek fancied themselves mighty hunters and flushed the pheasants and quail in our field. Unfortunately, the humans at Pryor Creek are not hunters so the dogs were never trained for this activity.

In addition to their hunting ability, Dals make excellent herding dogs. They have been used as cattle dogs in various areas of the United States. They nip at the heels of the steers who are being recalcitrant about returning to the barn. Several reports have indicated that Dalmatians have been seen sheep herding also.

A theory as to why the dogs were relegated to the stable and thus developed an affinity with horses is that the dogs were more difficult to train than the setters, retrievers, and spaniels. Pointers and setters were easily trained to handle their chores in the field. And this is not to say that training a Dalmatian for field work is especially difficult. Training a Dalmatian for field is slightly different from the usual training for hunting dogs.

In England the gun dog was the all important member of the squire's retinue. The Dal, resembling the pointer, was thought to be a pointer and was treated as such. Apparently, lacking imagination, no one wanted to take the time to make the discovery that the Dal is a better flushing dog than a pointer and so the dogs were sent to the stables where they became companions of the horses and developed their own thing, coaching.

When George Washington wrote to his nephew about his Dal he referred to it as a "Coach Dog." And Coach Dog it is.

Ch. Tally Ho Sirius

Ch. Beau of Hollyroyde

134

14

Breeders and Exhibitors

NAMES OF PEOPLE and names of dogs appear, from time to time, in pedigrees, stories, conversations, and the uninitiated are sometimes nonplussed and wonder who these people and/or dogs are. No story of any breed is complete without information concerning some of the breeders and their dogs who made substantive contributions to the breed either as sires and dams or as show dogs.

Tally Ho

A very important kennel of the past, one which contributed a great deal to the Dalmatians in the country, was Tally Ho, Mrs. L.W. Bonney's famous kennel. Mrs. Bonney started in Dalmatians when she was a young girl. Her home, located in Flushing, had been the family estate for three generations. In the late 30's with the coming of the World's Fair, Mrs. Bonney decided that her home no longer had a "country" feel to it and she selected some 90 acres at Oyster Bay as the site of her new kennel and moved to it in 1938. She named the estate Sunstar Hill. By this time Mrs. Bonney was also well-known as a breeder of fine Chow Chows and later became involved in Poodles.

Her kennels produced numerous champions and is one of the two kennels to have owned a three-time national specialty winner, Ch. Tally Ho Last of Sunstar.

Mrs. Bonney had a breeding program which followed closely that employed by many other great breeders of the world. This policy provides for the use of a distinct outcross every few generations. Mrs. Bonney felt that in

Ch. Elmcroft Coacher

Ch. Four-in-Hand Blackberry

136

this way a line would never really wear itself out. She made numerous trips to the British Isles, going every two years up until the outbreak of World War II, and she imported many good dogs. Her last import was the impressive Duxforham Yessam Marquis. Mark made his initial appearance at the national specialty in 1966. He did not win that day but managed to finish his championship quite handily within the next few months. He was to be Mrs. Bonney's last champion as she died in January 1967.

She was known world wide as an excellent judge of Dalmatians, Chow Chows, and Poodles. At her last assignment, Steel City Kennel Club, Gary, IN, she awarded Best in Show to a Dalmatian, Ch. Rockledge Rumble, owned by Gloria Schwartz.

As Secretary-Treasurer of the Dalmatian Club of America for more than 50 years, Mrs. Bonney was on top of all matters pertaining to the breeding, showing, and judging of Dalmatians. If anyone ever deserved the title, MRS. DALMATIAN, Mrs. Bonney did.

Her encouragement, advice and counsel were given freely to all who asked her. Anyone who has been in the breed for more than ten years is aware of the awe and respect in which Mrs. Bonney's memory is held.

We had a stunning experience concerning this great lady, however. A young man who became interested in Dalmatians in about 1970, came to our home in 1974 to breed his bitch to one of our studs. We were talking Dals and one of us remarked, "Mrs. Bonney did not destroy patched puppies" (we have a letter from Mrs. Bonney stating this practice). The young man looked at us and asked, "Who is Mrs. Bonney?" He knows now. Sic gloria transit mundi!

Although there had not been any dogs housed in the Tally Ho Kennels for a number of years, since Mrs. Bonney's death and the dispersal of her estate, it was shocking to know that this once great kennel burned to the ground in the spring of 1977. At the time it was built it was one of the most up-to-date establishments in America, providing indoor and outdoor exercise areas for the dogs, bathing and grooming areas, awninged runs, bathing facilities, everything necessary for the care and breeding of excellent specimens. The building itself was 134 feet long and the central portion was 45 feet wide. During Mrs. Bonney's lifetime the building was equipped with automatic fire extinguishers.

Four-in-Hand

One of the most influential early kennels was Leo Meeker's Le Mel later renamed Four-in-Hand. Mr. Meeker, who lived in California, imported the very best of English bloodlines and established a breeding program on the West Coast which has not yet been equalled.

As a child Mr. Meeker had had Dalmatians and in the mid-20's he decided to exhibit in the California shows. He found the entries very low and the quality of the specimens on exhibit poor. He purchased some dogs from the famous Cress-Brook Kennel in Michigan and some from Ruth Kane's Dal Dale Kennels in Illinois. He then imported a bitch from Mr. Wardell, the English champion, Queen of Trumps. She finished in the States easily.

Later he imported a fine dog, Four-in-Hand Mischief. This dog became an American and Canadian Champion. He was shown from coast to coast and established the record for Best in Show wins for a Dalmatian. His show record includes 50 Best of Breeds, 35 Group L's, 8 Group II's, 2 Group III's and 1 Group IV with a mighty 18 Bests in Show.

Many of the dogs in California at the present time are descended from the Four-in-Hand line established by Mr. Meeker. One of the dogs sired by Mischief, Ch. Four-in-Hand Athos, won an all-breed Best in Show at the age of 7 ½ years. The dog was owned by Dr. and Mrs. Zane Feller, Hackney Way Kennels, Citrus Heights, CA.

Four-in-Hand is behind the dogs of Rho Dal, El Tross, and can be found in the extended pedigrees of many established breeders today. Mr. Meeker also became a popular Dalmatian judge. Other famous dogs produced by the Four-in-Hand breeding program are Ch. Four-in-Hand Sparkletts, Ch. Four-in-Hand Tarberry, and Four-in-Hand Jookery.

Williamsdale

A kennel established in 1938 and closed in 1976 is probably the one which has had the most influence on Dalmatians throughout the United States. That kennel was Williamsdale in Cincinnati.The kennel was established by Charles Williams. He employed Martin Milet as kennel manager and handler. Together they instituted a great line of dogs. They imported a great many dogs and bred many great dogs.

In 1955 Mr. Williams sold his kennel to Martin Milet who continued to breed and show dogs until his death in 1969. The kennel continued under the management of his sister-in-law, Mrs. May Milet until the end of 1976. Because of illness Mrs. Milet discontinued the kennel.

Although most people import bitches for foundation stock Milet imported two great studs, Am. Can. Ch. Elmcroft Coacher and Ch. Igor of Kye of Williamsdale. The former was imported from England in dam by Ray McLaughlin of Stratford, Ont. After the dog had finished his Canadian championship Milet bought him and brought him to the States where he completed his American championship with all majors. An outstanding sire, he accounted for 27 champions, quite a record for a dog in those days, the late 40's and early 50's.

138

Igor sired 16 champion get. While a great dog and a fine sire he didn't seem to have the prepotency as a stud dog that marked Coacher's get although he sired Ch. Williamsdale Rocky, a national specialty winner.

In the days when handlers were permitted to judge specialty shows Milet was tapped to judge the DCA show in 1957. He had won the breed at the Specialty with his homebred Ch. Williamsdale Rocky in 1953.

He didn't limit his imports to males of course. He brought in a number of dogs from England and Canada. His great brace of imports was made up of Am. Eng. Ch. Penny Parade of Williamsdale and Ch. Colonsay Tantivey Claudia. Other imports included Eng. Am. Ch. Beau of Hollyroyde.

The foundation bitch of this kennel was Her Majesty of Williamsdale. Although she was never shown she was a great brood bitch and produced a number of champions.

Choice of the breed of dog one wants to buy is based on a variety of peculiar things. One Dalmatian owner purchased her dog because she liked the way a Dalmatian looked curled up before the fire. Another bought a Dal because she had black and white as a color scheme in her living room and she wanted her dog to match. And Juan Peron, the Argentinian dictator, rode an Appaloosa horse and wanted a dog to match the spotting of the horse's markings.

He wrote to Williamsdale to find a pup. At the time Milet had no puppies available but he had used Rocky on a very lovely bitch, Ch. Ser-Dals Lone Star, owned by Mrs. Victor Sachse of Baton Rouge. This bitch had won BIS at New Orleans at the age of not quite one year. Star's puppies were of the correct age so Milet made the arrangements for Mrs. Sachse to sell a puppy to Peron. The pup was named Vigilante Vic. In order to get his dog, Peron sent his personal plane to New Orleans to pick it up. Conversation concerning this transaction kept tongues wagging for days in New Orleans and Baton Rouge. This great event occurred in the spring of 1955.

Reigate

Reigate Kennels played a great part in the world of Dalmatians during the years it was active in breeding. Mary Leigh Lane and George Lane, and their sister, Billie Close, did much to keep the Dalmatian in the winners circle. Some of their greats include Ch. Reigate's Bold Venture, Ch. Reigate's All Clear, Ch. Reigate's Remus, Ch. Reigate's Native Dancer, Ch. Reigate's Double Trouble, Ch. Reigate's Flag Drill, Ch. Reigate's Miss Springtime, Ch. Reigate's Count Fleet, Ch. Reigate's Regimental, Ch. Reigate's Lothario, Ch. Reigate's Dress Parade, Ch. Reigate's Souvenir, Ch. Reigate's Dress Parade, and several Reigate dogs which were not finished as champions but which contributed a lot to the breed including Reigate's Tracery, Reigate's

Ch. Reigate Bold Venture

Ch. Reigate Hoedown. *Tauskey*

Daltina, Reigate's Flora Temple, and Reigate's Star Pilot, and many many more. All of these names pop up in extended pedigrees of many of the dogs of today. Somewhere the word came forth that they had bred over 2000 Dalmatian puppies at their kennels.

Mrs. Lane was great to talk to about Dals. If someone said that a particular bitch or dog did this or that, Mrs. Lane replied, "Must have such and such a dog behind her." And a careful check of the pedigree would reveal that Mrs. Lane's conjecture was correct. When the Lanes died and their kennel was closed the dog world lost a wonderful part of it, Reigate Kennels. Few, if any, domestic pedigrees are without at least one Reigate dog in the background.

Whiteside Sioux

A kennel name familiar to all is Whiteside Sioux. This prefix belongs to Mrs. Wilbur Dewell. Although no longer an active breeder and horsewoman, Mrs. Dewell is still very interested in her favorite breed of dogs. Having come from the midwest to Connecticut, Mrs. Dewell understood the difficulties of careful breeding when one lived far away from the center of the genetic pool. That she had a successful breeding program is proved by the use of her dog's picture in one of the popular encyclopedias written shortly after World War II, *The Modern Dog Encyclopedia* edited by Henry P. Davis. Mrs. Dewell was active in the road trials and in obedience and participated in many activities of the Dalmatian Club of America. She is eligible to judge Dalmatians at AKC shows.

Roadcoach

The turnover in the dog fancy is tremendous. Anyone who has been "in dogs" for five years is an old timer. Some people seem to remain fanciers, exhibitors, and breeders for a long time and they seem to be the ones who really contribute to the advancement of a breed.

In Dalmatians there are a number of breeders who started out "way back when," some before World War II, and they are still in the fancy. One such kennel is Roadcoach in Dover, MA. No one can remember Dalmatians without a Roadcoach Kennel in the picture.

Mary Powers was involved in horses, in fact, her family owned a stable of fine horses. Through the horses Mary met Alfred Barrett who later became her husband. Together they established Roadcoach Kennels. Looking through pedigrees one is impressed with the number of times the prefix Roadcoach appears. Although the kennel was established in the 30's the prefix was not registered with the American Kennel Club until 1945.

141

In the 1920's and the 1930's all fashionable stables had to have "Coach Dogs" and in 1931 Mrs. Christy of Worcester, MA, with a string of show hunters, was no exception. The only difficulty with Mrs. Christy's farm and stable complete with Dalmatian was that apparently the Dal was killing off the chickens. Alfred Barrett discovered that Maggie, the Dalmatian, was about to be destroyed because of the chicken activity. He took her to the Power's stables where he was boarding a horse. Mr. Powers, Mary's father, had shown a number of dogs so Mary and Mr. Barrett decided to register and show the Dalmatian. She was registered as Mistress Margaret. She came from Borrodale stock, the kennel owned by Mrs. Gladding of Providence.

She was entered at the Eastern Dog Show in February 1932 under Frank Addyman who encouraged them to continue to show the bitch. She was shown that spring at Morris & Essex and at other shows and was fortunate enough to win. She completed her championship March 20, 1933. She was bred to Ch. Gladmore Harper and later to Ch. Tally Ho Ian who produced Gambler's Luck, and she was also bred to Ch. Cress Brook Bang. This was the start of Roadcoach Kennels. Mary Powers became Mrs. Alfred Barrett in 1935. And, oddly enough, the chickens at Christy farm continued to be killed after Maggie left for her life as a show dog and brood bitch.

Mrs. Barrett reports that she did import a few dogs over the years which were not a great success. She found that Tally Ho, Tattoo, Hollow Hill and Reigate lines proved best for her.

Hugh Chisholm, who owned Strathglass Kennels, decided to go out of Dals and concentrate on his Welsh Terriers. The Barretts acquired the Strathglass stock and that year won their first Best in Show with Strathglass Cricket. Other Strathglass dogs which proved to be successful additions to the kennels were Ch. Strathglass Lady Dolly, a group winner; Ch. Strathglass Buttons; and a good liver, Ch. Strathglass Cherry Coke.

In 1954 a litter sired by Ch. Boot Black from Dalmatia out of Ch. Roadcoach Kittereen, a group winner, produced a dog destined to become one of the greats of the breed, Ch. Roadcoach Roadster. Kittereen was by Ch. Roadcoach Bandit out of Ch. Roadcoach Phaeton, a DCA specialty winner and a group winner. Bandit went back to Strathglass Buttons. Boot Black was owned by Wendell Sammet who bought his first Dalmatian from Roadcoach.

Roadster started winning in his first year. He was Best Dal from the classes at the Garden under Harry Peters and second in the group in 1955 with Mrs. Barrett handling. He won the group that year at Morris & Essex with Charley Meyer handling under judge Lew Worden. In December of 1955 Roadster was sold to Mrs. S. K. Allman (now Mrs. George Ratner), who campaigned him extensively. His greatest win, of course, was Best in Show under Margery Renner at Morris & Essex in 1956 over 2304 dogs. He also won the Group at Westminster in 1957. The total record on the dog was 176

Best of Breeds, 17 Best in Shows, 9 American Bred Best in Shows and 79 Groups.

So many of the New England breeders started with a purchase from Roadcoach that it is impossible to name them all. The Barretts both became breed judges and both passed on the entries of the national specialty twice. Mr. Barrett died several years ago and Mary has continued on alone. During the 50's the Barretts also became interested in Poodles and the Roadcoach prefix has become one to reckon with in that breed. At the present time Mrs. Barrett is eligible to judge the non-sporting breeds and group.

Dalquest, Miss Marjory VanderVeer's kennel, Dalmatia, Wendell Sammet's establishment, the Sittingers, and many others all were helped by Mrs. Barrett and Mrs. Bonney in the start of their kennels.

In 1979 we find Roadcoach Kennels still breeding and showing and quite successfully, too.

Coachman

Mr. and Mrs. William Fetner established Coachman Kennels in St. Louis in the late 1940's and registered their prefix with the American Kennel Club in 1951. Here is another kennel which had an interest in horses as well as in dogs. And the interest in both continues.

When Jean and Bill Fetner were married Jean had a Dalmatian which she had acquired from the Kingcrest Kennels, Dr. and Mrs. George King, Alliance, OH. They purchased several Dalmatians without a great deal of success until they found Chips. Chips was Ch. Fobette's Frishka CD and became the foundation of Coachman breeding. Chips is behind every dog they have ever bred.

Ch. Fobette's Frishka was a magnificent specimen of the breed and although she was not campaigned she managed to gain four Group I's and earned her Companion Dog title with Jean Fetner handling.

Coachman breeding has produced some of the top winners of the Dalmatian world. Four DCA specialty winners came from this kennel. They were Ch. Coachman's Classic in 1958; Ch. Coachman's Callisto in 1964; Ch. Lord Jim in 1970 with Best of Opposite Sex going to Ch. Coachman's Carte Blanche, a father-daughter combination; and Ch. Coachman's Canicula in 1973. Callisto is also one of the three Dalmatians to win the group at Westminster. A note of interest: Jean and Bill did not own any of these winners at the time of the win, the only Fetner name of ownership being on Carte Blanche who belonged to a Fetner son, Jay.

The breeding of Dalmatians started as a family hobby for the Fetners and looking at the list of exhibitors and DCA members today one could say that the hobby has continued to be a family affair. There are three sons in the

Ch. Roadcoach Tioga Too CD

Ch. Coachman's Colours

Family portrait: Ch. Coachman's Chuck-a-Luck, his son, Ch.
Lord Jim, and Jim's daughter, Ch. Coachman's Carte Blanche.

Ch. Coachman's Carte Blanche in an informal pose.

family, Jay, Christopher, and Kevin. Jay lives in the East where he breeds and exhibits Coachman dogs. He has served a term on the Board of Governors of the Dalmatian Club of America and is currently on the Standard Committee. Christopher, a surgeon, lives in Dallas with his wife, Phyllis and their two children. Although Phyllis had never owned a dog before she married Christopher, she is now actively exhibiting and breeding Coachman dogs. Kevin has moved to the Dallas area and he too, is active in exhibiting Dalmatians.

Coachman has placed a mark on its breeding. It is easy for anyone who knows Dals to spot a Coachman-bred dog as they are very typey, have good markings, are of correct size, move well, and have magnificent temperaments. No one has ever seen a Coachman dog which could be described as "too long" or "too tall." The careful breeding program which has been followed by the Fetners has paid off. Not every breeder is as fortunate as they were to get a foundation bitch such as Frishka. Bred any way, she produced well.

While the Fetners prefer to do line breeding they have used outcrosses from time to time. And in recent years they have had a number of successes with liver dogs as well as blacks. Mrs. Fetner has stated that she believes the best blacks come from livers, the liver factor seeming to make the black more intense. Other breeders have made this comment, among them Muriel Higgins of Pennydale Kennels. There is no scientific data to prove this idea but it seems to be true.

Pryor Creek

Pryor Creek, the Treen prefix, owes much to its association with Coachman Kennels. Ch. Fobette's Fanfare, later CDX, was acquired from a Louisville dentist. He had been previously owned and finished by the Fetners. He became the foundation stud of Pryor Creek.

A carefully worked out inbreeding program was used on Fanfare, call name "Pepper". This dog seemed to have prepotency in pigment as he never sired an unrimmed eye dog or an unfilled nose. Through a selective breeding program the great Ch. Coachman's Chuck-a-Luck was produced.

A son of Pepper and a daughter of Pepper out of different bitches were bred to produce a suitable bitch to be bred back to Pepper. To our consternation this second mating did not produce the great show winner and producer. It did, however produce "Rosie," Pryor Creek's Yaupon Rose, who was a delightful bitch to live with. Rosie preferred hunting or fishing to most activities but she was quite willing to have puppies also.

When the Treen family found that it had to move back to the Milwaukee area because Mr. Treen's employer so decreed, the number of dogs in the

Ch. Fobette's Fanfare CDX, as a young dog. He is the foundation stud of Pryor Creek Dalmatians.

Family portrait: Ch. Coachman's Chuck-a-Luck, having won the Veteran Dog class at the 1975 DCA specialty posed with his son, Ch. Lord Jim, his grandson, Ch. Coachman's Canicula, and another Jimmy son, Ch. Count Miguel of Tuckaway.

147

kennel had to be decreased. Rosie found a good home with the Smiths in St. Louis and she was left there on condition that she be bred to Coachman's Clotheshorse. This dog was an excellent coach dog whose mother had stepped on him when he was a tiny puppy. The resulting injury to his foot gave him a peculiar gait and he could not be shown. He did a fair amount of siring of excellent puppies, however. When the litter arrived Mr. Fetner chose a male as a stud puppy and sold it to the John Blairs as a pet. This pet, Brewster, Ch. Coachman's Chuck-a-Luck, became a winner in the show ring and at this writing has accounted for 27 champion get. There are still one or two of his children almost finished. Brewster died at age 12 from bloat. He had returned to the Treens as a beloved member of their household after his show career had finished. He is still the only Best in Show Dalmatian to have sired two Best in Show sons.

Pryor Creek has a modest record of show successes having produced over the years both group winners and Best in Show dogs. The breeding program was limited and the showing program has been negligible. Most of the winners from Pryor Creek breeding have had other prefixes. We have always felt that the name of the breeder will appear in the catalog as it really doesn't matter whose prefix the dog carries. It would seem that insecurity can be found among dog breeders also.

Pryor Creek became interested in Dalmatians after a dog of another breed had had an argument with our son and our son lost the debate. It seemed imperative to get a puppy far removed from the breed we had had so that our three-year-old child would not grow up with a great fear of dogs which his experience seemed to have left him. After careful study and consideration we decided on a Dalmatian. Not being expert in the breed we chose a bitch which was much too dark for the show ring. A year or so later we found our foundation bitch, Ch. Saint Rocco's Polka Dot, CD. We were living in Wisconsin at the time and then we were transferred to Houston. We remember quite well that even on the great Texas circuit in 1952 only one other Dalmatian was entered at the shows. He was an Ard Aven dog and was handled by Porter Washington. He won.

Later we found competition at some of the shows in Dallas and Fort Worth, but it wasn't easy to find points in Texas in Dals in those days. Eventually, we worked hard and built up entries. Now the Dalmatian entry at most Texas shows accounts for a major and at the specialty show of the Dalmatian Organization of Houston in the fall of 1978 there were 101 entries!

We acquired Ch. Fobette's Fanfare and through him, built a good breeding program. After about five years in Texas we were again transferred, this time to southern Illinois, near St. Louis. We established our kennel there and continued to exhibit and breed, both sparingly. In 1959 we were returned to the Milwaukee area where we have been ever since. Our breeding days are over, our schedule does not lend itself to breeding. It is impossible to carry on a program when you are not at home.

What about the boy's fear of dogs? He was completely cured and both he and his sister became excellent junior handlers. He was invited to compete at Westminster, unfortunately at the time we were moving north, so he was unable to go.

Greeneland

Greeneland, the Dalmatian breeding kennels of the Myron Greenes of Rochester, NY, was a popular name in Dalmatians for a time. A dog they purchased from Reigate was WD at the DCA specialty in 1955. This was Reigate's Native Dancer who went on to become one of the fine sires in the breed. The Dancer was used in a standard visualization of the breed as the ideal Dalmatian. Greeneland also accounted for a number of other stellar wins and dogs. Included in their records is another great stud dog, Ch. Reigate's Mr. Jive of Greeneland. The Greeneland Kennel has become inactive although Mr. Greene still retains his interest in the breed.

Quaker's Acre

Quaker's Acre has always been a kennel name to be reckoned with in either the obedience or the breed ring. Mary Munro Smith, owner of this kennel, started out in horses as did so many of the people who became involved with Dals. Mrs. Smith, a Canadian, moved to the United States, Detroit, in the late 20's as a secretary for an architectural and engineering firm. She progressed with the organization and became its public relations director. At this time she had a riding stable where she taught riding as a hobby.

As secretary of the Boots and Saddle Club of Rochester, MI, she visited a number of stables in the state and it was thus that she became acquainted with Dalmatians. In 1940 she acquired a Dalmatian from the famous Cress Brook Kennels in Michigan. She trained the dog for obedience but never showed him. In 1948 Mrs. Smith started breeding Dals. Her first bitch was purchased from the Quaker Oats Company. This was Quaker's Acre Pirette. By this time Mrs. Smith had moved to Florida.

Mrs. Smith then bought an Elmcroft Coacher son, Velvet Frank. She finished the championship on this dog quite handily. This, then, was her start. She started classes with Velvet Frank in obedience eventually becoming the founder of the Dog Training Club of Fort Lauderdale and Hollywood. Her activities in club work in the Florida area are well-known and are reported in the obedience section of this book.

Ch. Lucky Legend of Fyrthorne. *Brown*

Ch. Reigate Lothario. *Tauskey*

150

At this time there are Dals of Quaker's Acre breeding in 18 different countries. Mrs. Smith has returned to Canada and is no longer actively breeding Dalmatians.

Tomalyn Hill

Tomalyn Hill Kennels of Montville, NJ, now on the inactive list, was a family affair for the Nelsons. The TO was for Thomas Nelson, the MA for Mrs. Nelson, and the LYN for Evelyn Nelson. The latter is better known now as Evelyn Nelson White. She is a past president of the DCA, past secretary of the DCA, and editor emerita of THE SPOTTER. And she is an AKC judge of Dalmatians. Her most recent assignment was at the Dalmatian Club of Detroit's specialty show in June of 1979. She judged the breed at the 1976 national specialty of the DCA and immediately went to Mexico where she judged the national specialty of the Club Dalmata de Mexico, A.C.

For many years "Miss Nelson" wrote the column for the DCA in the GAZETTE. Tomalyn Hill dogs are well-known to older breeders. The Nelsons started exhibiting in 1940. The newer crop of breeders may not recognize the prefix until they get into extended pedigrees and there they will find numerous champions bearing the Tomalyn Hill name. At least thirteen of the dogs who made their titles were homebreds and most of the Tomalyn Hill dogs finished their championships from the Bred by Exhibitor class. Among the dogs to finish were Ibett's Toni, Lou-Ann Sinful of Tomalyn Hill, Tomalyn's Air Cadette, Tomalyn's Chieftain, Tomalyn's Daiquiri, Tomalyn's Martini II, Tomalyn's Rascality, Tomalyn's Black Jet, Tomalyn's Bonanza, and Tomalyn's Danny Boy, all home bred. Another Tomalyn Hill bred dog was Ch. Tomalyn's Gunsmoke, the first Dal to go Best in Show in Brazil. Blacky won a DCA specialty and Rascality and Air Cadette both gained a BOS win at DCA specialty shows. The Nelsons bought and finished Four-in-Hand Blackberry, Lorbyrndale Little Steeve, Tomalyn Kailana, and Dal Dunn's Royal Reward which had been sired by Black Jet.

Much credit is given to Mrs. Bonney for her advice and counsel in the breeding program conducted at Tomalyn Hill. An ad in a specialty catalog for this kennel states: "Over a quarter of a century of breeding Dalmatians to an ideal instilled by Flora M. Bonney that will always be upwards."

At the present time Mrs. White resides in Florida and her sister, Mrs. Kenneth A. Darling, remains at the New Jersey home of Tomlayn Hill Kennels.

Albelarm

For more than thirty years the prefix of Albelarm has been a winning one in the breed. And the name of Isabel Robson is very well-known both as a competitor and a judge. Not only has Mrs. Robson been a breeder of champion Dals, she has known when to buy from outside her line to get a winner.

Her introduction to Dals came through her association with horses. When she was a teenager she had hunters with a friend in Southern Pines, NC. Her friend had a pair of Dals and when there was a litter she insisted that Isabel take the pick of the litter. This was during the war years so showing the dog was not considered. Later she bought a daughter of Ch. Nigel of Welfield and Stockdale. This was the foundation bitch for Albelarm. Dr. Byron of Lorbyrndale Kennels, sold her Lorbyrndale We Hail. She showed him to his title, owner handled. Then We Hail was bred to the Nigel bitch to produce the A litter. Albelarm has used the alphabet system of naming dogs ever since, having reached the Z just a couple of years ago.

Ch. Albelarm Attention was the first home-bred champion. For several years Mrs. Robson continued to breed and show Dalmatians. She finished many champions and bought several top dogs. She imported Eng. Ch. Cabaret Charivaris and won WB at the DCA national specialty with her in 1952. She also imported Tantivvey Georgina who won the open liver bitch class at the same specialty. Charivaris won her championship easily but Georgina was never shown again as Mrs. Robson was too involved in showing horses to show dogs every weekend.

Later the Robsons imported Pateshull Pucelle, a liver. And in the early years of breeding Mrs. Robson had two home-bred group winning bitches. One was Ch. Albelarm Bewitched and the other Ch. Albelarm Joker.

A list of the dogs owned and/or bred by Albelarm which finished their championships reads like a history of the breed in this country. Along with numerous Albelarm prefixes we find Reigate, Willowmount, Blackpool, Colonial Coach, Coachkeeper, Quaker's Acre, and Green Starr.

The biggest winning dog in the list was Ch. Colonial Coach Son of York who managed to rack up 150 Best of Breeds. Ch. Coachkeeper Blizzard of Quaker's Acre, a liver dog, was the Robsons' first Best in Show winner. Ch. Coachkeeper Windsong of Quaker's Acre, also a liver, was a top winning bitch in the breed for several years.

At the present time Albelarm is campaigning Ch. Green Starr' Colonel Joe who not only won the national specialty in 1978 but has compiled a great show record along the way with 12 Best in Shows and 31 Group I's in 1978 and has continued his winning ways into '79.

For the last seven years Bobby Barlow has handled the Albelarm dogs.

Pennydale

Another kennel which has passed from the scene but which is well remembered is Pennydale, Arthur and Muriel Higgins' kennel in Syosset,

Long Island. Pennydale has the honor of having owned and shown one of the three group winning Dals at Westminster, Ch. Coachman's Callisto.

The interest in Dals at Pennydale came about through an interest in horses (the usual reason). Most of their dogs were owner-handled by Arthur Higgins. Over the years they finished over two dozen champions which they bred. They also retired the DCA challenge trophies at the national specialties with three time wins for Best of Breed, Best of Opposite Sex, Best of Winners, Winners Dog and Winners Bitch. They won two best puppies at National specialties with Ch. Pennydale Little Binge and Ch. Pennydale Star Sight. Three times the top win at the Chicagoland Dal specialty was won by Pennydale and the same record was made at the Dalmatian Club of Southern New England shows.

Their first dog was Head of the River Storm which they purchased from Annette Colgate Sanger. This is the only dog they showed which did not finish his championship.

After Arthur Higgins died Mrs. Higgins discontinued breeding Dals and now lives on the West Coast. She is still very popular as a judge of the breed and is eligible to pass on many of the non-sporting breeds.

Williamsview

One of the kennels which has been in Dalmatian breeding for a long time is Williamsview, owned by William Hibbler. Mr. Hibbler has been a serious breeder all through the years since his kennel was established in 1939. During the war years, of course, some of the breeding was curtailed but resumed after the war was over. Mr. Hibbler has never campaigned a dog but has finished eighteen of his dogs. His breeding is behind a good many of the newer kennels.

In looking at his dogs Mr. Hibbler stresses the importance of correct type, over-all balance and soundness.

Bill Hibbler has been an active Dalmatian exhibitor and a member of the Dalmatian Club of America. He is a past president of that organization and is currently serving on the standard committee.

Dalmatia

We have mentioned the "turnover" in the sport of showing dogs. We now have a primary example of this. In the fall of 1972 Wendell Sammet, well-known handler, entered a Dalmatian at one of the large Eastern shows. He entered his dog in the Bred by Exhibitor class and thereby caused much raising of eye-brows and questioning looks from the other exhibitors. Most of them had no idea that Wendell had ever had any connection with Dalmatians as in more recent years he has been seen showing Poodles and Yorkshire

Ch. Hackney Way Lady Athos, owned by the Zane Fellers.

Ch. Four-in-Hand Mischief

Terriers. Wendell's great bitch, Ch. China Doll of Dalmatia had won Best of Breed at the Dalmatian Club of America's specialty show in 1949. Ch. Colonel Boots of Dalmatia won the specialty in 1954.

His fine male, Ch. Bootblack of Dalmatia, sired one of the all-time greats of the breed, Ch. Roadcoach Roadster. And the name "of Dalmatia" has graced a number of top animals in the breed.

Wendell was also interested in obedience in the years after World War II. And he participated in the Road Trials. He is, of course, so well-known in Poodles and Yorkshire Terriers that it is startling to realize his early love was Dals. He acquired his first Dalmatian from Roadcoach. From time to time Wendell breeds a litter of Dals and if any look promising he will show them. He may not be among the most active in the breed but he is surely among the most loyal of Dalmatian fanciers.

Crestview

A neighbor's child, a litter of Dal puppies, and a Pointer which had to be put down, all combined to found Crestview Dalmatian kennels. Violet Montgomery (later McManus) was taking care of a little boy for her neighbor who needed help. The neighbor had a litter of Dalmatians and when Vi had to have her beloved Pointer put down because of illness, she gave Vi a puppy from the litter as a "thank-you." Knowing absolutely nothing about Dalmatians at the time, Vi chose what she thought was a beautiful animal, a heavily marked, patched Dal.

Someone invited Vi to attend the Golden Gate Kennel Club show, and as she had never been to a dog show before, she accepted the invitation. She saw the Dalmatians and felt they were certainly a pale lot compared to her puppy. She met Hazel Carroll, an early Dalmatian exhibitor in California, at the show and learned that patches were not considered comme il faut, and that a dog, too heavily marked, was not a show dog. In fact, Mrs. Carroll was extremely helpful to Vi and guided her in her choice of dogs.

About this time the neighbor had to move and could not keep her Dal bitch, the mother of Vi's patched puppy, so she gave Vi the dam, too.

Through Mrs. Carroll, Vi met Mr. Meeker and started breeding Dals. She is not truly a breeder, she says, as she bred her first litter in 1948 and to date had had no more than 30 litters. She considers herself a fancier.

The first champion at Crestview was Ch. Lady Victoria O'Carroll which Vi obtained from Mrs. Carroll. Her first home-bred champion was Ch. Esquire of Crestview. All of the Crestview stock goes back to Four-in-Hand Mischief, Meeker's great dog.

The success of the breeding program at Crestview, limited though it may be, can be gauged by the number of specialty wins the Crestview dogs have

Ch. Crestview Steal A Kiss,
owned by Vi McManus.

Ch. Boot Black from Dalmatia owned by Wendell Sammet.

156

Ch. Crestview Diamond Jim, owned by Vi McManus and handled by Jim McManus, winning the DCA specialty, Evelyn Nelson White judging.

Ch. Crestview Jaqueline, owned by Vi McManus.

157

scored. Ch. Crestview Diamond Jim won the DCA specialty in 1960 under Evelyn Nelson White. He managed to win four other specialty shows as well. Ch. Crestview Lisa, Ch. Crestview Prince of Beaux, Ch. Crestview Mr. Bently of Beaux, Ch. Crestview Domino Mischief, Ch. Black Eyed Susan, Ch. Crestview Poncho, Ch. Crestview Steal a Kiss, Ch. Crestview Barregan's Fido, and Ch. Crestview Dan Patch all won one or more specialty shows. Dan Patch won DCA in 1976.

Domino Mischief was Best of Breed at the Dalmatian Club of Northern California in 1963 and several years later won the breed at the New England specialty club's show from the Veteran's class. Lisa was BOS at the DCA in 1961.

Mrs. McManus is continuing to breed Dalmatians on a limited basis. Her latest achievement was Winners Dog at the DCA national specialty in 1978 with Crestview Rogue. We expect to see Crestview dogs in the ring for many years to come. Although she says she is not a breeder, Mrs. McManus has produced some fine Dalmatians. She is also a judge of the breed.

Altamar

When Maria Johnson moved from St. Louis to southern California she took with her the makings of a fine kennel. Her foundation dogs were all Coachman breeding. With this start she had the joy of winning the national specialty with her beloved Tack, Ch. Coachman's Classic, in 1958. This dog also won the Dalmatian Club of Southern California specialty show twice, in 1956 and 1958 by which time he had added Mexican and Canadian titles to his name. In fact, a challenge trophy was offered for Best of Breed at this specialty in Tack's name and Maria Johnson retired the trophy! She won the specialty with Ch. Altamar's Aristos in 1966, with Ch. Altamar's Acheson in 1972 and with Ch. Altamar's Adastar in 1976. Obviously, Tack was the foundation of the Altamar kennels of Maria Johnson.

Tack also brought fame to the Dalmatian breed in quite another way. When Dodie Smith's classic, 101 DALMATIANS, was purchased by Disney, Maria was contacted to help the studio in its drawings of Dalmatians, puppies and grown dogs. Tack was the model for the hero dog, Pongo. Puppies at Altamar were used by the Disney cartoonists for the various dogs in the film, one of the animated feature-length productions of Walt Disney Studios. The story of the production of this movie is half a book in itself. Suffice it to say that Maria and her Dalmatians, all from the goodness of her heart and a fondness for the breed, helped the studio immeasurably. She went on TV programs with her dogs to publicize the movie when it was released. Everything the studio needed to learn about the dogs, Maria supplied. During the sketching in preparation for the actual animation, Disney artists came to

Ch. Altamar's Aristos, specialty winner from the classes at DCSC 1966, owned and handled by Maria Johnson.

Maria Johnson's Am. Can. Mex. Ch. Coachman's Classic CD, winner of 1958 DCA specialty show.

159

Ch. Altamar's Acheson, another specialty
winner owned by Maria Johnson.

Ch. Altamar's Adastar, owned by Maria Johnson.

160

the Johnson home and observed and sketched puppies. Other times Maria took her dogs to the studio so they could be sketched. Tack posed for many publicity stills. It was a great experience for Maria and the dogs.

Almost all of Maria's breeding has been on the line with Coachman stock. Her foundation bitch went back to Four-in-Hand Mischief. She has imported several English dogs and has used them on occasion to introduce some feature she was looking for, but mostly her breeding and type is Coachman. And we continue to see fine Altamar dogs in the show ring.

Long Last

In the history of almost all the early Dalmatian kennels we find a reference to an "interest in horses" and "there were always Dals around the stables." The refrain of horses runs through the majority of the stories of "how I got my start in Dals."

The origin of Long Last Kennels is no exception. Lorraine Donahue spent the war years with show horses and noticed the pure-bred Dals around the stables, mascots who "helped" her with her stable chores. When a litter of puppies arrived she received a bitch puppy as a gift. The description of this puppy is anything but likeable. "She was overmarked, patched, and unregistered." This unattractive little gal became one of the top obedience dogs in the U.S. Her name was Spur of Victory, UDT. She was the first Dal bitch and the third Dalmatian to achieve the UDT title. She won numerous highs in trial prizes and four times she had perfect scores in both Open and Utility! She passed the tracking test six times just for the fun and exercise of it.

Mrs. Donahue became increasingly interested in show stock and in breeding quality Dalmatians. Early purchases were from Reigate, Lorbyrndale, Dal Duchy and Tattoo kennels. Her foundation bitches were sisters, a liver daughter and a black daughter of Ch. Reigate Bold Venture.

In 1947 Mrs. Donahue registered her Long Last prefix with AKC. This kennel bred, imported and owned more than 30 champions such as Ch. Long Last Kelso, Ch. Long Last Ripcord, Ch. Long Last Let's Pretend, and Ch. Long Last Limoge, all of whom were multiple breed winners and producers of group and Best in Show winners.

In the mid 1950's Mrs. Donahue became interested in some of the English bloodlines and imported several dogs. Am. Ch. Washakie Boldhills Barbara, a liver bitch, was the first one to join the Long Last ranks. She was later joined by Am. Ch. Washakie Regina and Washakie Destiny.

The greatest import Mrs. Donahue brought over was Eng. and Am. Ch. Colonsay Blacksmith. This dog was Best in Show at the British Dalmatian Club's 1957 national show. Blacksmith won many breeds in the U.S. after he

Ch. Long Last Kelso, liver dog, owned
by Long Last Kennels, Lorraine Donahue.

Ch. Long Last Living Legend, "Kojak," photographed
at three years of age, owned by Long Last Kennels.

became a champion and had a definite influence on the Dalmatian in this country.

Extended pedigrees will show that Long Last provided a solid foundation with the combination of American and English bloodlines and this can be found behind many modern-day kennels throughout the U.S. and Canada. Mrs. Donahue continues in Dals.

Colonial Coach

One of the oldest registered kennels still active in Dalmatians is Colonial Coach located in Wauconda, IL. Mr. and Mrs. William H. Knowles, Bud and Laura, founded the kennel in 1946 in Des Plaines, IL. Their start in Dals was not exactly promising. A fellow worker at Mr. Knowles' place of employment lived in an apartment in Chicago and was unable to keep his Dal, Dotty. Bud took her home with him with some misgivings. As a boy he had had Staffordshire Terriers but in Laura's family there had been no dogs at all. However, Dotty saved the day by winning over the entire household. After a time the family decided to buy a registered Dalmatian. They visited the Chicago International dog show and became interested in dog shows. They purchased a dog from a breeder in Michigan and named it Bozo. He became Ch. Knowles Bozo Boy. The next purchase was a bitch from Colorado, Ch. Ding Dong Dresden Doll. She was living in Kenosha, WI, with a young man who sold her and her litter of pups to the Knowles.

They attended as exhibitors the Skokie Valley Kennel Club show in Harms Woods Forest Preserve near Chicago, June 5, 1944, a cold rainy day. There the Knowles were fortunate enough to meet a number of Dal breeders and exhibitors, Ruth Kane, Dal Dale Kennels, Martin Milet, Williamsdale Kennels, Percy Omo of O'Dal kennels and Blanche Osborne of Oz Dal. As Mr. Knowles says "from then on we were hooked in the dog fancy."

All the people the Knowles met at the Skokie show became their good friends. When Mr. Omo passed away the Knowles puchased all of his dogs from his widow. The purchase advanced them about five years in their breeding program. Bud Knowles handled many of his dogs himself to their championships. They also used the late Larry Downey as a handler.

In 1964 Laura fell ill and was unable to continue to operate the kennel. Natalie and Ron Fleger took over for the Knowles. Laura died in 1965 and the kennel was moved to Wauconda where it is now. Bud Knowles passed on in April of 1979.

The Flegers have retained the high standards of breeding that the Knowles had established. Some of the great dogs from this kennel are Ch. Colonial Coach Devonshire, Ch. Colonial Coach Cheshire, Ch. Colonial Coach Brouette, and Ch. Colonial Coach Son of York, to name a few.

Ch. Colonial Coach Devonshire. *Tauskey*

Ch. Colonial Coach Cheshire, the beloved Toby. *Tauskey*

164

Ch. Colonial Coach Honey Chile. Colonial Coach Kennels was founded by the late Laura and Bud Knowles. Natalie and Ron Fleger are continuing the operation of his famous kennel.

Ch. Blackpool's Bullshott owned by Nick and Barbara Peters.

In the Valley

In the Valley, the prefix used by Sue Allmann (now Mrs. George Ratner) accounted for a number of dogs on the show scene. One ad from *Popular Dogs* pictures five champions, all but one homebred. That one was, of course, Ch. Roadcoach Roadster, the dog which made Dalmatian history by winning the group at Morris and Essex twice, Best in Show at that prestigious event once, and winning the group at the Garden.

But In the Valley had some outstanding dogs to its credit in addition to Roadster. Ch. Bootiful Doll in the Valley, Ch. Tin Lizzie in the Valley, Ch. Sweet Chariot in the Valley, Merry Olds in the Valley, Ch. Barney Oldfield in the Valley, and Ch. Dalquest Belle Charm, purchased from the Dalquest Kennels of Miss Marjorie VanderVeer.

Now that this kennel has closed its doors and the In the Valley dogs have vanished from the show scene, one can look back and see that all of Sue's dogs were coach dogs. She bred Dalmatians for only a few years but had a considerable impact on the breed as a whole. The In the Valley dogs can be found in many extended pedigrees.

Her foundation sire was Ch. Lucky Legend of Fyrthorne. And the foundation bitch was Williamsdale Allspice. Judicious purchases from other kennels such as Williamsview, Dalquest and others aided her plan of breeding.

Mrs. Allmann was able to buy Ch. Boot Black of Dalmatia from Wendell Sammet. When he bought Roadster she returned Boot Black to his breeder. Boot Black was Roadster's sire. Mrs. Allmann always had an interest in dogs but always said she was a "novice in Dalmatians." All novices should do as well.

The fame of the great Morris & Essex shows is still widespread. People still talk about them in somewhat hushed tones or at least with a touch of awe in the voice.

The shows were established by the late Geraldine Dodge of Giralda Farms. They were held on the polo field of her estate. Various breeds were invited to participate. Entries were not open to all breeds. Each year Mrs. Dodge added a breed or two to the roster and the shows which started in 1927 grew and grew. The first year the entry was 595. Dals were invited to show in 1931 for the first time. In 1939 the entry had worked up to a total of 4456, an enormous show. The entry of Dalmatians was 49 that year. In 1941 the Dal entry had reached a total of 61. During the years 1942 through '45 no shows were held by Morris & Essex because of the war.

When the shows resumed in 1946 there was an entry of 2086. There was no Morris & Essex show in 1954 because of a confusion of dates. The Dalmatian entry varied from a low of 34 to a high of 78. In 1955 the

Dalmatian, Ch. Roadcoach Roadster won the group. He was owned by the Barretts of Roadcoach Kennels, his breeders. Following the win at this show the dog was sold to Mrs. S. K. Allmann, Jr. and in 1956 Roadster went on to the Best in Show win at M & E. He also won the group at Westminster the following winter, one of three Dalmatians to have that honor. The M & E win was over a total entry of 2304 dogs. At this point Roadster took his place in canine history along with such prestigious names as Ch. My Own Brucie, the Cocker Spaniel; Ch. Nornay Saddler, the smooth Fox Terrier; Ch. Rock Falls Colonel, the English Setter; and Ch. Baroque of Quality Hill, the Boxer. In 1957, the last M & E show was presented. It was a great loss to dog shows as the late Mrs. Dodge made it truly a prestige event.

Green Starr

When he was serving his internship Dr. David Doane liked to take a walk on occasion to get away from the hospital routine and to fill his lungs with fresh air. Frequently, as he walked along he was joined by a friendly Dalmatian who lived in the neighborhood of the hospital. After a time it seemed that the Dal was waiting for him to come along the street and would wag his tail happily in greeting and join the intern on the balance of his walk.

After Dr. Doane had moved to Walton, NY, to establish his medical practice he decided that he had to have a Dalmatian as his companion of his walks had sold him on the breed.

His foundation stock is directly descended from the great Reigate Bold Venture. One of his earliest dogs was Ch. Beloved Scotch of the Walls. Dr. Doane says that this grandson of Bold Venture ''was a preponderant sire that far out-produced his own quality.'' His foundation bitch was Shad's Dotter of Whitlee. Scotch sired Ch. Green Starr's Darling Dotter, Ch. Green Starr's Dazzler, Ch. Green Starr's Masterpiece; Ch. Green Starr's King Pin and Ch. Green Starr's Undergraduate. Ch. Green Starr's Brass Tacks was one of the greats found in the Green Starr line-up as is Ch. Green Starr's Colonel Joe, the current Best in Show Dalmatian.

Masterpiece set the record of being the first liver spotted Dalmatian to win a Best in Show and then he won a second. His record has since been matched by Ch. Melody Dynamatic who goes back to Green Starr breeding.

The Doane children are also interested in breeding and showing Dalmatians. Now grown, they live in various sections of the U.S. Miss Leslie Doane is at home at the Green Starr farm in Virginia not far from where her father is stationed, Fort Belvoir, VA. Dr. Doane is now Colonel Doane and heads the hospital at Belvoir. Both Dr. and Mrs. Doane are popular judges.

The breeding program at Green Starr spans some thirty-five years. A check of the Westminster catalog of 1947 shows Dr. Doane as an exhibitor.

Over this period of time approximately 70 champions have been recorded from Green Starr breeding, an enviable record. The breeding program continues at Green Starr farm so we can watch for some more greats to come into the ring under the Green Starr banner.

Blackpool

Barbara and "Nick" Peters started in Dals via the obedience route. Their first Dalmatian was Sir Knight of Blackmail, CDX. They had worked him for Utility but never succeeded in qualifying for the third leg of that title. They purchased him in 1950. Having had a taste of the breed they decided to go into Dals in earnest and purchased some foundation stock. The Blackpool blood lines are basically a cross between the Willowmount and Crestview lines. Willowmount's Dainty Delite, while definitely named Willowmount, was unlike most of the Willowmount dogs according to her breeder, Kay Robinson. She seemed to be a throwback to the Reigate type of Dals. Willowmount Tommy Tailwagger was another Willowmount dog which the Peters acquired.

This combination of dogs, however, produced the top-winning bitch in the United States, Ch. Blackpool Crinkle Forest. Tommy Tailwagger was the sire and Dainty Delite was the dam. Dainty Delite, as do so many of the Willowmount dogs, goes back to Dalmatia, Ard Aven, and Of the Walls breeding. Tommy Tailwagger also goes back to the Reigate breeding which was behind most of the dogs.

Co-owned with Edward Jenner, Crinkle Forest had a tremendous show record. She was named Best in Show at six all-breed shows, a record for a bitch exceeded only by Ch. Swabbie of Oz-Dal's total of eight. She was named Best of Breed at the DCA national specialty in 1965 and again in 1966, and was Best of Breed at the Chicagoland Dal Club specialty in 1964. She had 114 Best of Breed wins, 33 Group I's, 30 Group II's, 21 Group III's, and 12 Group IV's. Based on the number of Best of Breed wins she is the tenth in the Dalmatian order and the top bitch, followed by Ch. Swabbie of Oz Dal in 11th place and Ch. Korcula Salona in 12th. These figures are from statistics compiled by Walter Johnson who handles the statistics for the Dalmatian Club of America's *Spotter*.

Blackpool and Edward Jenner imported the liver dog, Ch. Colonsay Olaf the Red. This dog is behind many of the winning liver dogs in the ring today. And later Mrs. Peters imported a puppy, Tantivey Nora. Nora is now co-owned with Robert Liggett of Dallas, Tx.

Dal Haven

Becoming acquainted with a Dalmatian while on vacation led to the founding of Dal Haven Kennels, Wally and Betty Back's Dalmatian home.

The Backs met a couple who were travelling with the family pet, a Dal. The dog impressed them so much they decided to acquire one. This was in 1950.

Wally was interested in a dog which would work in the field as well as in show and obedience. The purchased a fine young male who broke his leash in an attempt to go after another dog and when he dashed into the road after his prey, was struck by a car and killed.

The next purchase was a three-year-old bitch which had been abused, nearly starved, and not trained. She was touted as a great field dog. This latter statement seemed to be a joke as she was extremely gun-shy. Despite all these strikes against her the Backs worked hard to acclimate her to their way of life, to showing, working in obedience, and hunting in the field. Apparently love won out as this bitch became Ch. Little Miss Lucy UD. When she conquered her gun-shyness she was absolutely tops in the field.

She was bred once to Ch. Greenland Iron Liege. The resulting litter produced Ch. Dal Haven's Sweetheart, UD, Ch. Dal Haven's Debutante, UD, Ch. Dalmy of Ironliege, and Dal Haven's October Boy, CDX.

Over the years the Backs have bred perhaps ten litters and have produced eight champions.

The current dog at Back's is called Prima. She is following in her great-great granddam's footsteps (Lucy) as she is an outstanding field dog.

Willowmount

Although Willowmount Kennels was actually a Canadian kennel and when its owner speaks of importing dogs she is discussing importing to Canada from the United States, so many of the Willowmount dogs completed their American championships that people feel as though it is an American kennel. Kay Robinson (now, Maurer) is the person responsible for the success of Willowmount.

Again the connection with Dals came through horses. Miss Robinson was involved with teaching riding and hunters and jumpers. A friend gave her a Dal to keep her company. After a time Kay decided to breed this bitch and from her first litter had two champions. One was Am. & Can. Ch. Willowmount Lucky Climax, a group winner. He had a total of three group firsts, 27 Best of Breeds, a very fine record at a time when the Nonsporting group had some very consistent winners of other breeds.

Mrs. Maurer feels that her top winning dog was Ch. Willowmount Dashing Dogs. This dog won a Best in Show, eight groups, and 147 Best of Breeds. The dog the American fancy remembers best and which is really Mrs. Maurer's favorite among all her dogs was Am. & Can. Ch. Willowmount Fudge Fantasy. This was Willowmount's top producing bitch and much of her produce ended in the U.S. and did very well here.

Among the dogs imported to Canada were Am. and Can. Ch. Devonshire Duchess, Am. & Can. Ch. Reigate Double Trouble, Am. & Can. Ch. Red Label from Dalmatia, a liver, and Am. & Can. Ch. Green Starr's Enterprise. This last dog can be found in many of today's pedigrees. The last dog Mrs. Maurer imported was Am. & Can. Ch. Zodiac's Best Foot Forward.

Linda Cyopik, a well-known Canadian breeder and exhibitor both here and in Canada, has been fortunate enough to receive all of the Willowmount records, pictures and pedigrees. And Mrs. Cyopik is carrying on the winning tradition established at Willowmount with her own dogs.

Importing is a two way street. Many Willowmount dogs were exported to the United States and Willowmount took many U.S. dogs to Canada. When we speak of importing we usually are thinking of the overseas aspect of this but we must not forget that the Canadian dogs have contributed mightily to the development of the dog in America. Miss Robinson's dogs were certainly in the foreground of the importing picture from Canada.

Records on the dogs in Canada do not go back very far. There were several Dalmatians reported as having been shown during the years of 1916–1918. These reports were made by the Canadian Kennel Club Stud Book and appear in the department on Bench Show winnings. At that time it was not necessary to register a dog before showing it. Dalmatians had turned up in shows in Toronto, Winnipeg, Regina, Vancouver and Victoria.

Mr. J. R. Constantineau of Montreal was an early registerer of his Dalmatians. He had imported his dogs from England and from the U.S. And during the thirties a number of dogs were brought to Canada from England. The kennels represented include Kurnool, Phaeland, and Elmcroft. Tattoo Kennels in the U.S. was the source of stock also.

Four Dals were registered in 1935 by the Canadian Kennel Club. They were all imported to Canada, three from England, one with Silverden and Stubbington lines, one Ace of Trumps, Brown and Caefel lines, and the third, the Panworth line. Tanyo of Tattoo was the sole import from the U.S.

Several hundred Dals are registered each year in Canada at the present time.

Oesau

Loyal Oesau and his wife, Reba, visited the Golden Gate Kennel Club's benched show in 1951 looking for a dog to buy. They were impressed by the Dalmatian because of his size, temperament, and the short hair. (We feel sure that they found out about the short hair after they acquired their dog). So they purchased a Dal which, because it was too heavily marked, was a pet. Loyal soon decided that obedience was the field to follow with his Chief Mr. Black and trained him through a CDX.

Ch. Blackpool's Crinkle Forest, owned by Barbara Peters and Edward Jenner, top winning bitch.

Ch. Crestview Dan Patch, bred by Crestview Kennels, owned by Loyal and Reba Oesau during his show career. Now at stud with his breeders.

Am, Can. Bda. Ch. Spatterdash Coaltar Tobyson,
owned by Mr. and Mrs. Jay C. Sheaffer. *Ashbey*

Ch. Spatterdash Hucklberry Finn, owned by
Spatterdash Kennels, Jay C. Sheaffer. *Gilbert*

Through showing his Dal in obedience the Oesaus met other Dal exhibitors and decided they would like to try showing in breed. They imported a two-year old bitch, Widdington Kandy, from England. She had been bred to Ch. Amala Sahib just before she was shipped and about five weeks after her arrival she produced six puppies. The Oesaus kept three of them. All of them obtained their CDs and one went on to a CDX. Kandy finished her American championship without any difficulty.

Crestview Prince of Destiny was the next acquisition. He finished his championship in short order. Crestview Lady Luck moved in and earned a CD.

At the Dalmatian Club of Southern California specialty in 1972 Mr. Oesau handled Mrs. McManus' Crestview Dan Patch for her. He won the Sweepstakes and took first in the Puppy class. By January of 1973, Mr. Oesau knew he wanted that dog and so he purchased Dan Patch with two points on him. Loyal handled him to two more points at the Santa Clara show and then turned the dog over to a handler who finished him in April. The dog ran up a record of 29 Best of Breeds, 7 Group I's, 5 Group II's, and 7 Group III's, won the Northern California specialty and was listed as number 2 Dal in the country.

In 1974 Dan Patch continued to win, taking the DCSC specialty show and the next day winning Best in Show at the Santa Ana Valley show over an entry of 3200 dogs. He also won the Northern California specialty again and took Best in Show at Eugene, OR. His record for the year was 48 Best of Breeds, 2 Bests in Show, 14 Group I's, 16 Group II's, 6 Group III's, and 2 Group IV's and he became the number 1 Dalmatian which record he obtained again in 1975. Again he won the Southern California specialty and had 28 Best of Breeds, two Bests in Show along with 7 groups wins and numerous group placings.

The McManus's bought the dog back in 1976 and Mrs. McManus took him east for the DCA specialty show which he won. He has been retired from active showing.

Loyal now has a litter brother of Dan Patch, Crestview Mr. Godfrey, who has qualified for his CD and is working on his CDX.

Spatterdash

From a one-dog family in 1956 to a registered kennel in 1957 is the story of Spatterdash. The Jay Sheaffers decided they would like to have a dog to go with the new home they were building. They read about Mrs. Allmann's success with Ch. Roadcoach Roadster and decided to see if she had any puppies they would like to have. They had decided to get a pup and obedience train it and enjoy the companionship of a lovely dog. A picture of Boot Black

Am. Can. Bda. Ch. Spatterdash Coal Tar Tobyson, owned and handled by Jay C. Sheaffer, shown as a young dog. *Gilbert*

Ch. Labyrinth Sleigh Belle, owned by Christine Dyker.

completely sold them on the breed. They acquired Black Booty in the Valley. Black Booty was barely a year old when she entered her first obedience trial at Philadelphia where she won her first leg on her CD, and it led to a CDX.

The Sheaffers were so fond of Booty they decided they had to have another Dalmatian so they returned to In the Valley and bought a six-week old puppy, Linenduster. Mrs. Shaeffer trained Booty and Jay trained Duster. In 1961 Linenduster was the highest scoring Dal in obedience. She received her CDX that year. Spatterdash Bubbling Over also finished a CD that year.

Black Booty had a litter in April, 1957, sired by Ch. Lucky Legend of Fyrthorne. A second litter was whelped in January 1958 by Ch. Colonsay Blacksmith (English import) out of Linenduster. Bubbling Over, the true foundation brood bitch for the Sheaffers, was from that litter. The true foundation stud was Spatterdash Cirrocumulus. Over the next ten years the Sheaffers finished ten champions, all with the Spatterdash prefix.

They became so involved in breeding and showing Dalmatians they had to give up their home and build another. This time they moved to a more rural area, bought some acreage, and added a kennel building to the plans.

The Sheaffers were Dalmatian breeders for 16 years, having bred thirty-five litters. They did not confine their breeding to one kennel. They selected the studs used with care, fitting the dog to the bitch for a good mating. They also became interested in a new and different breed, one still not recognized by AKC but a breed which has received a great deal of publicity from time to time, the Canaan dog.

After Mr. Sheaffer started judging it became more difficult to continue exhibiting. In 1975 the Sheaffers sold their kennel property and moved into an urban home. Mr. Sheaffer is eligible to judge all Nonsporting breeds, Toy Poodles, and Great Danes.

Stablemate

In the late 40's and early 50's many kennels were changing the interests and habits of many people. Dal Duchy Kennels of Toledo, OH, owned by Mr. and Mrs. Earl St. Clair, had a great deal of influence on a number of people in the northern Ohio and Detroit, Michigan areas. The St. Clairs bred their Ch. Dal Duchy's Gay Lady to Ch. Ace of Fyrthorne. The result was an outstanding litter. Every puppy in the litter finished its American championship.

The St. Clair's favorite was George (Ch. Dal Duchy's Gorgeous George) which they kept. He sired many fine puppies and started many people on their way to being Dalmatian breeders. One such kennel is Stablemate, Sylvia Howison's kennel. Sylvia bought a daughter of Gorgeous George, Charlie's Pretty Penny, and she became the foundation bitch for Stablemate.

The Howisons, for Sylvia's husband, Harold, is also interested in dogs, have had great success with their breeding. They finished a number of champions in Dalmatians as well as in their second breed, Bernese Mountain Dogs.

Then the Cinderella dog came into their lives and things haven't been the same since. A fellow Dal exhibitor called to ask the Howisons if they knew anything about Willowmount bloodlines. A Canadian Labrador Retriever breeder had offered the Dal breeder a liver male Dalmatian of Willowmount breeding. Of course, Sylvia explained that Willowmount breeding was of the best and asked a few more questions concerning the dog. It seems that the Canadian was also the animal control officer for his district and had finally picked up this Dal which had been running loose for four months on an Indian reservation in his territory. The dog had obviously been abandoned. A check of his tattoo number was easily traceable through the Canadian Kennel Club to his breeder, Kay Robinson of Willowmount. By this time breeding activities at Willowmount had been discontinued.

The next day the same Dal breeder was on the phone asking if the Howisons could possibly keep the Canadian dog until a good home was found for him. The answer was "yes" and so Baron Brown came to live at Stablemate.

He was "a skinny looking scarred-up mess," recalls Mrs. Howison. "He was also the best liver Dal I have ever seen." The good home for the dog had been found. His travels were over.

It took months and about $300 in telephone charges to trace his line of ownership. At the age of two years he had had a total of six owners. The registration had never been transferred from the original owner's name and all the subsequent owners had to be contacted and had to sign off to the next in line. The dog arrived at Stablemate in October and the registration from Canada came through in March. The American Kennel Club took a mere 14 days to process the application for registration in the country.

Meanwhile the dog had been trained and temperament tested. He is somewhat stubborn but extremely stable. He would stand in a show pose for long periods of time and never flinch. He objected, however, to being put on leash. There was no way to force him to walk on leash. Suddenly, one day, Mrs. Howison *asked* the dog to walk with her while he was on leash and he did. He has had a wonderful home at Stablemate ever since and has accounted for at least fifteen champion get. He is also an American and Canadian champion. He loves dog shows, people, cats, kids, pups and bitches. He hates male dogs and detests riding in a car. But he is now a top sire, has contributed much to Dalmatians in the U.S., even though he is a dog that nobody wanted.

Mary Howison, the Howison daughter, has now become active in the Stablemate activities.

Sylvia is a founder of the Dalmatian Club of Detroit and has served the club as president, show chairman, and in other activities. This is a very active club which participates in community activities and holds a speciality show each year. One notable characteristic of the Detroit specialty is that a breeder judge is always selected to pass on the entry.

Tuckaway

Tuckaway Kennels, situated in the heart of the Kentucky blue grass country, is one of the more active breeding kennels in the fancy today. Dr. Sidney Remmele, a veterinarian, acquired his first Dalmatian in 1952. She was a daughter of Ch. Williamsdale Rocky, national speciality winner, out of Kinjocity Lady R. Dr. Remmele, however, was not able to do much breeding and showing while he finished his education. In 1963 he wanted another Dalmatian so he bought a $50 pet bitch. He became interested in showing and finished the pet in 13 shows with three majors. Her name was Ch. Garland' Pride, call name Tuck. It was from this bitch that the kennel took its name.

Dr. Remmele became an active breeder in 1965. He bought a male, Williamsview Shane, from Bill Hibbler's Williamsview Kennels in New Jersey, and in 1969 he purchased Ch. Coachman's Canicula from Coachman Kennels in St. Louis. Using Canicula on Shane daughters has been the best breeding program for Tuckaway. Ch. Lord Jim also lived his last years at Tuckaway.

Dr. Remmele was justly proud of Canicula, a son of Ch. Coachman's Chuck-a-Luck. The dog is a three-time group winner and a multiple speciality winner. His greatest win was Best of Breed at the 1973 DCA national speciality show. Canicula was the sire of 20 championships and won the Stud Dog Class at the DCA speciality show twice. He died in August 1978.

A Shane daughter, Ch. Labyrinth Sleighbell, has become one of the top producing bitches in the history of the breed. Her first litter by Canicula produced seven champions, six American and one Canadian. Three of her offspring have accounted for eleven group wins while one of the males, Ch. Tuckaway Gallant Man, is rapidly becoming an outstanding stud dog in his own right.

Labyrinth

Spanning a number of years we find the breeding of Labyrinth Kennels, Chris Dyker's Dals. Shortly after the war Christine became interested in Dalmatians when her then husband-to-be owned a bitch named Reveille Girl. When he moved into an apartment he placed the bitch with good friends, Teresa and Nick Nichols.

Labyrinth Oh Susanna, owned by Christine Dyker.

Ch. Labyrinth Tuckaway Julep, winning Best Senior in Sweeps at DCSNE specialty show, owned and handled by Christine Dyker.

178

When Reveille Girl was bred Christine selected a nice male from the litter and named him War Eagle Taps, call name Bugler. Chris says she will be forever grateful to this dog as he taught her many important lessons. She became involved in obedience and conformation showing. Bugler taught her to lose and to learn from the losses and in obedience that the work is for the good of the dog and not the glory of the trainer. This dog sired eight litters and eventually lived out his life on a farm with friends when Christine was married and unable to keep him.

As soon as she could have another dog she selected a daughter of the Nichols' second Reveille Girl. Ch. Poca Dot Salute to Reveille became one of the top producing dams of 1970 in the Nonsporting group. A daughter, Ch. Labyrinth Sleighbell, finished with four majors and followed in her dam's footsteps as a producer.

Labyrinth's foundation bitch Dot along with her daughters have been responsible for some 19 champions in the States. There are also Bermudian, Brazilian, Canadian, and South African champions from this breeding.

The prefix Labyrinth has an interesting background. In the 1700's this was an early designation of the farm property where the Dykers live near Washington, DC. It was part of a large parcel of land owned by George Washington.

Notable offspring from Labyrinth are the winning litter brothers, Ch. Tuckaway Bold and Brave, Ch. Tuckaway Gallant Man, and Ch. Tuckaway Jason James. These dogs were sired by Ch. Coachman's Canicula who was Best of Breed at the 1973 National Specialty. Mrs. Dyker is co-breeder of these dogs with Dr. Remmele who owned Canicula. All these dogs have been group winners.

Mrs. Dyker is continuing to breed on the same bloodlines and to show top Dalmatians. She is also a judge of Dals and Poodles and has had the honor of judging at the national specialty show of the Clube Dalmata do Brasil.

Crown Jewels

A mistake on an entry blank for an obedience class was the spark which founded one of the most active kennels in the midwest, Crown Jewels. In 1958 Norma Price purchased a Dalmatian bitch, Sophia of Glenwood, as a guard dog. Her choice of breeds was based on the fact that the decor of her apartment was black and white.

The bitch was trained and ready to enter Novice obedience classes. In making out the entry, the class entered by Mrs. Price was Novice, NOT Novice A or B. When she arrived at the show and discovered the error, Mrs. Price decided to stay and take her chances. This was a wise decision because she went WB for two points that day.

179

Sophia was bred to the top stud dog in the area, Ch. Colonial Coach Chesire. This litter produced Ch. Crown Jewel's Black Diamond who went on to become the producer of the most champion get in the breed to date. He sired a total of 42 champions.

Both Mr. and Mrs. Price have been active in Dalmatians. Mr. Price served several terms as president of the Chicagoland Club.

Dalmor

One of the early kennels well known to breeders and exhibitors was the Whitlee line of Dals which belonged to Mrs. Jean Whiting Verre. The line is behind a number of present day breeding programs including that of Green Starr.

In 1964 Patricia Borowiec decided she wanted a Dalmatian and bought a very nice pet but a couple of years later she decided to breed so she bought a five year old bitch for breeding. The important thing about the bitch was the fourth generation of her pedigree. It contained several dogs with the Whitlee prefix. Mrs. Verre was Mrs. Borowiec's mother and the daughter wanted to continue the same breeding program to some extent.

Mrs. Borowiec and her husband, Walt, breed just one litter of Dals each year as they also breed and show Pointers. To date they have had five champions carrying their Dalmor prefix.

One thrill for the Borowiecs was winning Best of Winners at Westminster in 1973 under Dr. David Doane because Mrs. Borowiec's mother had said she's always wanted to win something at the Garden. The dog was a descendant of Whitlee breeding, and the judge's foundation stock had come from Whitlee breeding.

The breeding program at Dalmor is very carefully thought out and planned. To date they have bred Ch. Shadodal's Showoff of Dalmor, Ch. Dalmor's Caesar Augustus, Ch. Dalmor's Emily Bronte, Ch. Dalmor's Euripidea, and Ch. Dalmor's Mike Finnegan.

Watseka

To win the national specialty must be one of the greater thrills in the life of any breeder-exhibitor. To win the national specialty (*three times with the same dog*) must be the consummate thrill. This feat was accomplished by Don and Carol Schubert with their great dog, Ch. Panore of Watseka. Panore was named Best of Breed at the national specialty held in California in 1972 by Dr. David Doane. In 1974 he again won the breed at the national show in Waukesha, WI, under Mrs. Winifred Heckmann. A short while later the dog was retired. In 1977, Panore was entered at the national specialty in Crete, IL, as a veteran dog. He won the veteran dog class judged by Mrs. Isabel Robson.

180

Ch. Colonial Coach Carriage Way, the "Cinderella" dog
owned by Watseka Kennels, Don and Carol Schubert.

Ch. Tamara of Watseka, owned by the Schuberts.

Best of Breed competition was judged by Alfred E. Treen. The dog looked superb and the longer the judging went on the better the dog looked. He won.

The Schuberts had always had some dogs around the house, mostly mixed breeds, just pets for their children. In 1960 their daughter Sherry wasn't feeling well so her father bought her a Dalmatian as a pet to cheer her. A neighborhood Dal had visited them frequently and they rather admired the breed. The Dal purchased for Sherry was Lola of Watseka. The Schuberts showed her a couple of times but she was too heavily marked to do any winning. They bred her to Ch. Colonial Coach Cheshire and from a litter of five puppies she produced two champions, one of whom was Ch. Tamara of Watseka, one of the leading dams of the breed.

In the spring of 1961 the Schuberts saw a young dog being shown as a puppy at the International Kennel Club show in Chicago. They were much impressed with this dog. Later when the dog was three years old, they acquired him. He became Ch. Colonial Coach Carriage Way.

The dog had been sold off the bench at the show that spring to a young couple who had, in turn, sold him, and he seemed to have disappeared. They continued looking for him and finally located him in a downtown Chicago slum area. They found that during the summer he was chained to a fence in a yard covered with glass and garbage. In the winter he was chained to a bathtub in the house. He was so filthy dirty that his spots were practically invisible. He was in terrible physical condition. This dog, however, was the one the Schuberts wanted to breed Tamara to. They decided to try to buy the dog as they certainly didn't want to take their bitch to the place where the dog was.

At first the owner was willing to sell but later called and said that he had changed his mind. A few months passed and the owner called Mr. Schubert at his office and offered to sell the dog. He was apparently in need of money. The banks had closed for the day by the time the owner made his call but Don was able to borrow cash from his friends so that he had tens, twenties, and other bills in his pocket. He went to pick up the dog before the owner had time to change his mind again. Don fanned out the cash money in his hand as one would a bridge hand. The cash must have looked very enticing to Carriage Way's owner as he handed the dog over to Don.

After the dog had been chained for so long no one could predict how he would react. He was turned loose in a fenced area of five acres. Sitting on a small hill entranced with his new freedom, the dog was unaware that one of the Schubert children was approaching him from behind. The child threw arms around the dog's neck and hugged him. The dog simply turned and "kissed" the child. He was a smiling, laughing dog.

After a thorough bathing he was taken to see a veterinary where he was given an anesthetic to take back his nails which were so long the dog could not stand on the pads of his feet.

Ch. Bob Dylan Thomas of Watseka, owned by the Schuberts.

Ch. Panore of Watseka, winner of 10 Bests in Show and three-time
winner of DCA specialty show, owned and handled by Carol Schubert.

183

Although the Schuberts had purchased this dog for a stud dog rather than a show specimen, he responded so well to good treatment that at three years of age he began a show career. He finished his championship in short order and went on to become a multi group winner and also won the breed at the Garden.

While his show career was quite grand, he excelled as a sire. He has sired 40 champions, many of whom are breed winners and including three specialty winners. Matings with Tamara produced thirteen champions including the great Panore. Panore, in addition to the specialty wins, has won ten all-breed Best in Shows. His son, Ch. Bob Dylan Thomas is third in a line of leading sires.

Over the years the Watseka line has produced more than thirty champions.

A few years ago Carol Schubert became a handler. A superb handler, she is difficult to beat and manages to get the most from any dog she shows. She also handles a number of other breeds including Akitas, Basenjis, Great Danes, Weimaraners, and German Shorthaired Pointers. She presents all of these dogs as expertly as she shows the Dals. Don has also entered the ranks of the handlers but does not show as often as Carol.

Melody

A decision to purchase a Harlequin Great Dane puppy is the reason Melody Dalmatian Kennels are in existence! Jack White (Dr. John V. White, Jr., DVM) had asked his father for a puppy. While looking for a suitable Harl to buy Jack came across a litter of Dalmatians and fell in love with them. Since his father was making the purchase, Jack had to be content with a puppy of pet quality. This bitch was Calculator's Miss Sincerity and while Jack was not aware of it, she came from show stock. Her background was Green Starr.

While stationed in Texas during his service days, Jack attended his first dog show. He was enthusiastic over the dogs and the competition. A breeder advised him not to breed "Sindy" as she was lacking in some nose pigment. Being a novice, Jack ignored the advice, bred Sindy and founded a kennel. One of the bitches from the first litter was Ch. Melody Sweet CD, an outstanding Dalmatian. Another champion produced in this first litter was Patrick Larabee. Ch. Long Last Ripcord, a son of Ch. Colonsay Blacksmith, a great import from England, was the sire of this litter. In a later litter Sindy produced two well-known liver bitches, Ch. Melody Crimson and Clover CD and Ch. Melody Up Up and Away CD.

After Jack finished his military service he moved to Colorado and attended veterinary medical college, graduating from Colorado State University, Fort Collins.

At first the going in Colorado show competition was difficult because there wasn't any to speak of. But Jack persisted, the numbers grew, and he managed to finish Sweet. He put points on Sindy but she didn't finish because one of her legs was broken in an accident and she was never sound after it healed.

While Sindy was actually the foundation bitch for Melody Kennels, the Whites' best known bitch is Sweet. After her start in Colorado Sweet went on to win six Group I's and various wins at regional and national specialties.

When Jack and Beth were married Beth had Collies but soon became interested in the Dals. They are both interested in conformation and obedience and nearly all of their own champions have a CD, but other interests—cattle and Appaloosa horses——take too much of their time for them to train for advanced degrees.

To date Melody has bred about 40 champions. They average a litter each year. Basically, their dogs are house dogs so they keep the numbers down. The dogs are very much at home on the ranch where the Whites live and run with the horses over the foothills of the Rockies.

Ch. Melody Ring of Fire of BB, CD, was a Best in Show dog winning Buckhorn Valley Kennel Club show in 1972, owner-handled. At DCA national specialties Ch. Melody Auntie Mame was WB in 1972; Ch. Melody Cat Ballou was RWB in 1973; Ch. Melody Up Up and Away, CD won Best of Opposite sex in 1974, and Ch. Melody Moon River was RWD at the same show; Ringer, the Best in Show dog, was Best of Breed at the DCA in 1975; Melody Kiss Me Kate was Best in the 1977 Futurity; Ch. Melody Penny Lane was Best of Opposite Sex at the 1978 DCA specialty. Ch. Melody Dynamatic, a liver, won Best in Show at Buckhorn Valley Kennel Club show in 1973 and tied the liver Best in Show record by winning the top award at the Colorado Kennel Club in 1975. The 1977 specialty show of the Detroit Dalmatian Club saw WD, WB and BW taken by Ch. Melody Steppin' Out and Ch. Melody Joleen of Croatia.

In 1978 Ch. Melody Sweet CD was named the top-producing bitch of the breed. She is the dam of 15 champions with two more pointed and close to finishing. Sadly, the Whites lost Sindy in December of 1978 at the age of fifteen years.

Rho-Dal

Frequently, so many times that it becomes almost commonplace, top enthusiasts of the breed come into it in quite strange ways. Rho-dals came about in an odd way. Shortly before the attack on Pearl Harbor, someone gave the Rhodas, Louis and Connie, a mixed breed dog, part English Setter and part Dalmatian. The dog was named "Poncho" and seemed to be more Dal than Setter. Mr. Rhoda was called back to the Navy for the war effort and shortly after he left for service someone stole the dog from the yard.

When the Rhodas decided to get another dog they, of course, chose a Dalmatian. Their daughter was then five months old and, as anyone wanting a dog will tell you, needed the puppy for companionship. They purchased a very heavily marked bitch named Rhoda's Sue. A friend of Sue's breeder talked them into breeding the bitch and through this introduced them to the Dalmatian Club of Southern California which they later joined.

The Rhodas had never seen a liver Dalmatian and they heard that one was being boarded by a veterinarian near where they lived so they went to look at this dog and were very impressed. She was Four-in-Hand Copper Queen and belonged to Leo Meeker. Mr. Meeker asked if they would like to lease the bitch and Mr. Rhoda said, "Yes." This was their advent into livers. Later on they were talked into taking another bitch on lease, a black and white, Maal's Velvet and Lace. These two bitches, the liver and the black, were the foundation of the Rho-Dals. With limited breeding they have produced four champions. Two other dogs were almost finished when ill luck befell them, one with 10 points and both majors being paralyzed after being hit by a car and the other with 15 points, lacking a major, dropped dead with heart failure.

For some time the Rhodas have not been breeding although they kept up their interest in the breed. They now have an English import, Bridalane Mace for Rho-Dal, a liver dog, and plan to campaign him in the near future.

Pepper Spattered

When a beloved child pesters the life out of you to buy a particular breed of dog you eventually will give in to the demands. At least most indulgent parents will and the Dalmatian fancy is fortunate that Jane Helms Venes' parents were indulgent.

When Jane was about seven or eight years old she attended a dog show and decided that showing dogs was the greatest thing on earth. After she attended a second show a couple of years later she started a campaign for a show dog. Since she had horses, she chose the Dal, although she had investigated numerous other breeds, weighed the pros and cons of each, before she finally settled on the Dal.

Her parents took her to Colonial Coach kennels in the nearby Chicago area (the Helms were living in Elm Grove, WI, at the time) and she looked at the Dalmatians. Jane had saved a portion of the purchase price and made arrangements to buy the bitch from the Knowles. The bitch was 2½ month old puppy so the decision was for the Helms to pick her up in June after school was dismissed a month or so later.

This bitch was Ch. Pepper Spattered Sunshine, Jane's foundation. She was sired by Ch. Colonial Coach Cheshire out of a Tioga Sports Car bitch, beautiful line breeding.

Jane showed the bitch herself and had the honor of winning Winners Bitch at the national specialty under Mrs. Bonney on August 23, 1962. This date is important as it was Jane's fifteenth birthday and the trip to the specialty was a birthday present. Sunny was bred to Ch. Coachman's Colours. The resulting litter produced four champions: Ch. Pepper Spattered Myrosa Mia, CD, Ch. Pepper Spattered Teddy Bear, Ch. Clipper Ticonderoadster, and Ch. Pepper Spattered Remember Me, CD.

At the national specialty in 1966 Pepper Spattered Teddy Bear finished his championship and was named Best of Opposite Sex to the great Ch. Blackpool's Crinkle Forest over fifteen male specials by Louis Murr. Two days later Sunny was Best of Opposite at Gary, Indiana (Steel City) to the eventual Best in Show winner, Ch. Rockledge Rumble, under Mrs. Bonney.

When Jane married Robert Venes after she graduated from university she had to dispose of her dogs. They were entirely too jealous of this interloper in their family, Bob. And Robert Venes had never had a great deal of interest in dogs. Life was quite difficult when the spotted beauties refused to let him in the house unless Jane came to oversee his entrance. She placed her dogs in carefully selected homes. Teddy Bear went to live at Crosspatch Ranch where he became the king pin of Beverly Keller's kennel.

Jane had piloted this young male to a group win and Best of Breed win at the Chicagoland specialty. Beverly Keller showed him to top veteran dog at that same specialty several years later. Jane has now acquired a new bitch, Ch. Coachman's Curtain Call, which she finished with all majors. "Ceci" has been bred once and some of her get are being shown successfully.

Jane has two children now, a girl, Katie, and a boy, Jimmie. We expect to see them all in the ring in the future. And now that the dogs are not jealous of him, Bob is beginning to enjoy them, too.

Korcula

When the Garvins' pet Collie died their son, Charles, not yet in his teens, asked to have a different sort of dog. He had decided on a Dalmatian and so his parents bought him one for a pet. The pet turned out to be Ch. Korcula Salona, CD, the top winning bitch in the breed for several years and an outstanding producer. Charles learned to handle and to show and eventually won the coveted trophy at Westminster for top junior handler in 1969.

"Korky" became the foundation bitch for the Korcula kennels. Since they started breeding the Garvins have finished more than twenty champions and have earned CD titles on many of them.

Ch. Wyckliffe's Beau Brigand owned by Charles Colling.

Ch. Pill Peddler's Chuck Wagon, owned by Al & Peg White.

188

Charles, as children do, grew up, graduated from college and medical school, taking time out along the way to marry Lynn Oliver and now there are four Garvins involved in showing Dalmatians. And Charles has started to do a little judging, having handled the sweepstakes assignment at several regional specialty shows and at the DCA national specialty in 1978. He has truly grown up in Dalmatians.

The entire Garvin family is active in Dalmatian activities, club and show. At the present time Mrs. John Garvin is secretary of the DCA and writes the Dal column for the *Gazette*. Dr. John has served as obedience chairman for DCA shows. While in medical school in California, Dr. Charles served as president of the Dalmatian Club of Southern California and Lynn was trophy chairman for the group.

A son born to the young couple in April 1979 will probably join the ranks of junior handlers as soon as he is old enough.

Dottidale

Amy and Elli Lipschutz's interest in the breed was practically inherited from their father who used to run for blocks following the horse-drawn fire engines with the Dals flying at their heels when he was a boy. They acquired their first Dalmatian in 1947 when they were children. Their interest has never flagged.

Their greatest Dal was Ch. Dottidale Jo Jo, who, in 1967 was the top winning liver Dal in the U.S., rated #4 in the Phillips ratings, and won the breed at the Kennel Club of Philadelphia, Eastern Dog Club, Westchester, and Greater Pittsburgh Dal Club. He also won the veteran dog class at the Dalmatian Club of Southern New England specialty in 1970 and the veteran class at the DCA national specialty in 1971.

He has also acquired a record as a sire. In 1969 Dalhalla's Thunder Bolt, Winners Dog, and Dottidale's Cedelia, Winners Bitch, Best of Winners and Best of Opposite Sex at the national specialty, were sired by him. Thunderbolt was named Best of Breed at Westminster in 1972.

Jo Jo's daughter, Dottidale Elizabeth, is another of this kennel's outstanding Dals. For three years in a row, '75, '76, and '77 she was the winner of the veteran bitch class at the Southern New England specialty and she captured the same win at the DCA show in 1976.

Most of the Dottidale dogs are owner handled in the ring and they continue to produce good specimens, usually placing or winning each time they are shown.

Pill Peddler

Pill Peddler is the prefix used by Alberta Holden for her dogs. Mrs. Holden and her husband, Dr. Eugene Holden, have been breeding Morgan

Ch. Ye Dal Dark Brilliance, owned by Nina Asner.

Ch. Igor of Kye of Williamsdale

190

horses and Dalmatians for many years. Much of Mrs. Holden's breeding stock is from the now inactive kennel of the Lloyd Reeves' Rabbit Run. Mrs. Reeves, who winters in Florida and spends her summers in New England, is no longer active as a breeder but has retained her interest in the breed. Mrs. Holden, with judicious use of other lines, such as Dalquest, Roadcoach, and Tuckaway, has developed a very fine breeding program and had great success with her dogs. The Holdens have now closed the kennel in New Hampshire and moved to the sunny South where they are involved in breeding horses for harness racing. Their plans to continue breeding Dalmatians are still alive so we can look forward to seeing the Pill Peddler dogs in the ring for some time to come.

Migatz

For a brief time Bob and Roz Migatz and their daughters, Margo and Marcia, were interested in Dalmatians. They purchased a nice male from Dal Haven kennels and finished him to his championship. Later Bob put a CD on the dog. This was Ch. Dal Haven's Oliver Twist CD. They purchased a bitch and did a little breeding going so far as to erect a kennel as an adjunct to the garage of their new home which they built in 1971.

Margo, however, found that she enjoyed her horses more than she did her dogs and the family interest soon followed her lead. To say that she has been successful in the realm of equines is to give an understatement as she was National 4H Champion Rider one year and has numerous other awards on her horses.

Bob Migatz still holds a soft spot in his heart for Dals. He was elected president of the Dalmatian Club of America and served the club well. He continues to attend shows from time to time and watch the judging of his favorite breed.

Oliver Twist, at the age of 14, was hit by a commuter train and instantly killed. He was chasing a bitch in season at the time. Age apparently hadn't bothered him and so intent on his quarry was he that he failed to obey the rules of the house and left his yard.

Paisley

Paisley Dalmatians are really founded on obedience interests. Sue MacMillan (then Sue Reinarz) had trained the family Beagle in obedience and decided she would like a smart looking, flashy dog for obedience and breed competition. She acquired a Dalmatian after learning of the remarkable record of Belle Monti's Mr. Mickey, the Dal with so many high scores on the West Coast. She acquired a lovely liver bitch from Blackpool, Ch. Blackpool's Red Nora. This bitch finished her championship with several Best of Breeds over specials and won four consecutive High in Trial awards from the Novice class. The two times she was shown in Canadian obedience trials, she won HSDT. When she had achieved her CDX she was bred. Unfortunately Sue lost her in whelping the litter.

For a time college intervened but since about 1972 Sue and her husband, David, have been back in the Dalmatian picture. They have finished some 20 champions, 16 of them home-breds, and most of them owner-handled. Among others they are the breeders of Ch. Oak Tree of Gypsy Rose VII, a specialty and multi-group winning dog in Brazil before coming to the U.S. to do his winning. His dam, an American champion, was shipped to Brazil in whelp. She finished her Brazilian championship in four straight shows.

Probably, the most famous of the MacMillan's dogs is Pooka, Ch. Melody Up Up and Away, CD. This lovely liver bitch has more than 40 Best of Breeds and more than 25 group placings. Twice she was among the top ten Dals. When Paisley Dalmatians were revived Sue wanted to continue with liver Dals and worked with Jack and Beth White of Melody Dals in Colorado to get the bloodlines required, hence the Melody prefix.

Pooka has produced a number of champions, some of whom have also produced champions which is the type of breeding we all would like to achieve.

Of Croatia

What a change there must have been in the life-style of the Forrest Johnsons when they made the switch from Chihuahuas to Dalmatians!

Audrey and Forrest had bred and shown Chihuahuas for about ten years when they decided to go into Dals. They had admired the dogs for some time, having been attracted to the breed by their flashy appearance. And every encounter they had with a Dalmatian was a pleasant experience.

In the summer of 1967 while visiting relatives in Massachusetts they found two puppy bitches in a litter and had them shipped to Iowa. Two Dal puppies in a house accustomed to Chihuahuas and an occasional miniature Poodle was too much, so they sold one of the pups and kept the other. Unfortunately, Lady did not turn out to be show quality nor was she a brood bitch. So she was sold and new stock was introduced into the picture. The Johnsons named their Dalmatian breeding ''of Croatia.''

They are the breeders of Ch. Mr. Diamond Chips of Croatia, co-bred with Norma Price; Ch. Miss Nadana Topaz of Croatia; Ch. Mr. King Hill of Croatia, Ch. Christophers Duke of Croatia, Ch. Miss Dolly of Croatia, Ch. Mr. Frosty Boy of Croatia, Ch. Sylvann's Roadking of Croatia, Ch. Miss Tiffany of Croatia, Ch. Contessa of Croatia, and Ch. Mr. Paul Revere of Croatia.

Ch. Fobette's Frishka CD, the foundation bitch of Coachman's Kennels. She is behind every Coachman Dalmatian.

Their first home-bred champion, Mr. Diamond Chips of Croatia, finished his championship under a year of age with a Group I and a Group IV from the classes. He finished with all majors and was always Best of Winners. He was named Best Puppy at the national specialty in 1970. His first litter sired at Croatia was out of Ch. Crown Jewel's Nadana Topaz. Her sire was Ch. Crown Jewels Black Diamond and her dam was Ch. Crown Jewel's Black Agate. This litter produced four champions.

Another of the young champions at Croatia promises to contribute excellent qualities to the breed. She was bred by Dr. and Mrs. Jack White of Melody Kennels, sired by Ch. Sugarfrost out of Ch. Melody Crimson and Clover. She is Ch. Melody Joleen of Croatia and finished her championship at the Dalmatian Club of Detroit specialty where she was Winners Bitch and Best of Opposite Sex defeating 56 bitches.

The Johnsons are founders of the Davenport Dalmatian Club and are very active in dog activities. They are also members of the Tri-City Kennel Club, the Scott County Kennel Club, the DCA and the Chicagoland Dal Club. Mr. Johnson has served as trophy chairman and as show chairman for the national specialty. He is also a judge of Dalmatians and Poodles.

Hopi Kachina

Hopi Kachina in the Land of Enchantment, the Nogars' Dalmatians in New Mexico, is not really a kennel at all. As they put it, "We are really not breeders—only pet owners of a few extra nice Dalmatians."

The Nogars were from the Chicago area. Their first Dal, Dawn, was an unregistered bitch which they felt was the greatest. At that time the great obedience enthusiast Oscar Franzen conducted obedience classes for children on TV. The series was shown weekly with the home viewing audience invited to train their dogs at home. The Nogar son trained Dawn. At the conclusion of the series the audience was invited to come to the Lakefront to participate in a graduation. To their great surprise and delight, the Nogars' young son Nick and his Dawn won first place over a very large class. Mr. Franzen was most complimentary of the Dal's benevolent cooperation with her young owner. Says Mr. Nogar, "Dawn was everything a dog could be—baby sitter par excellence, super guardian, and loyal friend."

The Nogars acquired another bitch, a registered one this time. In the middle sixties they moved from the Chicago area to the southwest. Since they have lived out there they have finished five champions and continue to produce good stock. They started out with Colonial Coach breeding stock and have worked with Melody and Newsprint bloodlines to produce their own bloodline. Their last two champions were sired by the Best in Show liver dog, Ch. Melody Dynamatic.

Bespeckled

Dog affairs are a family activity at the home of Nan and Ken Nagler. Nan is the handler in the conformation ring and daughter Susan and Ken are the trainers in the obedience ring.

Some years ago Nan decided she wanted a dog. She knew she wanted a Dalmatian as she had seen one in the neighborhood and felt that it was the most beautiful animal she had ever seen. But she is a diplomat and rather than force her personal desires on her family she was willing to look at other breeds. The first litter of puppies they saw was a Beagle litter. Unfortunately for the little hounds, they had just been fed and they looked grotesquely fat. The second litter to be viewed was a litter of Dalmatians. The Naglers came home with a puppy. This dog became Lightening Sparks UD. He was mostly Never Complain breeding, Emily Lennartson's stock.

The UD title on the dog started Ken on obedience work to the point that he is now a judge of all obedience classes. The second Dalmatian was Ch. Princess Lois of Loki UD. Do notice that we are now up to champion-UD in this household. Lois was mostly Reigate and Byrondale breeding. A male out of Lois which finished his championship and UD title was Ch. Charcoal Chips UD. And they have Ch. Bespeckled Becky UD. The Naglers are now using the prefix Bespeckled on all their breeding.

It is difficult to imagine achieving a championship UD on a Dalmatian but the Naglers have had three Dalmatians which are Ch-UD, and several dogs which have had CDs and CDXs. This is a lot of canine intelligence in one household.

Shawnee

Ch. Jameson of Shawnee has won two specialty shows two times each! He was named Best of Breed at the Chicagoland Specialty show in 1974 and 1975 and he won the same award at the Dalmatian Club of Detroit specialty show in the same years. In addition he accumulated 43 Best of Breeds including Westminster Kennel Club in 1975. He was always owner handled.

Jamie is owned by Bill and June Dahn of Ohio. In 1965 the Dahn's decided that it would be nice to have a dog for championship and protection for June who was going to stay at home rather than pursue a career. They were sure they wanted a purebred and studied books which they found in the libraries and pet shops. They were having difficulty finding a Dal so they contacted Maxwell Riddle, then the Pet Editor of *The Cleveland Press*. He gave them the name of Elizabeth Doyle, a local breeder. A litter was expected shortly in the Doyle household and although Mrs. Doyle gave them the names of other breeders in the area the Dahns waited for her litter. In May 1966 they acquired a bitch, Brigadier's Jubi of Shawnee. Brigadier was the prefix Mrs.

Ch. Coachman's Lucky Cuss as a puppy.

Ch. Coachman's Lucky Cuss as an adult dog.

196

Doyle used on her dogs. Jubi is a combination of June and Bill. The Dahns lived on Shawnee, thus the name came into being. The Dahns, through Mrs. Doyle and Betty Kilfoyle, another Dalmatian fancier, became interested in the emerging Western Reserve Dalmatian Club and also became interested in showing their dog. They soon found that Jubi was not going to be a champion so they decided to breed. They chose Ch. Koko's Mr. Copper, a liver, for a sire. The resulting litter gave them Ch. Marvelous Maggie of Shawnee CD. She finished on her second birthday having picked up the obedience title along the way. Maggie was bred to Ch. Lord Jim and Jamie was pick of that litter. However, there was a bitch which the Dahns liked very much so they kept her too. She is Ch. Chiquita Coqueta of Shawnee. The Dahns have owned four Dals and have three champions. Jamie has sired eight champions of record and there are more well on the way. The Dahns intend to continue showing and breeding Dalmatians as a retirement hobby. They are, however, extremely concerned with the betterment of the breed and feel that the local clubs should do more to face up to the problems the breed is heir to, such as deafness, uric acid and dermatitis.

Piasa

Ch. Lord Jim, owned by Bill and Carol Victor of St. Louis, had a remarkable show career. Handled by Bill Kramer, the dog won the national specialty in 1970. He was shown 78 times in 1971 and won Best of Breed 77 times, Group I 42 times and went on to the top award at thirteen all-breed shows. He was named the winner of the Quaker Oats award in Nonsporting dogs for 1971. He was sired by Ch. Coachman's Chuck-a-Luck who is the only Dalmatian to date to have sired two all-breed best in show dogs, Ch. Lord Jim and Ch. Roadking's Rome.

Lord Jim has sired some excellent dogs including the specialty show winner, Ch. Jameson of Shawnee.

"Jimmy" spent his last year at Tuckaway in Kentucky living with a number of other Dals. He, however, ruled the roost at Tuckaway and was given freedom of the house and yard. The other dogs are kenneled. Some of his get are still being shown and he will have a number of champions sired in another year or two.

The Victor's Piasa Dalmatians are not active at this time but they are watching for another good Dal so they may continue breeding and showing.

Reicrist

Chris and Ron Zemke decided that dogs were fun and they would like to enjoy the company of a dog, possibly show it, and certainly wanted to get a dog which was nice to look at. They attended shows and considered breeds for two years before they decided on a Dalmatian. Earlier Ron had had a well bred Boxer bitch but had not shown her. He had, however, been involved in showing Holstein cows, pigs, and chickens. Chris had had an Afghan but felt the amount of grooming required was too much to make showing the animal fun. She also did not like ear and tail cropping which ruled out many breeds.

The decision was not an easy one. Ron liked the Dal and the English Setter. Chris was interested in terriers. They compromised and purchased Calgary of Watseka in 1969. The decision was made after they had seen some very good Dals in the ring for the two years before their purchase.

Their intention was to show their bitch. Cal hated the ring. And anyone can tell you that a dog or bitch which hates to show is a difficult proposition.

In 1970 the Zemkes had an opportunity to buy Ch. Crown Jewel's Oriental Pearl CD, a top brood bitch. Gem, as she was called, had won their hearts with her smile and personality.

Gem was bred to Ch. Jack Daniels of Watseka and produced Ch. Woodlyn's Shagbark Tipsy Topaz. Tipsy was co-owned and handled by Lynn Wood. She was sold to the Ericksons of Washington State. They bred Tipsy to Ch. Panore of Watseka. Pick of this litter was Ch. Woodlyn Reicrist the Tippler, was co-owned by Lynn and Chris Zemke. Lynn handled Doxie, as she was called, to her championship. This bitch was Winners at the national specialty at six months of age. She had finished by the time she was 10 months old.

All told, Gem produced seven champion offspring and is the foundation bitch of two kennels, Reicrist and Woodlyn.

At first the Zemkes used the name of Shagbark but after registering two litters with this name, AKC informed them that the name was not open. So now the Zemkes register their dogs with a prefix of Reicrist. Ron's first name is actually Reinhold and Chris is really Christabel; the combination is simple to figure out.

In 1974 a two-year-old liver Dal needed to be rescued from an unfortunate home. The Zemkes bought her. The original owners had purchased a potential show animal and then discovered that dogs shed. The poor bitch was tied to a post in the back yard on good days and to one in the basement in inclement weather. The bitch is now Ch. Ponypacer Caramel Candy, call name Dulce. Bred to Long Last Kelso she produced Brazilian Ch. Reicrist Tia Maria. Tia finished in four straight shows in Brazil and won her first Gold Medal Excellent at age six months.

The Reicrist Dals continue to be seen in the ring and the Zemkes continue to be active in Dalmatian affairs and clubs. Ron has served as president of the active Dalmatian Club of Detroit.

Ch. Coachman's Chuck-a-Luck as a young dog.

CHICAGOLAND
DALMATIAN CLUB
SEPT. 20, 1969
BEST OF
BREED

JUDGE
MR. M. BAKER L'H FRANK

Ch. Coachman's Carte Blanche.

Thad-dan

Reared by her grandparents, Jane Schenn was not permitted to own a dog because her grandmother suffered from asthma and dogs and their dander are bad for people with that disease. As a child Jane used all her pocket money to buy collars for stray dogs. She believed that if they were wearing collars the dog-catcher wouldn't pick them up. After she was grown and in her own home she purchased a Dalmatian.

She had always felt these were the most beautiful of animals. This Dal, however, was not registered. Several years later Jane bought Crown Jewel's Flawless Emerald. The call name on this bitch was Lady. Lady was struck by a car when she was about six months old. Her hip was smashed. The veterinarian felt that she would never walk normally but she managed to heal well and Jane finished her and earned her CD degree as well.

Jane has had her share of problems with the dogs. She bred Lady to the great Ch. Rickway's Topper, her grandsire. A few days after she returned home from the breeding one of the children forgot to close the door securely and Lady went for a walk with a Poodle. The litter was one of Poo-Dals and could not be registered. Then Jane's dogs had a siege of demodectic mange. This was followed by the discovery of hip dyplasia in one of her dogs. Despite the set-backs and the struggles Thad-dan Dals have continued to be produced. Jane accounts for nine champions with several more almost finished and others just starting out. Two of the nine were specialty winners, Ch. Thad-dans Beau Brummell CD, and Ch. Thaddan's Treasure of GT.

Homestead

Homestead is the name the Stoltings have given to their dogs. Before they became interested in Dalmatians they had Dobermans. They prefer the short-haired dogs because they enjoy seeing the structure and muscle of the animal rather than the long coat. Peggy Adamson, well-known Doberman breeder, is a close friend. It was through her that they became interested in showing Dobermans. Later they decided to get a Dal. Although they are a small kennel they have had great success on a limited basis.

Their foundation bitches are Ch. Homestead's Peppermint Cane (Peppy) and her daughter, Ch. Homestead's Peppermint Stick (Pudge). Both bitches have done well as producers.

The Stoltings, Bob and Evelyn, have bred and raised four litters. They were co-owners and co-breeders on two. They have finished seven breed champions plus Peppy for a total of eight and have obedience titles on two. One litter produced three champion bitches and another litter produced two.

Caution is the keynote of the breeding program here. Space is at a premium and four dogs fill it. It is possible that a fifth dog could be accommodated but they are more comfortable with four so that each can be given adequate attention and time.

The basic Homestead pedigree is filled with Chuck-a-Luck, Canicula and Lord Jim with a sprinkling of Crown Jewels, Blackpool and Pill Peddler shown as the outcrosses.

Currently the Stotlings are showing a young male who is just coming into his own.

JaMar

President of the Dalmatian Club of America at this writing is Jack Austin of Canton, OH, who with his wife Marcella has JaMar Dals. Jack and Marcella have had Dals for a number of years but confined most of their activity to the obedience ring. When they decided to go in for conformation showing they acquired Pacifica's Maid of the Mist as their foundation bitch. They finished her easily.

She had a single litter which produced Ch. JaMar's Magic Lady of the Mist, Ch. JaMar's Minnie Dixie Belle, and Ch. JaMar's Dusty Boots, and Annle's Dipper of JaMar. Lady was bred to Ch. Blackpool Ironstone and produced Ch. JaMar's My Gypsy Rose. All of the breeding has been line breeding on the Blackpool lines.

Jack Austin had the distinction of being chosen to judge the first futurity in the history of the Dalmatian Club of America in 1977. He drew an entry of 88 which will stand as a record for a first time event.

He and Marcella are quite active in the all-breed club in their home town and have served in various capacities at the Western Reserve Dalmatian Club. For many years Jack was president of the Canton Humane Society. He is now a popular Dalmatian judge.

Deltalyn

A pet Dalmatian which did not have enough quality for the show ring led Bob and Judy Rivard to buying a quality bitch. When the Rivards bought their own home Judy thought she wanted an Afghan but Bob, who had had a pet Dal when he was a child, convinced her she really wanted a Dal. The pet Dal came to live with them and although they tried showing her a few times they realized her shortcomings. Someone referred them to Crown Jewels in Chicago and they bought an eight week old bitch who later became Am. Can. Ch. Crown Jewel's Delta Diamond. They also bought a 12-week old male from Alberta Holden's Pill Peddler kennels. Delta Diamond finished in August of 1972 and the male, Am. Can. Ch. Delta Dals Mr. D, finished in July 1973.

Am. & Cuban Ch. Quaker's Acre Young Bess,
Am. & Cuban UD, owned by Mary Munro Smith.

Mary Munro Smith's great liver dog, Ch. Storm King of Quaker Acre.

They decided to breed Delta Diamond to Ch. Coachman's Canicula and are very pleased with the results. Two pups from the litter were shown and both finished. One was Ch. Deltalyn's Mystic Brandy and the other is the Best in Show dog, Ch. Deltalyn Decoupage. Decoupage, or Cooper as he is known, finished owner-handled at 14 months, having taken 9 points from the puppy class. In 1975 he was the #3 Dal and in 1976 he was #2. Both years he was the #1 owner-handled Dal in the U.S.

In addition to the Best in Show win at Vacationland Kennel Club Cooper has at least 10 Group I's and numerous other group placings. He was also best of breed at the Dalmatian Club of Southern New England in 1975; at the Western Reserve Dalmatian Club in 1975 and 1976, and the spring specialty show of the Dalmatian Oraganization of Houston. He was breed winner, too, at Westminster 1976.

A repeat breeding of Diamond to Nicky took place. The results from this second breeding are also pleasing. Among the puppies we find High Jinks Leila of Salimar, Deltalyn Debonaire Daymon and Deltalyn the Deacon.

Bob and Judy are very active in Dalmatian affairs having served the New England club in various capacities. Judy spent a number of years as editor of *Coaching Lines*, the bulletin of DCSNE. We will look forward to seeing them with more Deltalyn dogs in the future. They are conscientious breeders and careful trainers and their Cooper should contribute much to the future of the breed.

Roadking

About ten years ago Dianne and Ray Burnett started breeding Dals drawn to the breed by their clean cut appearance and very flashy coat. They bought a bitch from Jane Helms Venes, "Mimi," who, at the ripe old age of five, became Ch. Pepper Spattered Remember Me. She was their foundation bitch. Bred to Chuck-a-luck she produced, among others, Ch. Roadking's Rome, a Best in Show winner, owner-handled. The dog had multi-group wins and ranked in the top ten for two years.

Now living in Florida the Burnetts have finished several champion Dals including Ch. Roadking's Remark, Ch. Roadking's Raindrop, and Ch. Little Slam's Good Earth. In recent years the Burnetts who also breed thoroughbred horses, have become interested in terriers and have had a great deal of success with their Sealyham, Ch. Sherwood Hill Juggernaut.

Best in Show Liver dog, Ch. Melody
Dynamitic owned by Ed Flock.

Ch. Melody Sweet, CD, owned by Dr. & Mrs. John White, Jr.

15

More Breeders and Exhibitors

ALTHOUGH THE HOBBY of breeding and showing dogs attracts more and more people each year the figures on Dalmatians have remained constant in the ratio of dogs registered to dogs shown. This is a plus because when too many people start breeding the quality of the dogs usually deteriorates. Without pointing a finger at any breed, we all know how popularity and backyard breeding have caused several breeds to worsen. Our breed has been lucky. Our breeders, so far, all seem to have the welfare of the breed at heart and are trying to improve their stock with each mating.

Coachmaster

Breeding to the great Ch. Roadcoach Roadster gave the Coachmaster Dals a great start on winning and producing. Bob and Shirley Hays bred their bitch, Black Baby of Tarzana, to the great winning Dal and produced a great winning bitch, Ch. Coachmaster's Roadette. Roadette in turn became a great producer for the Hayes. She was bred to Ch. Colonial Coach Carriage Way and produced the winning bitch, Ch. Coachmaster's Bernadette.

Among other wins, Roadette was Best of Breed at the Dalmatian Club of Northern California from the veteran bitch class at 8½ years of age in 1971. She was named Best Brood Bitch at the Southern California specialties in '70, '71, and '72. Six of her produce from two litters were show winners. Bernadette finished her championship in Mexico as well as in the States and won numerous groups and Best of Breeds here.

The Hayes have continued to breed and have produced a number of champions including Ch. Coachmaster's Impresario who was sired by Ch. Rickway's Topper, sire of Carriage Way, and Ch. Dandy Dan of Coachmaster as well as the current specialty winner, Ch. Coachmaster's Tycoon, owned by the Sachaus.

Tosland

Although Dalmatian activity in California is so widespread it would be impossible to mention all the breeders there and in the Pacific northwest, we cannot overlook Tosland. Almost all of the Tosland dogs are from imported British stock. This is because Sylvia Tosland Cox, owner of Tosland Dalmatians, is herself, a British import. Mrs. Cox has been breeding Dalmatians all of her life and when she moved to the States she continued her hobby with a great deal of success. Special dogs which come to mind are Ch. Tosland's Tarr Baby, Ch. Todd of Tosland who is also a Canadian champion, Ch. Tosland's Inga Ya Mandoa CD, Ch. Tosland's Billie Bandit, Ch. Tosland's Autumn Chelsea, and Ch. Tosland's Tammy True who is also an international champion, having finished in Belgium for this title.

Hapi-Dals

Hapi-Dals is another California kennel which has been breeding Dalmatians for a number of years. Ralph and Margaret Schools are the guiding lights of these dogs. Over the years they have finished about 20 champions. The foundation stud was Ch. Blackpool Lancer, a son of the great winning bitch, Ch. Blackpool Crinkle Forest. This dog sired a number of champion get including Ch. Cal Dal Chocolate Chip UDT, the second male in Dal history to have both a championship and a UDT title. He is owned and handled by Jon Mett. Many of the Hapi-Dals are behind some of the winning dogs of the present time.

West Coast

Other west coast breeders who are showing and breeding with success include the Barnetts of Drumhille, the McCluer's Spottsboro Dalmatians, Patsy Wallace with Chalkhill Dals, Ed and Carol Petit with their Hansom Dals, Dalwood Dalmatians owned by the Lloyds and their daughter Jean, a threat in the Junior Showmanship ring at all times, John and Irene Brink and the Cinder Dals. The Brink's daughter Pam, after competing most successfully in Junior Showmanship, is now a judge of that class. The Sanchez' Whinemaker Dals, Fred Klensch and his Pacifica Dalmatians produced a Best in Show winner, Ch. Pacifica Pride of Poseidon, also a specialty show

Ch. Melody Ring of Fire of BB, specialty winner, owned by Dr. & Mrs. John V. White, Jr.

winner, and a Best in Show dog, Ch. Beaumont of Pacifica. Few kennels produce two top award winners.

Dalwood Dals owned by Georgiann Rudder and Carol and Diane Haywood have produced a number of very fine dogs but they are, at the moment, proudest of the Dalwood's Knight Edition, who finished in the States and then went to Mexico City for four international shows returning home with the International, Mexican and World Show titles, winning best of breed at all four shows and a Group I, II, and IV. His junior handler, Diane, is also a threat in the Junior Showmanship classes. The younger generation is filling the ranks of superb handlers.

Little Slam

A kennel which built its reputation for having fine Dals in California, now moved to Arizona, is Little Slam. Lita and Bill Weeks founded this kennel with English imported stock. Lita is British. Ch. Little Slam's Major Game is one of the outstanding sires in the breed as well as a winner in the ring. He won the DCSC specialty show in 1971 and was rated the number 1 Dalmatian in the west. One daughter, Ch. Little Slam's Club Finesse, known as Solo, was sold to John Ed Lee of Houston. Her show career in Texas was an enviable one. She was the top winning bitch in the U.S. in 1973, always expertly handled by Adelene Pardo.

In addition to being an American champion Major Game also finished in Canada and Mexico. He has sired a number of well-known dogs such as Coachman's First Class, High Jinks Illustrated, Stoney Run Ace of Little Slam, Am. & Can. Ch. Polka Dot Satin Doll, and Dalwood's Waggon Master to name a few.

The sire of this dog was an Ascotheath dog imported from the Cudds in England. He was Ch. Calash Fife Major of Ascotheath who was sired by Eng. Ch. Hot Brandy of Ascotheath, a liver dog. Earlier the Weeks had Ch. Little Slam's One Club, Ch. Little Slam's Quick Trick CD, a liver. Their breeding program, which they are continuing in their new home in the Phoenix area, continues to produce both quality blacks and livers.

Arizona

In the Phoenix and Tucson areas we find Van Dals, Tucwinn, and Wee Ranch. Van Dals owes its fine reputation to Crestview foundation stock. Three champions were produced in one litter sired by Ch. Crestview Thunderstar ex Dono Perro del Punto CD. Ch. Van Dals Raisin in the Sun, Ch. Van Dals Puddin Pie CD, and Ch. Van Dals Whipper Snapper were all handled to their titles by Bonnie VanDervort. This young lady also had the honor of handling Ch. Crestview Rogue to his impressive win of Winners Dog

Rho-Dal Ginger Snap owned by Louis J. Rhoda.

Jane Helms Venes' Ch. Pepper Spattered Teddy Bear.

at the DCA specialty in 1978 in California for his owners, Jim and Vi McManus.

At Tucwinn we also have a young lady handler for most of the times the dogs are entered. She is Sarah Simaan, daughter of Constance Simaan, the actual breeder and owner of Tucwinn dogs. The foundation stock for this breeding kennel is Melody and the breeding program is built from line-breeding to the Melody status.

At Wee Ranch Navona Ouimette has foundation stock of Green Starr and Melody and has bred very carefully to carry on these lines. Just recently she moved her kennel from Arizona to Idaho.

In Wyoming we find the Jalonens with Khaseyno Kanines, and in Nevada we find Coachwyn, Karen Barthen, who has been successful with Ch. Coachwyn's Chevy and Ch. Coachwyn's Color Me Candid, and has more on the way.

Maricam, Marian Witherspoon, started her Dalmatian career in Colorado and now lives in the Pittsburgh area where she continues to breed and show. Ch. Maricam's Sassie Lassie, Ch. Maricam's Sundance Kid, and Ch. Thaddan's Challenger are among the Maricam dogs.

Caravan

The feeling strikes us at times that the entire population of the United States is transient. People in this country seem to move and do it frequently. The Heriots who own Caravan Dals have just completed a long distance move from the Washington DC area to the middle of Iowa, Iowa City to be exact. They have reported that they were unprepared for the friendliness which greeted them in dog circles in this area of the country. They have not been breeding and showing for very long but have had some success in the short time they have been in dogs. They started out with Snowcap and Green Starr stock and have finished several champions and bred a few litters. When they started showing in the middle west they were delighted to be greeted by friends in the dog fancy whom they did not know were their friends. And when they were fortunate enough to win a group with their home-bred bitch, Ch. Caravan's Campaign Promise, they were delighted to receive notes and cards of congratulations from their competitors.

Dog activities are a family affair for the Heriots as both of their children, Russell and Megan, are also interested in the dogs and the dog shows.

Range Trail

Jean Bass and her parents, the Dudleys, have a fair sized kennel of dogs near Madison, WI. From time to time the Dudleys visit in England and usually bring home a nice Dalmatian. The latest import is Sydon Starlight who

Ch. Clipper Ticonderoadster,
a litter brother to Teddy Bear.

The great Ch. Korcula Salona winning Veteran Bitch class at the
1975 DCA specialty in Kentucky, owner handled by Charles Garvin.

was sired by Eng. Ch. Washakie Bamboo of Marzelina. Among other dogs on the Range Trail list are Ch. Range Trail Maple Tree Flagg, a group winner, and his brother, Ch. Range Trail Maple Tree Maham. These dogs were bred by Robert Slater, Maple Tree Farms. Flagg spends some of his time with the Roadrunner dogs in Florida. Range Trail Road Runner Mimi is one of the bitches currently being shown by Jean.

Indalane

Indalane Kennels in Ohio belong to Eleanor Hilen who has finished a number of dogs, notably Ch. Korcula Kerry of Indalane, Ch. Tuckaway Traveller Indalane, and Ch. Indalane's Korcula Kristebel. The combination of names reveals the background on the dogs. Mrs. Hilen is a serious breeder and continues to bring out good dogs. Her husband collects antique fire engines which go well with Dalmatians.

Hobnail Farms

In the "far north of the middle west" we find two well established kennels that have been breeding for years. Hobnail Farms is one of them. This kennel is owned by Bill Cornelius and Fred Brandt. In addition to the Dalmatians Hobnail Farm is noted for its chickens and for magnificent antiques. Over the years this kennel has accounted for 27 home-bred champions.

Maranan

The other kennel in the north which has been well-known for years is Maranan. This is owned by Marion O'Hara and Ann Gross. The kennel was established in 1947. Among the champions to their credit are Ch. Act of Stock-Dal (1945-1959); Ch. High Brow Peggy (1947-1962); Ch. Chief Cormac of the Isles (1950-1967); Ch. Maranan Big Wheel (1951-1964); Ch. Maranan Dauntless (1955-1968); Ch. Maranan Debonaire (1957-1969); and Ch. Maranan Mellow Mood (1955-1969). Ch. Maranan Dauntless won the Chicagoland specialty from the veteran class in 1963. At that time he was owned and handled by Irma Gibson of Omaha.

Maranan has not been in the show ring as frequently in recent years and have been missed. They are, however, continuing to breed fine Dalmatians and we expect to see them back in the ring in their usual style.

Tollhouse

Toll House, Emily Westervelt's prefix, has accounted for a few young dogs which have some fine winning to their credit. Basically she has had Coachman-Pryor Creek breeding. Her foundation bitch was Coachman's

Ch. Korcula Midnight Margie, breeder-owner-handled by Charles Garvin.

Ch. Dottidale Jo Jo, owned by Dottidale Kennels, Amy and Ellen Lipschutz.

Credentials which was out of the magnificent Ch. Coachman's Carte Blance and was sired by Ch. Dalhalla's Thunderbolt. Two champions from a litter sired by Ch. Coachman's Chuck-a-Luck were Ch. Tollhouse Traffic Stopper and Ch. Tollhouse Top of the Mark. Tollhouse is on Long Island.

Crosspatch

Crosspatch Ranch Dals are firmly based on Coachman and Pryor Creek breeding. Beverly Keller, president of the emerging Aztalan Dalmatian Club of Southern Wisconsin, started with a bitch sired by Ch. Pryor Creek's Charlie Brown. Eventually she acquired Ch. Pepper Spattered Teddy Bear and used him on the bitches she had. Teddy Bear was sired by Ch. Coachman's Colours. His dam was Ch. Pepper Spattered Sunshine who was a Cheshire daughter. Presently she is showing a bitch from Tollhouse, sired by Mark out of Tollhouse Hat Trick. This is Tollhouse Daisie Don't Tell.

Coachkeeper

In the Houston area a breeding kennel which has produced a number of champions is Coachkeeper which belong to the Romeros. Among the champions they have produced we find Ch. Coachkeeper Quaker Queen, Ch. Quaker's Acre Coachkeeper CD, Ch. Coachkeeper Mocha Mist, Ch. Coachkeeper's Pamela Sue, Ch. Blizzard of Quaker's Acre, Ch. Gale Storm of QA and Mex. Ch. Coachkeeper's Prince of La Mancha. Again, the names indicate the background of these fine animals.

Houston

Other breeders and exhibitors in the Houston area who are coming to the front in Dalmatians include Tim Robbins with Robbsdale Kennels. Basically, his foundation stock is Crown Jewels. Carolyn Diehl and Eva Biering are also well-known breeders in the Texas area. Mrs. Diehl now lives in Louisiana but co-owns dogs with Mrs. Biering under the Cardhill prefix. Both are quite active in the Dalmatian Organization of Houston as is Tim Robbins who has served as president of the club a number of terms. And another active breeder in Texas is Judy Box who shows both blacks and livers. Ann Harris Jones started out with a Crown Jewels dog and now is a successful breeder on her own. She showed in both conformation and Junior Showmanship as a very young girl and has more or less grown up with the dogs. She is now married and has a daughter who will probably join the ranks of junior handlers.

In Louisiana the Applewhites have the Tippin In Dogs which are founded in Colonial Coach and Watseka bloodlines and the Mexics of New Orleans have group winners of their credit based on Rolenet breeding. In the Dallas

Ch. Pill Peddler's Christmas Holly owned by Teresa Vila and Alberta Holden.

Ch. Melody Up Up and Away CD "Pooka," owned by David and Susan MacMillan, bred by Dr. and Mrs. John V. White, Jr.

215

area the Landal dogs of the Bynums are also to be reckoned with. These are basically Blackpool breeding and are generally owner-handled.

Rolenet

Doing a favor for a friend introduced Bob and Lenor Liggett to the world of Dalmatians. For some time the Liggetts had been showing Boxers in the Texas area with little success. One day, Mrs. Chester, Shiloh Dalmatians, asked Bob to handle a Dal for her at a show. Bob agreed to help her out and so found the Dal to be a great breed.

Mrs. Chester was pleased with Bob's handling and consulted him on finding a study for her bitch. Together they wrote to numerous kennels and finally decided to use Ch. Blackpool's Bullshot. Mrs. Chester gave Bob a bitch from the ensuing litter.

Through this breeding the Liggetts became acquainted with the Peters of Blackpool Kennels. Later Bob acquired a fine animal from the Peters, now Ch. Blackpool's Ironstone. Stoney is the foundation stud of the Rolenet Dalmatians.

Rolenet is a combination of RO for Robert, LEN for Lenore and ET for the last syllable in Liggett. And the Rolenet prefix has produced 15 champions as well as the top producing dam in 1976.

Shiloh

Mrs. Sarah Chester's Shiloh Dalmatians are also among the outstanding ones in the Texas area. Shiloh is a prefix found on many of the winning dogs today. The present start of the kennel is Ch. Shiloh's Beau Chet who has managed a fine record of wins, ranking #8 in the United States with group wins and placings in 1977. He ranked #11 in 1978 with 22 Best of Breeds, one Group I, three Group II's, one Group III, and five Group IV's.

The friendship between the Liggetts and Mrs. Chester has remained firm even though they frequently compete with each other. Stoney (Ch. Blackpool's Ironstone) is the sire of Beau Chet.

Breeders in the Northwest

In the Northwest Marie Kirk is one of the leading breeders with her Paisley and Watseka stock. She obtained her foundation stud from a litter sired by Ch. Panore of Watseka ex Ch. Melody Up Up and Away, CD. The dog is Ch. Paisley's Firechief of Siview. She is also the breeder of "Torch," winner of the first specialty show of the Dalmatian Club of Greater New York. "Torch" is Ch. Paisley's Torch of Kirkland, a fine liver dog who is now at home with his owner Senhor Saber in Brazil. He also won the breed at

Ch. Melody Joleen of Croatia owned by Forrest and Audrey Johnson.

Ch. Mr. Diamond Chips of Croatia owned by Forrest and Audrey Johnson.

217

Channel Cities and Santa Barbara during the DCA week in California in 1978. The dog was sired by Ch. Paisley's Five Card Stud ex Ch. Melody Bobby McGee CD.

Toleak kennels is another successful one in the Seattle area. This belongs to Pete and Lois Erickson. They have concentrated on Woodlyn dogs which are basically Watseka breeding.

The Strands, Rod and Patti, and the Williamsons, John and Ethel, are also involved in Dalmatians in the Pacific northwest. MGR is the prefix or suffix used by the Strands. It stands for "Merry-Go-Round." And Karastella is the prefix used by the Williamsons. Sometimes the names are combined as in Ch. Karastella Cadilla of MGR, the current top winning dog in the Puget Sound locale. Ch. Orion of Karastella is one of the dogs making a name for them on the West Coast, too. He was sired by Ch. Coach Lane Duke CD ex Ch. Karastella Flash of Electra. Electra was sired by the great Ch. Pacifica Pride of Poseidon, specialty show winner and breed winner at the Garden. Another dog in their stable is Ch. Karastella Panda Pacific. The Strands started with Am. & Can. Ch. Dandy Dan of Coachmaster.

Considering the proliferation of Dalmatian Clubs throughout the United States and the fact that we register approximately 5000 Dals each year AKC, it would be impossible to cover everyone involved in breeding and showing Dals whether in conformation or obedience. Some of the newcomers who have been extremely successful early on in their Dalmatian activities include Mona Dill and Pic-a-Dilly Dals and the Newmarks with Pepper Pike Dals. Both of them are involved in both phases of showing and both have been very successful, having chalked up specialty show and group wins with their dogs.

In the St. Louis area we find a group of breeders who are most active in breeding and showing. Steve Finkel and his Warlord Dalmatians has made a number of contributions to the breed through his "Newsy" and careful breeding. Newsy was Ch. Newsprint Bronze Newsgirl. She was the foundation bitch of Steve's kennel. Using Ch. Panore of Watseka, Steve produced Ch. Warlord's Glory Bound. Newsy was also the dam of Ch. Warlord's Call Me Deep. Newsy was line bred to Green Starr's Masterpiece, a great liver dog.

Tamarack is another successful breeding kennel in the St. Louis area. Bob and Sharon Freeman are the proud directors of this kennel. The foundation bitch for Tamarack came from Warlord, Ch. The Warlord's Night Hawk, out of Newsy. Ch. Tamarack's Tapestry was the first big winner with the Tamarack prefix but Ch. Tamarack's Tailor Maid is the bitch which really brought fame to this kennel. Tailor Maid was entered at the Chicago weekend, the first futurity of the DCA, a DCA Sweeps, the DCA national specialty, the Chicagoland Sweeps, and the Chicagoland specialty all on one weekend. She was named Best Junior in the Futurity, Best in Sweeps at both specialty

Ch. Bespeckled Becky CDX owned and trained by the Kenneth Naglers. *Gilbert*

Ch. Jameson of Shawnee, specialty show winner, owned by Bill and June Dahn.

219

shows, and first in the 9-12 month puppy bitch class at both specialty shows. She finished her championship quickly and has done some spectacular winning since then. Plans to repeat the breeding which produced her, Ch. Green Starr's Colonel Joe ex Ch. The Warlord's Night Hawk, are made and the Freemans hope to have some more fine Dals to show.

Centurion Dalmatians have moved from the St. Louis area to central New York State. The Lindhorsts were highly involved in the working of the Dalmatian Club of Greater St. Louis. They have bred several champion Dals including Ch. Centurion Celestial Seraphim, a specialty winner. And the Nichols are also actively breeding in the St. Louis area. Their prefix is Saratoga, the foundation of their kennel is Watseka bloodlines, and they are the proud owners of Ch. Saratoga of Santana.

The Willeys have renamed their kennel Thorntree. They are best known for Ch. Count Miguel of Tuckaway, a Canicula son, who has won groups and specialty shows without much trouble and is now siring interesting puppies.

Dr. Robert Schaible, a geneticist with the University of Indiana, became a Dal enthusiast through research programs. As a highschooler he became interested in Cocker Spaniels and bred several good ones which he showed. He was also involved in Dachshunds and showed a number of them. When he became interested in some of the genetic problems found in the Dalmatian he started in that breed.

Dr. Schaible's research efforts are concentrated on eliminating deafness, dermatitis and urinary calculi from the Dal genetically. Feeling that if he is at all successful in doing this with his own stock it will not help the breed unless his animals are of show quality which breeders desire. So some of his Stockore dogs are shown from time to time. His show career is limited to just twelve shows a year but this is enough to tell him whether his stock is measuring up to the show quality desired.

His studies on urine, deafness and dermatitis have appeared in scientific journals and he has been a regular contributor to the *Spotter* magazine. The Dalmatian Club of America is fortunate to have Dr. Schaible as one of its members. Not all scientists recognize the need to see what breeders are interested in. Some simply go their merry way on research projects which do not aid breeders in their efforts to improve their stock.

Currently Dr. Schaible is making a survey concerning deaf puppies through the Dalmatian Club of America.

As founders of the Indianapolis Dalmatian club we find the Leonard Siegels have done some fine breeding along with their club activity. They have recently moved to Lafayette, IN, where Dr. Siegel is in practice as an optometrist. Wedgewood is the name they give their Dalmatians and they usually show in the Bred by Exhibitor class at specialty shows.

Ch. Lord Jim owned by Mr. and Mrs. William Victor, Piasa Dalmatians.

Ch. Deltalyn's Decoupage. Cooper, owned by Bob and Judy Rivard, was the leading winner, owner handled, for a number of years.

Cincinnati is now the home of Limestone Kennels owned by Cindy Ingalls. Her top dog is Am. & Can. Ch. Limestone Zara Padaric. He sired a fine dog ex Am. Can. Ch. Camosun's Kate Dalrymple, a liver, which was sent to Brazil. Other dogs in her kennels are Limestone Nell of Raintree, a liver, Benjamin of Bay Colony, also a liver, Limestone Lexington and Limestone Counterpoint, all of them winning Dalmatians.

At one time Cincinnati was the home of the de Montjuic dogs. They have since moved to the New England area. Benito Vila and his wife, Teresa, are the proud owners of this kennel. They have used a combination of Pill Peddler and Coachman (Altamar) to produce a group of fine dogs, most importantly, Ch. Iman de Montjuic and Ch. Frazata de Montjuic. They are continuing in the same breeding program and are always a challenge in the ring.

In Florida where many people have moved either to escape the dreaded northern winters or for retirement, the outstanding breeding kennel in Dalmatians is Road Runner. This is owned by the Gambles of Fort Myers. Their first great dog was Ch. Richard the L.H. Roadrunner, CD. Richard finished by winning the group at the Augusta Kennel Club. He has done his share of siring and some of his get are going very well in Colombia, Venezuela, and Brazil. The Gambles were helped on their way by the advice and counsel of Mary Munro Smith and Bob Einig who used to handle for them.

Another of their winning dogs is Ch. Range Trail Bunker Hill. They also have Ch. Pill Peddler's Roadrunner Jane and Ch. Roadrunner's Love Bug. Both the Gambles show dogs. At the moment Ch. The Roadrunner's Mickey Finn is ranked #16 in the list of winning Dals.

Susan Brooksbank is a relative newcomer with her bearded Oaks Dals. She has based most of her breeding on Roadking stock with a slight sprinkling of a few other bloodlines. Her Ch. Roadking's Raindrop was named best Brood Bitch at the first Atlanta specialty show. Another dog, Ch. Bearded Oaks Roadking finished with three four-point majors on the Florida winter circuit. Another winner is Bearded Oaks Rascal who took a five pointer from the Bred by Exhibitor class at the Atlanta specialty under Edd Bivin. She is located in Sarasota.

Breeders in the Chicago Area

The breed is in a healthy state in the Chicagoland territory. Home of some of the earliest breeders and winners, Chicago is still the center of many fine young breeders, the hope of the future of the breed. Of course, Watseka, Colonial Coach, and Blackpool are in the Chicago area and are still actively breeding. But coming along are some new kennels, new meaning about five or six years in the fancy.

Ch. Roadking's Rome, owned by Raymond
and Diane Burnett, a Best in Show winner.

Ch. Count Miguel of Tuckaway owned by the Michael Willeys.

223

Norma Baley, presently president of the Chicagoland Dalmatian Club and a member of the Board of Governors of the Dalmatian Club of America, is one of the newer breeders. Norma has a fine blend of Crestview and Dalmatia as her basic stock. The latest champion to finish is Chrestview Spark o'Firesprite. Firesprite is the name the Baleys used on their dogs. Sparky joins other champions in the kennel including Ch. He's So Handsome from Dalmatia.

Another active and progressing kennel is Coachlite owned by Monte and Shiela Wymore. They are using basic stock from Paisley and Melody and being careful to linebreed for future competitors.

Woodbury Dalmatians, Susan and Ernie Schuenaman and Fran Schuenaman, is another name which will continue to be seen in the ring in the future. These three young people, brother, sister and wife, are producing fine black and liver spotted dogs. Ch. Woodbury's General Jeb Stuart finished his championship by taking BW at the 1976 Chicagoland specialty show. Ch. Woodbury's Stonewall Jackson was Best of Winners at the Chicagoland specialty in 1977, taking five points at 7½ months. He then won Winners Dog at the same specialty in 1978 for a second five pointer, and finished by winning the third five point major at the Houston specialty in 1978, all three wins under breeder judges. Basically the Woodbury Dals are from Blackpool stock with a mixture of Crown Jewels and Melody worked in to develop the Woodbury line.

Diamond D, owned by the Lesters, will probably make a good contribution to the breed in the future. The breeding at Diamond D is basically Pryor Creek and Coachman. The Lesters have purchased judiciously and breed carefully and have sent some fine dogs into the ring.

Many other kennels are starting out in the Chicago area and are doing their share of winning. Firewag'n, Teaka, Running Iron, Val Dals, and Longhi are the names of some of them. Several have been in the breed for a number of years but have not been active recently. Together, however, they are building a good base for the future of the breed.

Atlanta

Atlanta offers a number of good breeders. The Dalmatian fanciers in that area have just succeeded in bringing the Dalmatian Club of Greater Atlanta to show-giving status and have held two specialty shows. Active among the breeders in the Atlanta vicinity are Sally Koehl whose Ch. Kale's Cracker Jack is a group winning dog, the Williams with a number of fine dogs, and the Bellringer dogs owned by Artur and Marie Zorka. One of their dogs, Ch. Bell Ringer's Caballa has accounted for a number of champion get. Very recently

Ch. Homestead's Peppermint Cane owned by the Robert Stoltings. *Ashbey*

Ch. Spatterdash Zodiac, specialty winner,
owned by Mr. & Mrs. Richard Price.

225

they imported Duxfordham Aladdin, a liver dog, from Catherine Gore in England. He is a proven OFA sire and garnered points his first time out in the states.

Canalside

Helene and Pauline Masaschi have Canalside Dalmatians and have the honor of winning Best of Breed at the first Dalmatian specialty show ever held in Canada. It was the Dalmatian Club of Quebec's first show. Their dog, Ch. Pacifica's Boston Bandit, an American, Canadian, and Bermudan champion, won the specialty last spring. He is sired by Ch. Merithew Grand Slam ex Heidi of Edmonton. Another of the Dals which they have shown is Ch. Coachman's Chocolate Soldier. He was sired by Blackpool Copper Courier ex Coachman's Coffee Break and is a fine liver dog. These young ladies have been very active in the affairs of the DCSNE and are also very proficient in the saddle, having won numerous awards at horse shows.

Snowcap

For years Diane Reimer and her Snowcap Dalmatians were located in the heart of the Bronx. Recently she has moved both her stable and her kennel to a more suburban area. She has been doing some serious breeding for a number of years and has produced some top dogs. Among the champions to be found in the Snowcap roster are Ch. Snowcap's Intrepid, Ch. Snowcap's Hannibal Hayes, Ch. Snowcap's Iago of Annle, Ch. Snowcap's Idle Dice of Annle, Ch. Snowcap's Sympatico, a specialty winner, and Ch. Snowcap's Never on Sundae, a group and specialty winner owned by Luisa and Michael Weinstein. Charles Kidd handled this lovely bitch until her retirement in 1978.

Enchanted

In the Carolinas the Enchanted prefix is well known. This kennel is owned by Al and Midge Brown and is located in Darlington, SC. They have accounted for a number of winning champions including Ch. Enchanted Even Par, Ch. Enchanted Play Boy, Ch. Good Grief I'm Enchanted, and Int. Ch. Regina's Enchanted Rio, the second Dalmatian to go Best in Show in Brazil. The foundation bitch for this kennel was Enchanted Dee Dee Girl, a Cheshire daughter.

Summerhill, Jim and Edith Vogel in Winston-Salem, NC; Islandia, Linda Diehl, Richmond, VA; Dazdell, Bill and Mary Jo Weimer, Howell, MI; Double O, Brenda Osborn, Houston, TX; Betty Hardee, Houston, TX;

Ch. Highlight's Sequin.

Ch. Coachman's Canicula, DCA specialty winner.

227

Dr. Billie Ingram, Brio Del Rey Kennels; Ravenwood, Lee and Kathy McCoubrey, Orlando, FL; Repeatwyn, Jerry and Bea O'Steen, Tallahassee, FL; Ron and Jean Smith, Mt Bryton Dals, Brighton, MI; Rainbow Acres, Margaret McCune, Vida, OR; Dashway, Delores Logan, Sumner, WA; Advocate, Jean and Granville Meador, Ridgewood, NJ; Proctor, Ken and Eva Berg, Moraga, CA; and Clockgate, Mary Lou Volz, Detroit area are just a few of the newcomers who are showing, breeding and doing some fine winning with their dogs. Seaspot kennels of Mark and Karen Sachau, Soquel, CA., had the distinction of winning both the Southern and the Northern California specialty shows in the same year with their Ch. Coachmaster's Tycoon. They have continued to show and to breed with a great deal of success in a short period of time. Among other dogs they have Ch. Seaspot's Swashbuckler and Ch. Seaspot's Punctuation, CD. They are both quite active in the Northern California Dal Club. Mr. Sachau conceived the idea of the special theme for each year's specialty catalog making these books collector's items with pictures of old time dogs, Dals in action, etc.

Lancer

Owner-handled Best in Show is the record Ron Brooks achieved with his Ch. Lancer's Sir Lancelot, a liver dog. He attained this honor on April 24, 1976. This typey dog has done some other good winning such as taking the Pittsburgh specialty show, and placing in the group after numerous Best of Breed wins. The dog was bred by John Yama sired by Ch. Lancer's Royal Lancer ex Ch. Lancer's Lady of the Lake.

Yama's breeding goes back to imports, Ch. Ragged Robin of Kurnool and Willowmount dogs. His Dals are all liver factored. Some of his dogs are either sired by or are grandsons of Ch. Coachman's Chuck-a-luck. His foundation bitch, Lancer's Queen of Chips, is the dam of Ch. Lancer's Cinnamon Snow, Ch. Lancer's Royal Lancer and Ch. Snowcap's Lancer Red of Annle.

A family picture of part of the famous Canicula-Sleighbelle litter. From left to right, Canicula, Ch. Tuckaway Bold and Brave, Ch. Tuckaway Gallant Man, Ch. Tuckaway Jason James, Ch. Labyrinth Tuckaway Julep, Ch. Tuckaway Dinah, and Ch. Labyrinth Sleighbelle.

Ch. Labyrinth Sleighbelle winning the Brood Bitch class at the 1977 DCA national specialty show. Jason James and Bold & Brave were shown as produce.

Queen Victoria had a Dalmatian to accompany her on her drives.

The famous Ch. Snow Leopard

230

16
Around the World with the Dalmatian

ALTHOUGH HIS PLACE OF BIRTH may be uncertain, there is no doubt the coach dog was adopted and developed by the British. England became his mother country.

Early writers put him in Great Britain more than four hundred years ago. His use to symbolize the Church of Rome when Oliver Cromwell was in power (1649–1660) place him there more than three hundred years ago. By 1665 he was coaching on English roads. By 1790 his likeness was engraved on wood by Thomas Bewick and published in London. While previously he had been referred to as the Coach dog, Carriage Dog, Spotted Dog, Plum Pudding Dog, "Spotted Dick," Danish dog, Harrier of Bengal, Braque de Bengale, Canis variegatis, or Little Danish dog, Bewick called him the Dalmatian.

By 1860 he was offered classes at a dog show in Birmingham. He arrived as a show dog in England more than one hundred years ago.

Before that his job had varied. He was used as a gun dog, a badger and bull-baiting dog, a coach dog as a guard and companion for travelers and mail, a promenade dog, a protection and attention getting dog for elegant carriages, a "pack" or watch dog for farmers' wives going to market, a music hall entertainer, a gypsy trick dog and as a heraldic symbol. He proved that in addition to being one of the best looking of all dogs, he had intelligence, versatility and charm, and was a good companion.

The British loved him. They defined his type and brought him closer to perfection. They drafted his standard which later became the foundation for the standards of all other countries. They organized clubs for his promotion and protection.

From England he was exported to most of the rest of the world where he was received with considerable enthusiasm. The British type was used to improve the breed on the continent and overseas. Imports from Great Britain have been the foundation stock for important kennels the world over.

Agitation in England for a Dalmatian club was started by Hugo Droesse. Mr. Droesse had promoted twenty-one Dalmatian entries for the Crystal Palace Show in 1889. There had been none the year before. With the enthusiasm generated by this support Mr. Droesse wrote to the dog papers, "At the last Crystal Palace show several exhibitors and gentlemen interested in Dalmatians expressed their willingness to support a special club for the breed, and urged on me to take the matter in hand, acting in the meantime as hon. sec. pro tem. As the proposal is a most welcome one to me, and has my full approval and support, I shall be pleased to hear from anyone favorable to the object, and trust that not only lovers of the breed in Great Britain, but also those residing abroad, will communicate with me. At the same time I shall be glad to have any propositions and suggestions, in regard to the club to be formed, which are likely to be of value and good for the furtherance of the object."

As a result of this start The Dalmatian Club was founded in 1890 with W. B. Herman as secretary. A standard was formulated that same year. It was the fourth for the breed. Previous standards had been unofficial descriptions written by Vero Shaw in 1882, Stonehenge (John Henry Walsh) in 1886 and a translation from *Der Hunde Sport* published in the *Fanciers Gazette* in 1889. When the North of England Dalmatian Club was formed in the Manchester area in 1903 it adopted the 1890 standard with only a change in the weight of bitches.

World War I almost annihilated the breed. To counteract government pressure to destroy all dogs, the Kennel Club of Great Britain stopped all registration for the duration. Added to the deprivations due to the war was a general muzzling order lasting until 1922 because of rabies brought in by imported dogs.

Without horses it seemed the coach dog was also losing friends. The Crystal Palace show in 1920 had only one Dalmatian. The single exhibitor, Mr. Fred Kemp, thought something should be done about it. In 1925 a group of enthusiasts met at Crufts and from that meeting the Southern Dalmatian Club was formed. Mr. Kemp became and remained its president for twenty-two years. The Dalmatian's fortunes began to change.

The Southern Dalmatian Club grew rapidly. It soon became national in scope. In 1930 it changed its name to the British Dalmatian Club. The All Ireland Dalmatian Club was formed in 1934.

232

"Goworth Victor" model for the Royal Doulton Dalmatian figure.

Famous imported Ch. Nigel of Welfield owned by Stock-Dal Kennels. *Reeves Studios.*

World War II played hob with the entire dog fancy. Little breeding took place. "Radius shows" were instituted by the Kennel Club. Only dogs living within 25 miles of the show site were permitted to enter. When peace was achieved dog activity began again. The three Dalmatian clubs and the British breeders made a fresh start. Apparently the enthusiasm and know-how had survived because when the first post-war specialty show was held on October 2, 1945 by the British Dalmatian Club there were 263 entries.

By 1947 the British Dal Club was publishing *Spots of News,* a newsletter edited by Leighton Yeomans, to keep members informed. The Club engaged in many kinds of varied activities, educational and social. It developed a rescue service "dedicated to helping needy dogs to find kindly humans and happy homes." Membership in other countries grew. *Spots of News* from the start reported exported dogs becoming champions in many other countries. That same year the original Dalmatian Club phased out.

The British Dalmatian Club *Handbooks* which had been published from 1934 through 1938 were reinstated in 1949 and published every three years since. The Dalmatian continued to hold his own in Britain despite some economic ups and downs. The breed became better known and loved when Dodie Smith's *One Hundred and One Dalmatians* was published in England in 1956. Five years later movie goers were charmed by Walt Disney's version of the story as an animated cartoon in color.

When the British Dalmatian Club leadership became concerned about a twenty per cent drop in registrations in 1954 they could not anticipate the future effect of the efforts of Dodie Smith and Walt Disney. The delightful book and the animated feature length movie had considerable impact on the popularity of the breed around the world. Mrs. Smith's book was first published serially in *Woman's Day* magazine under the title, "The Great Dog Robbery".

In commenting on this in 1977, Mrs. Cooper, editor of the British Dalmatian Club's monthly newsletter, wrote "Obviously nobody at that time would have believed a time would come when the club was seriously asking members to try to restrict breeding, or that several hundred pounds a year would need to be spent in rescuing and rehabilitating dogs which were in need of homes."

The British Dalmatian Club continued to grow. Its Golden Jubilee Championship show in April 1975 pulled an entry of 99 dogs and 140 bitches, total number of entries 464. By 1977 when the Queen's Silver Jubilee was being celebrated the Club had 1079 members, 887 at home and 192 overseas. It had overseas representatives in seven countries: Australia, Canada, Holland, India, Sweden, United States of America, and New Zealand. There were overseas members in twenty-one countries: Australia, Brazil, Belgium, Canada, Finland, France, Germany, Holland, Hungary, Kenya, Liberia, New

Ch. Widdington Kandy, English import, owned by Mr. & Mrs. Loyal Oesau.

Am. & Can. Ch. Colonsay Blacksmith. *Tauskey*

Eng. & Am. Ch. Colonsay Storm owned by Mr. & Mrs. Phillip Chancellor, Mexico City. Handled by Jim McManus.

Ch. Colonsay's Olaf the Red imported by Mr. and Mrs. Dominic Peters. This was a liver Dalmatian.

Ch. Washakie Malteser, imported liver bitch, owned by Louis C. Furniss, Sr. *Tauskey*

Ch. The Lash, Dr. Josiah Harbinson's great liver dog.

Zealand, Nigeria, Norway, Portugal, South Africa, Spain, Sweden, Switzerland, United States, and Yugoslavia.

Whether the official regulatory bodies of these far-flung nations were affiliated with the Kennel Club of Great Britain or more recently with the F. C. I. (Federacion Cynologique Internationale) founded in 1911, or independent of either, the British standard became the basis for judging the breed. It has been translated into many languages. While the standard has been rewritten in some countries, particularly the United States and Canada, the Dalmatian dog remains remarkably the same around the world. This we have found to be true when judging in South Africa, Mexico, Canada, and South America. There are some discussions about size and length and blue eyes, but the friendly, dignified, beautifully spotted dog is universally loved as a companion and guard.

Dalmatian owners in many countries gather together to form clubs to further the breed and their own enjoyment of the world of dogs. One needs to list them to realize how many have grown up over a period of time in many parts of the world. Where known we have included the year of their origin.

Great Britain

The Dalmatian Club, 1890–1947
North of England Dalmatian Club, 1903
Southern Dalmatian Club, 1925–1930
British Dalmatian Club, 1930
All Ireland Dalmatian Club, 1934
Dalmatian Club of Scotland 1970

Europe

French Dalmatian Club, 1951
Dalmatien Club Luxembourgeois
Nederlandse Club Voor Dalmatische Honden, 1947
Klubben for storre Selskapshundraser (Norway)
Deutscher Dalmatiner Club, 1920
Finnish Dalmatian Club
Swedish Dalmatian Society, 1962
Swiss Dalmatian Club

Africa

Dalmatian Club of South Africa, 1961
Southern Cross Dalmatian Breeders Club
Dalmatian Club of East Africa

Asia

Indonesia Dalmatian Club
Dalmatian Club of Japan

Australia and New Zealand

Dalmatian Club in Australia, 1943
Dalmatian Club of South Australia
Dalmatian Club of Victoria
Dalmatian Club of New Zealand

North America

Dalmatian Club of Canada, 1966
Club Dalmata de Mexico, 1975
Dalmatian Club of America, 1905 (25 local clubs mentioned in Chapter 5)
Dalmatian Club of Quebec

South America

Dalmata Clube do Brasil
Dalmatian Club of Trinidad and Tobago, 1958

Foreign registrations at the American Kennel Club indicate Dalmatians have been imported from eight other countries in the last ten years. While they were principally from the United Kingdom and Canada, there were also dogs from Germany, Australia, Italy, Ireland, Holland, and Sweden.

Sweden

One of the European countries where Dalmatians are a popular breed is Sweden. The Dalmatian Club there was founded in 1962 and has about 500 members. The breed has grown from practically no dogs at all to a fairly large segment of the dog population.

In the early part of the century there were a few Dalmatians in Sweden, mostly of German and English stock. These seem to have died out.

In the early thirties two dogs were imported from England. They were Marjo of Elk Isle and Dotty of Elk Isle. A few years later a bitch named Princess Polly and a dog named Duff were brought in from England. These four were used for breeding and all the Dals in Sweden descended from them. The breed went into a sad state as all the dogs were inbred without any infusion of new blood to help the situation. Mrs. Anna Hammarlund had a good Dal puppy from this original line. She called this dog Kief. He was an

Camp. Mex e Int. Queene Victoria de La Mancha and Camp. Mex e Int. Don Benjamin de La Mancha win breed and best of opposite sex at the International show in Mexico City under English judge, Thelma Gray. Raymond Fitzsimmons and Alejandro Gonzalez are the proud owners.

Camp Duca di Mantua, owned by Raymond Fitzsimmons winning Best of Breed in Mexico.

International, Norwegian, and Scandinavian champion. She then imported some English bitches and established a great stock of Dals in Sweden. Kief was about the last Dal from the original stock established in the thirties. Mrs. Hammurlund also imported a male from America, Ch. Fleetwood Nu Boot of Dalmatia, a son of the famous Boot Black out of Ch. Fleetwood Farms China Doll. With this infusion of blood from the States and the English imports, the Dalmatian in Sweden is now well established. Pictures of the Swedish dogs show them to be sound, well-boned, and well-marked animals.

Mrs. Hammarlund is the author of a book on Dalmatians published a few years ago. She deals mostly with breeding the possible genetic combinations, and how to handle puppies. The book, a fascinating one, is written in Swedish, of course. Natalie Fleger of Colonial Coach met Mrs. Hammarlund when she visited the States a few years ago. Mrs. Hammarlund gave her a copy of the book. Several breeders were able to find someone to make a translation of it. We have enjoyed reading about the Swedish dogs.

Mexico

In Mexico until recently Dalmatian breeding has been done pretty much on a hit and miss basis. At one time, however, for a brief period, there was a major kennel known as Dalmex and owned by Dr. Phillip Chancellor. He purchased a number of top winning dogs and bitches in both England and the United States in order to produce good Dals. At one time he had at least 80 dogs and produced about 14 litters each year, all well-thought-out breedings.

One of his dogs which had won an all-breed Best in Show in the States was declared ineligible by the AKC to win this award. This triggered a disastrous reaction in Dr. Chancellor's kennel. He discontinued all Dalmatian activity, dispersed his kennel, and the careful breeding disappeared into mediocrity.

A number of other breeders were known to be producing some Dalmatians in Mexico. Among them was Manual Avila Camacho, president of Mexico from 1940 to 1946; the Beteta family, Ramon and his nephew, Mario Ramon, both of whom were Ministers of Finance under different presidents; the Rivera Torres family; Manuel Buch, a Senor Jaurequi; and Luis Garcia Maurino.

Dr. Chancellor's dog CAMP. Dalmex Chicharrin won an all-breed Best in Show in Mexico in 1961. The only other all-breed Best in Show win for Dalmatians was in Mexicali in 1976 when an American bred liver Dal, Am. Mex. Ch. Little Slam's Jack of Hearts, won the honor.

In 1975 the Club Dalmata de Mexico A.C. was incorporated. It is the official club for the breed in Mexico and presently has as members most of the serious breeders and exhibitors of Dalmatians in Mexico. It has held four specialty shows. The first show in April 1976 was judged by Ing. Robin Hernandez. The second assignment for the specialty in November 1976 was given to Dr. David Doane of the U.S. Mrs. Evelyn Nelson White judged the third specialty in November 1977 and Alfred E. Treen passed on the dogs at the fourth specialty in 1978. Mrs. Marjorie Doane has been tapped to judge the fifth specialty show for the breed.

The Mexican Kennel Club (Asociacion Canofila Mexicana AC) is affiliated with FCI and so all the standards used in Mexico are approved by that body.

The Mexican Dalmatian Club, however, has submitted a different standard which is being discussed by a committee of FCI. The Mexican Kennel Club has accepted the standard and is championing the cause of the Mexican Dal Club with the FCI. The former president of FCI is Mrs. Thelma Von Thaden who is also a past president of the Mexican Kennel Club. She is still the representative of Asociacion Canofila Mexicana A.C. to Federation Cynologyque Internationale. It is hoped that she will be able to help in this matter.

The Mexican Dalmatians are certainly under greater influence of the Dalmatians from the United States than from those in England, Germany, Sweden, Luxembourg, and other European countries. It is logical that the Mexican standard would resemble that of the Dalmatian Club of America. The point of contention is, of course, the blue eye, perfectly acceptable in the U.S. and Mexico, frowned on in European countries.

The original officers of the Dalmatian Club of Mexico were Raymond F. Fitzsimmons, president; Emilio Barajas, vice president; Rodolfo Saldana, secretary; and John Hogan, treasurer. Enrique Castillo was a director. Current officers of the club are Raymond Fitzsimmons, president; Enrique Castillo, vice president; Rodolfo Saldana, secretary, and John Hogan, treasurer. Lic. Jaime E. Gallestegui, MVZ Ezequiel Galindo E; Sra Isabelle Miranda, Lic. Alejandro Gonzales, and Ernesto Macip serve as members of the board.

Mr. Fitzsimmons has been a leader in the Dalmatian community for a number of years. The National Breeders Association named him the Distinguished Breeder of the Year in 1976, a highly coveted honor.

Early in the decade there was little or no usuable stock in Mexico. The La Mancha line (Fitzsimmons and Gonzales) went to the U.S. to improve the quality and provide a reasonably acceptable gene pool available for serious breeders. The La Mancha line has accounted for 13 champions so far and about 10 more dogs which are in the process of attaining championship status. All three of De La Mancha's imported dogs have achieved Mexican championships. All three are International Champions and one of them has won an American championship. The third imported dog was a liver male, CAMP Coachkeeper Prince de La Mancha, sired by Ch. Storm King of

Quaker's Acre ex Ch. Cinderella's Coach Keeper, and litter brother to the Best in Show Ch. Coachkeeper's Blizzard of Quaker's Acre. This dog was involved in a serious car accident which eliminated any further showing.

The outlook for Dalmatians in Mexico is quite rosy at this time. More people are joining the Dalmatian Club there and more and more of the Mexican judges are studying the breed to learn what is expected in a good Dal. Educational programs are presented by both the Mexican Dal Club and the ACM.

South Africa

The South African Club was formed on the 11th of December in 1961 by the leading Dalmatian breeders in the Transvaal, namely Mesdames Bell, Hoggard, Peacock, Popham and Roseveare, and Messrs. Aronson, Bell and Peacock. Mr. Aronson was transferred overseas shortly after the forming of the club but the other members built the organization into a fine group of fanciers.

Mrs. Peacock remembers the days when only 3 or 4 Dals would be entered at a show. The British Dalmatian Club offered a silver spoon to be awarded to the first Dal to win Best of Breed over an entry of at least six dogs. After a four year struggle the target number was reached and the spoon was awarded to Mrs. Peacock's Ch. Judith of Yumbani.

The Club held its first specialty show in October 1976. It was judged by Captain E. E. Adams, a Boxer breeder and a judge of a number of breeds under the Kennel Union of South Africa aegis. Chairman of the specialty show was C. E. McDonald. Serving with him were Mrs. McCallum, Mrs. J. Davies, Mrs. S. McDonald, and Miss McCallum, Mr. E. Davies, and Miss J. Maltman.

The Southern Cross group were originally an off-shoot of the Dalmatian Club but whatever caused the divergence has been lost in the limbos of the past. Now the membership of the two groups overlaps and each club supports the efforts of the other.

At the Goldfield's Kennel Club Show in 1977 there were nearly sixty Dalmatians entered and the two clubs banded together to host a delightful dinner party for the American judges at that show.

Canada

Although the membership of the Dalmatian Club of Canada is not large numerically it is large in enthusiasm all the way across the Dominion.

Founded in 1966, the organization has held two specialty shows, one in 1978 and the other in 1979. The first was judged by the late Joseph Faigel, an American all-rounder. The second assignment was handled by Mrs. Phyllis

M. Piper, Kent, England. Mrs. Piper is widely known for her Greenmount Dalmatians.

The Club has published an informational booklet on the breed and the club with a cleverly arranged title. All the As in the word Dalmatian have been dropped to the line below to emphasize its correct spelling. The spots decorating the cover are in two fields, one liver and one black, emphasizing the two possible colors of the breed.

The booklet mentions Catherine Blinko, Jean Hallett, Hannah Pentland, Joan Pollard, Don Simpson, Vivian Sterne and Joan Waterfield as staunch supporters of the Club. We would add to that list of distinguished people John and Monica Brooks, Jackie Hastings and Linda Cyopik.

Dalmatian Club of Canada members are well acquainted with many members of DCA as so many of our members exhibit in Canada and so many Canadians exhibit in the States. There is a feeling of mutual respect.

The Club publishes a monthly newsletter, *Transcanadals,* and is in the process of preparing a book on the breed.

Luxembourg

Although the Grand Duchy of Luxembourg is tiny in area the Luxembourg Dalmatian Club is not. It is a very active group of people working hard to promote Dalmatians all over Europe. The guiding light of the group is Barbara Kacens who acts as the secretary and the "responsible" editor of the *Spotted News,* the monthly publication sent out by this club. It contains information from all over the world concerning the breed and lists the coming shows and the results of important ones.

This club is in the process of publishing *Dalmatians in the World,* an informational book concerning all the clubs and countries in which there is any activity in Dalmatians. The Club has also published a Dalmatian Handbook for 1978.

The beginning of Dalmatians in Japan stems from the above pictured dogs. The male is owned by Major & Mrs. G. H. Fisher. His name is Conquest of the Wells and was purchased by Major Fisher in England during WWII. The dog flew 38 missions over Germany sitting beside the tail-gunner, was wounded in the back, and carries a decoration given by the British government. The puppy is Ard Aven Tipperary Mix, sired by Ch. Williamsdale Sunstar ex Ch. Princess Meekers. Major Fisher bought the little bitch from Dr. and Mrs. Harbinson's Ard Aven Kennels.

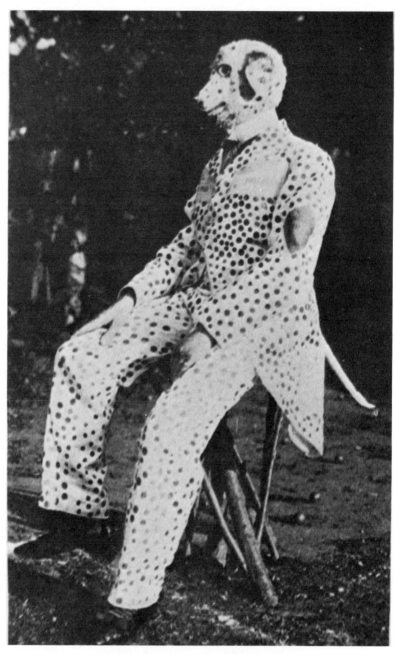

Dr. Wheeler-O'Bryen in Dalmatian Fancy
Dress for Ball at turn of century, London.

17

Fun Things and Side Effects

ALMOST EVERY BREED can point with pride to celebrity owners but the Dalmatian seems to have collected a great number, particularly in the movie community of Hollywood and Beverly Hills. A short time ago the singer, John Davidson, acquired a puppy to accompany his Arabian horses so that his children could grow up surrounded by the same type of animals he had had as a child.

Darrin McGavin has a Dal and went so far as to have a jogging suit made to match his dog so they will look well together as they run each day.

Glenn Ford has a number of Dals and amuses himself and his friends by training them to do a number of tricks. His Dals have appeared on national television doing their thing.

There are others, of course, of whom we have not learned but we doubt if any other breed has its own fancier who is an Oscar winner. Daniel Taradash won an Oscar for the screen play of "From Here to Eternity" in 1953. At that time he was actively engaged in exhibiting his Dalmatians. And while he is no longer active in the show ring he remains a member of the DCA.

The late Adlai Stevenson, former Governor of Illinois, Democratic candidate for President, and Ambassador to the United Nations, had a Dal named Artie with him in the Governor's Mansion in Springfield. A full page picture of the Governor and the dog appeared in *Life* magazine.

The great operatic basso, Ezio Pinza, later known to millions for *Some Enchanted Evening* in South Pacific, contributed his two Dalmatians to the war effort in 1942.

Arthur Fiedler, founder and conductor of the Boston Pops, pictured with his Dalmatian, Sparky, at a Boston Fire Department rally.

Arthur Fiedler and his "Sparky" as a puppy.

248

And we all know about George Washington and his "coach dog." The late Arthur Fiedler, that musical institution of the Boston Pops Orchestra, always had a keen interest in fire fighting, fire fighting equipment, and the like. Over the years he was made honorary fire chief of more than 400 fire departments. So when he decided to get a dog there was only one breed which appealed to him, the Firehouse dog of course. Mr. Fiedler obtained his Dalmatian from Roadcoach Kennels and named it (what else?) Sparky.

Sparky was a beloved member of the Fiedler household for a number of years and was sadly missed by the entire family.

In an interview on the CBS program, *60 Minutes,* Mr. Fiedler was asked about an analogy to W. C. Fields who is frequently quoted as having said, "Anyone who hates kids and dogs can't be all bad." Arthur Fiedler said he didn't think it applied. He said, "I like dogs . . . . and I have children of my own."

The well-known oil man from Fort Worth, TX, E. E. "Buddy" Fogelson, husband of movie star Greer Garson, owned a fine obedience Dalmatian named Axel of Hillview UD. Axel was shown in competition by Cal Boykin, an active kennel man from the Dallas-Fort Worth area.

Axel was bred by Carl and Marly T. Frisby in Georgia and was sold as a pet puppy to Mrs. Riley B. Roberts in 1951. Shortly thereafter Mr. Roberts was called into service leaving Mrs. Roberts with three small children and Axel. The entire situation was too much for Mrs. Roberts to handle and she finally gave the dog to the Sullivans who were stationed nearby. Bob trained Axel and completed his CD title. He had trained the dog for Open work and had one CDX leg on him when Mr. Fogelson bought him and turned him over to Cal.

Together Axel and Cal were a great team to watch. They obtained the Utility title in short order and continued to compete for a number of years. The dog won numerous High in Trials for his owner. Occasionally Axel would go to the office with Mr. Fogelson where he spent most of his time under the executive's desk. He was a credit to the breed, a fine obedience showman.

In Bennington, VT, there is a tourist attraction known as the "Lawn of Dogs." The lawn was established by Millie Matteson, nee Amelia Armbruster, and married to Peleg Austin Matteson, a dentist. Her interest in antiques was encouraged by her husband. In the 30s Mrs. Matteson saw a cast-iron statue of a Dalmatian. It was life-sized and stood near an iron foundry at Poultney, VT. It was about 100 years old then. The foundry is still in business but no longer casts the dogs.

The Mattesons bought the dog. Later on they found another Dalmatian statue which had also been cast at this foundry. They acquired this dog too. They decided to collect cast-iron animals. They found a finely detailed life-size Newfoundland. In 1940 they found a statue of a very large dog which

Willy Necker's troupe of Dalmatians.

Willy Necker's leaping and stunt-performing Dals.

250

they thought was a statue of a Mastiff. It wasn't a mastiff but a giant dog, breed unknown. This statue had been an important feature in a canine cemetery and had once stood on the estate of Commodore Vanderbilt before its use at the cemetery. The Mattesons have an iron deer which weighs about 700 pounds. They have two iron Whippets and a small 12-inch long setter not found on the lawn but used as a desk ornament. During the Victorian era these life-sized statues of dogs were in great demand. At first they had to be imported from England but later the American foundries cast their own models.

In the 1930s Mrs. Bonney found a pair of Dalmatian statues which she had shipped to her Sunstar Hill estate at Oyster Bay, Long Island. After her death, Mr. and Mrs. Arthur Higgins acquired the statues to flank the entrance to their Pennydale Dalmatians' home at Syosset. Today, Dr. and Mrs. Doane have one of Mrs. Bonney's statues and have acquired another statue.

In Oklahoma City there is a pair of Dal statues guarding the driveway of a home in the exclusive residential area of Nichols Hills. As far as can be determined the owners have no connection with the breed.

Today the antique dogs have a market value of $1500 to $3000. The price of the statue is only the beginning. Transportation and labor to set up the animals cost almost as much as the statue itself. And these dogs must be maintained; painting each year is almost a necessity. But they seem to be so lifelike that live dogs have been known to bark at them.

It seems natural that the hearty-eating, highly visible Dalmatian frequently turns up in dog food advertising and TV commercials. It is a little startling to know that a picture of a Dalmatian with a green collar was used to promote Fatima cigarettes in the spring of 1927.

A Dalmatian's portrait is part of the design of a stained glass window of a church in Bolinbroke, Lincolnshire, England. The two-light window is based on a Benedictine theme depicting the seasons of the year and some of the lovely things man had cause to be thankful for. The dog was one of them. Mr. Skeat, the artist, obtained his Dal, Widdington Dannilad, from Mrs. Hayman in the early 1950s.

Most of us are familiar with collective nouns and their use. Some are a bit amusing, such as a gaggle of geese, a pride of lions or a bevy of quail, but a dilly of Dalmatians?

Readers of the British Dalmatian Club's *Spots of News* had their chuckles as members contributed a ''dally-rally'' of these expressions:

A wagging of Dalmatians; a dapple of Dalmatians; a smiling of Dalmatians; a bother of Dalmatians; a rampage of Dalmatians; a rash of Dalmatians; a delight of Dalmatians; a garnishing of Dalmatians; a constellation of Dalmatians; and, finally, a delight of, a damnation of and a dither of Dalmatians.

Silent sentinels of a driveway in Oklahoma City.

Oros II, owned by Lois Meistrell, at a political rally.

Meanwhile, back in the States, the Dalmatian Club of Greater Atlanta members staged a contest to find the Dalmatian with the most spots on its tail. The winner was a champion, William's Apollo Moon Robber. The committee lost count at fourteen spots.

Spotted Verse

Over the years the character and stamina of the Dalmatian has become the subject of poetic inspiration many times. Some of the verses have made it to the printed page without recognition of the author. Where the author is unknown we have indicated the earliest source in which we have found the piece.

The Coach Dog

Long legged, loppy eared, his which and liver
    Dulled with the highway's dust, between the wheels
He lopes along, tail softly wagging, ever
    Proclaiming the contentment that he feels.
Philosopher of dogs—no cynic this!
    Well satisfied, be progress slow or fast,
To follow with no simulated bliss
    The lumbring vehicles of ages past
Uphill and he labors, low of nose
    His brown eyes straying neither left nor right.
Unwilling, 'til the journey nears its close,
    To falter, to philander, or to fight.
Methinks—though far be it for me to preach—
    A top hole lesson doth the coach dog teach!

Harold Willard Gleason

Willock 1927

The Spotted Dog

"Spotted like the Leopard, I
Live my days at Dobbin's heels.
Let the hastening pack go by,
With tooting horn and bellowing cry;
I am content between the wheels."

F. C. Hignett

The New Book of the Dog, 1907

A litter of Altamar puppies posing for Walt Disney artists in the making of "101 Dalmatians." Production supervisor Ken Peterson is shown sketching.

Ch. Williamscrest Dainty Dancer and Ch. Coachman's Classic CD modeling as Perdita and Pongo respectively for "101 Dalmatians." Ken Anderson is the artist.

Tack, Maria Johnson's Ch. Coachman's Classic CD, modeling as Pongo for Disney studio artist, Ken Anderson.

Tack shows his prowess as a musician for Disney studio Art Director, Ken Anderson.

Dan

I must tell you of Dan
It was love at first sight,
With his little brown nose,
and his ears set just right.

We had wanted a black,
But a black wouldn't do,
It just had to be Dan,
He was too good to be true.

We were new to the dog world,
and had taken advice,
From Dalmatian Club colleagues,
So helpful and nice,

Long letters and phone calls,
had brought us to Dan,
But this feeling of joy
Was not part of the plan.

They were only just puppies,
All faint spots and tails,
with snapping of teeth,
and scratching of nails.

There were twelve in the litter,
some walked and some ran,
But just one for us,
and his name would be Dan.

We had wanted a black but
a black wouldn't do
It just had to be Dan.
He was too good to be true.

This story took place,
some twelve months ago,
and now Dan has grown
As Dalmatians will grow.

He's done all the things
to which Dallies are prone,
Eaten odd objects,
Dug plants freshly sown.

But this love affair flourishes
As love affairs can,
Between one ordinary family,
And a liver dog DAN.

J. Tolliday

Spots of News #275

256

Dalmatians love to play Frisbee.

Seen at dog show. *Martin Booth*

257

Some British figurines pictured in the BDC yearbook, 1934.

George Jessel clowns with the Dalmatian, Kotor, at one of the early Texaco shows.

Dressing up the fire-plugs. *Bill Bond*

Oros II CD posing with a Girl Scout at the New York City Fireman's Museum in Greenwich Village, for Fire Prevention Week.

Fire Department float in a Florida Christmas parade.

260

"Vanity" license plates attract Dalmatians.

Two of the Anheuser Busch Dals, Bud and Michelob, watch as the Clydesdales are harnessed to the beer wagon.

Mike Callea's dog is mascot of the City of Davis, California, fire department. *Callea*

The Dalmatian

Of all the breeds of dogs I see
Just one spotted fellow appeals to me
There are many kinds of dogs in our nation
To me, there is just one, the Dalmatian
    Bold black spots on a field of white,
    That field of white so sparkling bright.
    Two eyes so filled with love for man,
    A heart that serves your every plan.
The size is right for one and all,
Not too short, not too tall.
Happy when you're smiling,
Droopy when you're sad.
    So, once you have owned a Dal
    You'll say there is no finer pal.
    He'll stick with you through thick or thin,
    A friend to please your every whim.

Lois J. Thiesen

The Spotter, June 1967

262

King George's Dalmatian A.D. 1822

Yellow wheels and red wheels, wheels that squeak and roar,
Big buttons, brown wigs, and many capes of buff . . .
Someone's bound for Sussex in a coach-and-four;
    And, when the long whips crack,
    Running at the back
    Barks the swift Dalmatian
Whose spots are seven score.

White dust and grey dust, fleeting tree and tower,
Brass horns and copper horns blowing loud and bluff,
Someone's bound for Sussex at eleven miles an hour;
    And, when the long horns blow,
    From the dust below
    Barks the swift Dalmatian,
Tongued like an apple-flower.

Big domes and little domes, donkey-carts that jog,
High stocks and low pumps and incomparable snuff,
Someone strolls at Brighton, not *very* much incog.;
    And, panting on the grass,
    In his collar bossed with brass,
      Lies the swift Dalmatian,
The King's plum-pudding dog.

DOROTHY MARGARET STUART: in Punch, 1925

Dalmatian head belt buckle. A series of these were numbered and the mold was destroyed. The numbered heads can become collector's items.

Dalmatian postage stamps from far places. Provided by Harold Schlintz, Bert Schoof and Stephen Berman.

"Mr. Hathaway," a Dalmatian miniature figurine, shown at the art display at Madison Square Garden during Westminster 1976.

264

Mosaic panel used as an ornament on the facade of the Home Savings & Loan in downtown Los Angeles.

Ch. Green Starr's Colonel Joe, owned by Mrs. Alan Robson.

18

Top Spots

$\mathbf{W}$HEN DR. LEON SELIGMAN chose Ch. Green Starr's Colonel Joe for Best in Show at the Spartanburg Kennel Club's July 1979 show he was unaware that the choice would break all BIS records in the breed. That win marked the 19th Best for Colonel Joe and placed him above all other Dalmatians in the history of the breed in this country for top honors. The next day at Asheville Kennel Club "Cass" again won the big rosette and his BIS win record stood at 20.

Best in Show records on the Dal are well known to Dalmatian enthusiasts as each year Walter Johnson compiles the list for the DCA *Spotter*. Records are made to be broken. Ch. Four-in-Hand Mischief's record of 18 Best in Shows stood from 1941 to 1979 and Ch. Roadcoach Roadster's record of 17 top awards remained untouched from 1959 until 1979. Mischief was English bred and Roadster was an American bred dog.

Colonel Joe has won the DCA National specialty two years in a row and will undoubtedly exceed the 20 Best in Show mark as he continues to win groups frequently. He has also topped the Best of Breed number of any Dalmatian ever shown.

Ch. Lord Jim is in fourth place with 13 Best in Shows and Ch. Panore of Watseka holds fifth place with 10 top awards.

Top winner in bitches is Ch. Swabbie of Oz Dal who had a total of eight Bests. Second among bitches is Ch. Blackpool Crinkle Forest with six.

Other multiple Best in Show award Dals include Ch. Ye Dal Dark Brilliance with seven top awards; Ch. Ard Aven Shamus, five; Ch. Crestview

Dan Patch, four; Ch. Coachman's Chuck-a-Luck, three; Ch. Green Starr's Masterpiece, two; Ch. Melody Dynamatic, two; and Ch. Rovingdale's Impudent Ingenue, two.

Those dogs who have won one Best in Show are Ch. Beaumont of Pacifica, Ch. Coachkeeper's Blizzard of QA, Ch. Colonsay Storm; Ch. Dalabra Star Dust of Ragusa, Ch. Deltalyn's Decoupage, Ch. Four-in-Hand Athos (at the age of seven years!), Ch. Gladmore Guardsman, Ch. Gren's Coal Tar, Ch. Lancer's Sir Lancelot, Ch. Melody Ring of Fire of BB, Ch. Nigel of Welfield and Stock Dal, Ch. Pacifica Pride of Poseidon, Ch. Reigate Bold Venture, Ch. Roadcoach Post Parade, Ch. Roadcoach Spice, Ch. Roadcoach Tioga Too, Ch. Roadking's Rome, Ch. Rockledge Rumble. Ch. Ser Dals Lone Star, Ch. Strathglass Cricket, Ch. Tally Ho Sirius, Ch. The Lash, Ch. Williamsdale Rocky, Ch. Williamsdale Michael, and Ch. Willy Overland in the Valley.

In an article in the summer 1975 issue of *The Spotter* Walter Johnson remarked that it had been fifty years since the present system of Best in Show, Group and Best of Breed had been in effect. During that period, 35 Dalmatians receive the distinction of a Best in Show award and only a total of 116 Best in Shows were won by them. Seven were bitches and 28 were dogs. By color out of that total of 35 BIS Dalmatians, 29 were black spotted and 6 were liver spotted.

Since then three more Dalmatians have won Best in Show rosettes. They are Ch. Lancer's Sir Lancelot, a liver dog, Ch. Deltalyn Decoupage, and Ch. Green Starr's Colonel Joe.

Liver spotted Dalmatians, once not as popular as black spotted dogs, are now in the limelight. It is a rare entry of Dalmatians in any show without at least one liver specimen being shown. The color choice is a matter of taste. At one time people would comment, "He is a well-marked dog *for a liver.*" No longer does one hear comments of this nature. The liver Dalmatian has come into its own and its breeders have developed spotting patterns equal to those in the black and white dogs. Some people feel that livers should be forgiven lack of pigment in eye rims and noses. No Dalmatian should be forgiven lack of pigment in our estimation. This is a serious fault for without proper pigmentation we will lose the main characteristic of the breed, the markings.

Over the years the statistics show that approximately 18 percent of the Best in Show Dalmatians have been livers. The first to achieve this honor was Ch. Colonsay Storm, an import, owned by Mr. and Mrs. P. M. Chancellor, at the Peninsula Dog Fanciers Dog Show, Bremerton, WA, March 30, 1952. The judge was the late Alfred LePine. The win was over an entry of 554, a good sized show in those days. Ch. Green Starr's Masterpiece, owned by Dr. and Mrs. David Doane, was Best at Duso Kennel Club, Narrowsburg, NY, June 30, 1956 over an entry of 323. The judge was Mrs. L. St. George. Masterpiece was also named Best at Carroll County Kennel Club, North

Ch. Swabbie of OzDal, the first Dalmatian and only bitch to win the group at West-minster. Owned by the late Blanche Osborne and always handled by Jack Funk.

Ch. Roadcoach Roadster, the second Dalmatian to win the group at Westminster. He was bred by the Barretts and owned by Mrs. George Ratner (Allman) and handled by Charley Meyer.

Conway, NH, on July 29, 1956 over an entry of 220 by the late Mrs. L. W. Bonney.

Ch. The Lash, owned by Ard Aven and El Tross, beat out 484 dogs at Vancouver Kennel Club, Vancouver, WA, January 27, 1957 under judge G. D. La Monte.

Ch. Roadcoach Spice topped 553 dogs at Rhode Island Kennel Club, Cranston, RI, April 8, 1962 under Mrs. L. S. Davy. She was owned by Roadcoach Kennels and is the only liver bitch to have won a Best in Show.

Ch. Melody Dynamatic was named Best at the Colorado Kennel Club show in Denver September 15, 1973 by judge Henry Stoecker over 1002 entered dogs. "Johnny," as he is called, is owned by C. E. Flock, Jr. He tied the record for liver Best in Show wins by repeating at the Buckhorn Valley Kennel Club show, Fort Collins, CO, March 8, 1975 under judge Herman G. Cox over 730 dogs.

And judge R. C. Graham awarded the top place to Ch. Coachkeeper Blizzard of QA at the Susque-Nango Kennel Club, Green, NY, June 28, 1974. The dog is owned by Mrs. A. R. Robson, Albelarm Kennels, and was handled by Bobby Barlow.

Ch. Lancer's Sir Lancelot, a liver dog, owner-handled by Ron Brooks, was named Best in Show at Progressive Dog Club in Wayne County, April 24, 1976 by judge John Honig over 1059 dogs.

Over the years three Dalmatians have won the non-sporting group at Westminster. The first to do so was a bitch, Ch. Swabbie of Oz-Dal in 1949. Swabbie was shown extensively, handled by the well-known Jack Funk. Although she was bred a couple of times and had one or two champion get, she is not remembered as a producer and cannot be found in many extended pedigrees. Blanche Osborne, her owner, was a registered nurse which probably gives a clue to the meaning of Swabbie. She was a lovely bitch and because she was so good and did so much winning very few champion Dals were entered against her at the outlying shows. As her show record piled up most exhibitors decided not to campaign their champions against her.

The second group winner at the Garden was Ch. Roadcoach Roadster in 1956. He was owned by Mrs. S. K. Allmann (now Mrs. George Ratner). His record of show wins at that time was unheard of. Mrs. Ratner campaigned him extensively with Charley Meyer handling.

Ch. Coachman's Callisto is the third Dal to win the group at Westminster. Bred by Coachman Kennels in St. Louis he was purchased by Arthur and Muriel Higgins of Pennydale Kennels, Syosset, New York. Arthur Higgins handled the dog to his great win at the Garden in 1963. In fact, Arthur handled the dog most of the time using a handler only when it was impossible for him to get to the show.

Those of us in Dalmatians are hoping for lightning to strike again. There are some great dogs being shown at this time so we can continue to hope.

Ch. Coachman's Callisto, the only owner-handled Dalmatian to win the group at Westminster. Bred by the Fetner's Coachman Kennels, he was owned and shown by the late Arthur Higgins.

19

Dalmatian Fancy's
Book of Records

DALMATIAN FANCIERS like to challenge each other's knowledge or memory of facts or events. Some discussions appear destined to last forever. In the interest of harmony and fun it seemed worthwhile to create a book of records for the Dalmatian fancy.

Selected events are listed in order of occurrence. Some of these landmarks are negative and reflect the need for the support to the breed which earlier fanciers provided. For instance neither England nor the United States had a Dalmatian present at its first dog show.

Records of "firsts" and "mosts" attained over the years in the United States also appear in this chapter. Additional charts are in other parts of the book. There is no attempt to weigh the importance of these highlights and milestones of the breed history, but only to gather them into a single reference source. This in itself may be an all-breed record. It could develop into a treasury of information about the Dalmatian. If any reader has knowledge of additional highlights or achievements which might interest Dal fanciers, the authors would be delighted to learn of them.

Milestones

1780   First printed use of word "Dalmatian' in the English language to describe a breed of dogs was in a translation of *Natural History* by Count de Buffon, published in Scotland.

1787   George Washington reports the purchase of a Coach dog stud for Madame Moose, his wife's pet.

272

1790	First English writer to use the word "Dalmatian" to designate the breed, Thomas Bewick in *A General History of Quadrupeds*.
1829	First reports that the practice of cropping ears was dying out.
1859	First dog show held in Newcastle on Tyne, June 28 and 29. Sixty entries, no classes for Dalmatians, only Pointers and Setters.
1860	Practice of ear flap removal discontinued in England.
1860	Dog show classes for Dalmatians, one of five breeds scheduled, included at Midland County Repository, Cheapside, Birmingham, England on December 3 and 4, 1860. "No prizes awarded."
1861	First record of Dalmatians being shown in England at Leeds, North of England Exhibition of Sporting and Other Dogs, July 16, 17, 18, 1861. First prize to "Ceasar" (2550), owned by Mr. G. Hutchinson of York.
1873	The Kennel Club founded in Great Britain.
1874	First dog show in America held at Memphis, Tennessee, October 8, 1874. No Dalmatians competed.
1877	Westminster Kennel Club held first show without Dalmatians.
1880	Captain (5394) and Crib (2557) became first two Dalmatian champions in England.
1882	Vero Shaw produced the first unofficial standard, a formal breed description under systematic headings with numerical standard of points in *Illustrated Book of the Dog*.
1884	American Kennel Club founded on a non-profit basis.
1886	Stonehenge (Dr. John Henry Walsh) published the second unofficial standard, a detailed description of the breed in his *Dogs of the British Islands*, fourth edition.
1888	First Dalmatian registered with AKC.
1888	Canadian Kennel Club formed.
1889	Twenty-one Dalmatians entered at Crystal Palace show in London.
1890	First club formed in England to support Dalmatians. Disbanded in 1947.
1890	First official standard published in England.
1895	The practice of cropping dogs' ears was prohibited by The Kennel Club of Great Britain.

1904   Dalmatian Club of America formed with 26 Charter Members. Membership limited to fifty.

1905   DCA elected member of AKC.

1906   First Road Trial for Dalmatians at Wissahickon, PA.

1907   Inception of Best in Show at AKC events.

1920   First official FCI Dalmatian Club founded in Germany.

1924   Alignment of breeds into five groups started at AKC shows. Became six in 1930.

1930   South of England Dalmatian Club became the British Dalmatian Club.

1930   Record entry of 458 at first specialist show (limited) in England at Tattersall's in Knightsbridge.

1931   Morris & Essex Kennel Club agreed to hold classes for Dalmatians at its May 23 show.

1933   British Dalmatian Club achieved championship status in April.

1934   AKC granted permission for two preliminary obedience trials.

1936   Obedience trials made a formal part of AKC's purebred dog program. The first AKC licensed Obedience test held at the North Westchester Kennel Club, Mount Kisco, NY, June 13, 1936. Twelve entries, no Dalmatians.

1937   Restriction limiting DCA membership to 50 lifted.

1956   Dodie Smith's *One Hundred and One Dalmatians* published

1961   Walt Disney's animated cartoon *101 Dalmations* released.

1962   Dalmatian Club of America revised description and standard of the Dalmatian February 12, 1962, approved by American Kennel Club December 11, 1962.

1968   Ch. Fanhill Faune, owned by Mrs. E. J. Woodyatt, became Supreme Champion at Crufts, London.

1971   *The Spotter* of the Dalmatian Club of America changed from a newsletter to a magazine format.

1975   Golden Jubilee Championship show of the British Dalmatian Club held April 5th with an entry of 239.

1976   Dalmatian Club of American membership reached 516.

1977   50th Specialty Show of Dalmatian Club of America presented September 23 with 327 dogs entered in conformation and obedience. On September 22 the first Dalmatian Futurity was held as well as the annual Sweepstakes. The two day event was held at Crete, IL.

Conformation Firsts

First Dalmatian registered in the American Kennel Club Stud Book, Bessie (10519) whelped October 1887. Owned by Mrs. N. L. Havey, San Francisco, CA. She was recorded as white, black and tan—breeder and pedigree unknown. Bench Show-2nd, San Francisco, 1888. Walter Johnson reports, "Bessie appears in Volume 5 of the Stud Book but has no progeny registered with AKC. Her fame appears only in her timely registration."

First Dalmatian registered as the result of completing a championship was Ch. Hoyt (82449) in 1905. Breeder, N.R.F. Roges, New Castle, PA., owner J. M. Schontz, Sharon, PA.

The first Dalmatians recorded as being shown in the United States were shown at the San Francisco Dog Show, April 27-May 2, 1883. The record is in the July 1883 issue of the *American Register*. The two males were owned by Dr. E. H. Woolsey with Spot placing first and Speck, second. There were two females, Nellie Dodge owned by A. J. Kelly placed first and Ruby owned by H. B. Slocum placed second.

The first Dalmatian champion confirmed by AKC was a male, Ch. Edgecomb D'Artagnan (80503) owned by Miss M. W. Martin, Philadelphia, PA., breeder, J. S. Price, Jr., Black and White, whelped June 9, 1902. Recorded November 1904.

The first bitch confirmed as a champion was the second Dalmatian to win this honor. She was Spotted Diamond (80504) owned by Miss M. W. Martin, Philadelphia, Pa., breeder, Mr. Berkholder, black and white, whelped November 1901.

First imported Dalmatian champion, Ch. Windy Valley Snowstorm (87741), White, black markings, dog whelped May 1, 1903. Breeder W. B. Herman (England), owner Windy Valley Kennels, NY.

Tally-Ho Last of Sunstar was the first Dalmatian to take the Non-Sporting Group. He came out of American-bred at the Nassau County Kennel Club's May 17, 1924 show.

First all breed Best in Show under the group system was Ch. Gladmore Guardsman at the Valley Kennel Club, New Kensington, PA. under Judge G. V. Glebe. He won over 179 dogs shown at the two day event, April 27-28, 1928.

The first DCA National Specialty was won by Ch. Tally Ho Last of Sunstar at Mineola, NY, on June 26, 1926. He won it again the following year and in 1931 becoming the first three-time winner. This record remained for 46 years. It was tied by Ch. Panore of Watseka in 1977. Ch. Tally Ho Last of Sunstar and CH Panore of Watseka each came out of Veterans to win their third National Specialty.

First bitch to win the National Specialty was Ch. Tally Ho Fore Thought at Forest Hills, NY on May 18, 1928.

First liver spotted Dalmatian to win a national specialty, Ch. Tally Ho Samson at Florham Park, NJ, on May 26, 1950.

Obedience Firsts

First Dalmatian entered in an Obedience class was Captain Fiske, exhibited by Louise Geddes Fiske in the Novice A class of the Eastern Dog Club, Boston, MA, February 21 and 22, 1937. The Obedience Test Club of New York (Mrs. Whitehouse Walker, Secretary, Bedford Hills, NY) offered both cash and special prizes for Novice, Open and Utility "Obedience Test" classes.

First Dalmatian to earn a Companion Dog degree, Meeker's Barbara Worth owned by George S. Walker, January 10, 1939.

First male Dal to earn an obedience degree, Blotter's Boy CD in February 1940.

First Dalmatian to earn Companion Dog Excellent (August 20, 1940) and Utility Dog (November 1, 1940) degrees was Io, not registered, owned by Harland and Lois Meistrell.

First Dal bitch to earn a Utility Dog degree, Spur of Victory, UD, Long Last Kennels.

First Dal Champion to win a CD degree May 1, 1940, Ch. Byron's Penny, owned by Robert Byron.

First and only Dalmatian recipients of the shortlived UDT title were Roadcoach Tess (N4258) and Dickie's Candy (N134720) both confirmed in the January 1956 AKC *Gazette*. Previously a dog was required to pass a "tracking test" before being permitted to use the title of "U.D." signifying "Utility Dog". These tests were given in connection with what was then called an Obedience Test Trial or at another time. The American Kennel Club issued a "Tracking Test" certificate for dogs successfully passing this test. For a brief period this became a UDT title. Later Tracking Trials evolved as separate events with the resulting "Tracking Dog" title. Now the owner of a dog holding both the "U.D." and "T.D." titles may use the letters "U.D.T." after the name of the dog signifying "Utility Dog Tracker".

First Dalmatian to achieve both Championship and Utility Dog degrees, Ch. Duke of Gervais, UD, owned by Maurice Gervais, December 8, 1944.

276

First Champion Dalmatian bitch to earn a Utility Dog and a Tracking degree, Ch. Dal Downs Dicie of Shadodal, owned by Bob and Marge Sullivan in 1976.

First 200 score by Lady Jane owned by Naomi Radler at Garden City, NY.

Mosts

The most Best in Show awards to date, 20, were won by Ch. Green Starr's Colonel Joe (NS 187661).

The most BIS awards won by an English import were 18 won by Ch. Four-in-Hand Mischief (A204760).

The most BIS awarded to a bitch, a total of 8, went to Ch. Swabbie of OzDal (N32668).

The most BIS awards won in a single year totaled 13 won by Lord Jim (NA 619679) in 1970.

The most prolific Dalmatian is probably Vimey owned by Mrs. Freda Hayman of Prestwood, Buckinghamshire, England. According to the 1968 *Guiness Book of World Records* he fathered 637 puppies between 1957 and October 1965.

Youngest

The youngest Dalmatian to win Best in Show was a bitch, Ch. Ser Dals Lone Star, at the age of 1 year, 2 months and 27 days.

The youngest Dalmatian to finish its championship is Ch. Crown Jewel's Hope Diamond II (NA371586) at the age of slightly over 7 months. Born June 9, 1965, he finished on the Florida Circuit in January 1966 and was confirmed in the March, 1966 AKC GAZETTE.

Oldest

The oldest Dalmatian Best in Show winner was Ch. Four-in-Hand Athos (A424221) at the age of 7 years, 5 months and 2 days.

Envoi

An art exhibition in London was held during February 1977 at David Messum's Gallery in Drury Street. Naturally this attracted some of the visitors to the Crufts dog show. Among them was Enid Aldrich-Blake who commented, "I had, of course, hoped to see some pictures of Dalmatians but there were only two. One, a head study of a dog painted in 1886 was rather heavy by present-day standards but he had an endearing glint in his eye and the name engraved on his broad brass collar was 'Spot,' The other was the original pen and ink drawing of The Dalmatian by Arthur Wardle, one of his studies of all the breeds which were reproduced in *Our Dogs* in 1910-1912. His Dalmatian will be familiar to many; it is shown on the cover of Milo Denlinger's book *The Complete Dalmatian*.

"An Exhibition such as this shows that the dog has always had a place in the everyday life of this country and I believe that this always will be so. It is something no anti-dog campaign will ever destroy."

Eugene O'Neill and Blemie.

EUGENE O'NEILL, whose plays won four Pulitzer Prizes, was called the American Shakespeare. He wrote more than 30 plays including *Anna Christie, Strange Interlude, Ah Wilderness, The Iceman Cometh* and *Long Day's Journey into Night* which was not to be produced until 25 years after his death.

"The last Will and Testament of an Extremely Distinguished Dog" is a touching tribute to the Dalmatian "Blemie" owned by the playwright and his third wife, the lovely actress Carlotta Monterey. O'Neill wrote this gem as a comfort to Carlotta a few days before Blemie passed away from old age in December 1940.

Blemie's will epitomizes the love between Dalmatians and their owners and serves as a fitting *finis* to this book which has also been written with love by its authors.

The Last Will and Testament of an Extremely Distinguished Dog

I, SILVERDENE EMBLEM O'NEILL (familiarly known to my family, friends and acquaintances as Blemie), because the burden of my years and infirmities is heavy upon me, and I realize the end of my life is near, do hereby bury my last will and testament in the mind of my Master. He will not know it is there until after I am dead. Then, remembering me in his loneliness, he will suddenly know of this testament, and I ask him then to inscribe it as a memorial to me.

I have little in the way of material things to leave. Dogs are wiser than men. They do not set great store upon things. They do not waste their days hoarding property. They do not ruin their sleep worrying about how to keep the objects they have, and to obtain the objects they have not. There is nothing of value I have to bequeath except my love and my faith. These I leave to all those who have loved me, to my Master and Mistress, who I know will mourn me most, to Freeman who has been so good to me, to Cyn and Roy and Willie and Naomi and—But if I should list all those who have loved me it would force my Master to write a book. Perhaps it is vain of me to boast when I am so near death, which returns all beasts and vanities to dust, but I have always been an extremely lovable dog.

I ask my Master and Mistress to remember me always, but not to grieve for me too long. In my life I have tried to be a comfort to them in time of sorrow, and a reason for added joy in their happiness. It is painful for me to think that even in death I should cause them pain. Let them remember that while no dog has ever had a happier life (and this I owe to their love and care for me), now that I have grown blind and deaf and lame, and even my sense of smell fails me so that a rabbit could be right under my nose and I might not know, my pride has sunk to a sick, bewildered humiliation. I feel life is taunting me with having over-lingered my welcome. It is time I said goodbye, before I become too sick a burden on myself and on those who love me. It will be sorrow to leave them, but not a sorrow to die. Dogs do not fear death as men do. We accept it as part of life, not as something alien and terrible which destroys life. What may come after death, who knows? I would like to believe with those of my fellow Dalmatians who are devout Mohammedans, that there is a Paradise where one is always young and full-bladdered; where all the day one dillies and dallies with an amorous multitude of houris, beautifully spotted; where jack rabbits that run fast but not too fast (like the houris) are as the sands of the desert; where each blissful hour is mealtime; where in long evenings there are a million fireplaces with logs forever burning, and one curls oneself up and blinks into the flames and nods and dreams, remembering the old brave days on earth, and the love of one's Master and Mistress.

I am afraid this is too much for even such a dog as I am to expect. But peace, at least, is certain. Peace and long rest for weary old heart and head and limbs, and eternal sleep in the earth I have loved so well. Perhaps, after all, this is best.

One last request I earnestly make. I have heard my Mistress say, "When Blemie dies we must never have another dog. I love him so much I could never love another one." Now I would ask her, for love of me, to have another. It would be a poor tribute to my memory never to have a dog again. What I would like to feel is that, having once had me in the family, now she cannot live without a dog! I have never had a narrow jealous spirit. I have always held that most dogs are good (and one cat, the black one I have permitted to share the living room rug during the evenings, whose affection I have tolerated in a kindly spirit, and in rare sentimental moods, even reciprocated a trifle). Some dogs, of course, are better than others. Dalmatians, naturally, as everyone knows, are best. So I suggest a Dalmatian as my successor. He can hardly be as well bred or as well mannered or as distinguished and handsome as I was in my prime. My Master and Mistress must not ask the impossible. But he will do his best, I am sure, and even his inevitable defects will help by comparison to keep my memory green. To him I bequeath my collar and leash and my overcoat and raincoat, made to order in 1929 at Hermès in Paris. He can never wear them with the distinction I did, walking around the Place Vendôme, or later along Park Avenue, all eyes fixed on me in admiration; but again I am sure he will do his utmost not to appear a mere gauche provincial dog. Here on the ranch, he may prove himself quite worthy of comparison, in some respects. He will, I presume, come closer to jack rabbits than I have been able to in recent years. And, for all his faults, I hereby wish him the happiness I know will be his in my old home.

One last work of farewell, Dear Master and Mistress. Whenever you visit my grave, say to yourselves with regret but also with happiness in your hearts at the remembrance of my long happy life with you: "Here lies one who loved us and whom we loved." No matter how deep my sleep I shall hear you, and not all the power of death can keep my spirit from wagging a grateful tail.

Tao House, December 17th, 1940